MAITLAND'S DARK AGES.

THE DARK AGES;

ESSAYS ILLUSTRATING THE

STATE OF RELIGION AND LITERATURE

IN THE NINTH, TENTH, ELEVENTH, AND TWELFTH
CENTURIES.

By S. R. MAITLAND, D.D., F.R.S., F.S.A.,

SOMETIME LIBRARIAN AND KEEPER OF THE MSS. AT LAMBETH.

VOLUME
ONE

WITH AN INTRODUCTION BY FREDERICK STOKES, M.A.

KENNIKAT PRESS/Port Washington, N.Y.

THE DARK AGES

First published 1889
Reissued 1969 by Kennikat Press

Library of Congress Catalog Card No: 68-8242
SBN 8046-0297-2
Manufactured in the United States of America

✓ 3/70

INTRODUCTION.

It is by no means easy for even impartial men to arrive at clear and accurate knowledge of the social and mental conditions of peoples and classes living under different conditions from themselves. Even a selected body of men like a Royal Commission often ends by presenting widely different conclusions, drawn from precisely the same evidence as to the same facts. The actual condition, for instance, of the Irish peasantry is a subject of hot dispute among men of education and intelligence living under the same laws at the same time. When the class under consideration differs from its critics, as in the case of a foreign country, the difficulty is greatly increased. How many Englishmen are qualified to pronounce upon the social and economic conditions of Russia, or China, or, one might even add, of Ireland ?

In truth, the judgments which men form are to a large extent subjective, and are determined not merely by evidence which may be the same for all, but by training, inclination, prejudice, sometimes even by heredity. In religious matters an impartial critic is the exception. The great majority of men inherit their faith, as they do their physique, from their parents. Hence it may be assumed as fairly certain that a Protestant writer dealing with the Dark Ages—a period when Christendom was Roman Catholic—will have a tendency to deal out something less than justice. Even if he be fair-minded —and many ultra-Protestant writers are not—there is the danger of what may be called involuntary bias. For most men unconsciously set up their own standards of happiness and enlightenment as the test by which others are to be judged. Rich men, as a class, take it for granted that their less favoured fellow creatures are necessarily miserable. Poor

men too commonly accept the deplorable fallacy
that to be rich is to be happy. The man of the
world regards monastic life as a species of voluntary
penal servitude. The monk, as a rule, assumes that
there is no real happiness or virtue outside the
cloister. Each decides not according to the objec-
tive truth of the matter, but more or less conform-
ably to his own mental sympathies and tastes.

Perhaps no period of Christianity has been more
misjudged than the Dark Ages—an epoch which, in
the present work, is taken as comprising the ninth,
tenth, eleventh, and twelfth centuries. The general
tradition when Maitland wrote—a tradition which
has been greatly modified by later historians like
Hallam and Gasquet—was that these ages were
almost wholly barbaric; ages of ignorance, superstition, oppression, and general misery. Perhaps
writers of the twenty-first century will take a
similar view of the nineteenth, and regard it as a
time when the world was desolated by famine, war,
pestilence; when the condition of the poor was as
harsh as it has ever been; when men were subject
to conscription, invasion, misgovernment. The
writers of the first half of this century looked down
with scorn upon the centuries before the Reformation, yet historians like Walpole pronounce an
almost equally severe verdict upon the times when
George the Third was king. The Anglican Churchmen of the last century were emphatic in their
denunciations of the abuses of pre-Reformation
times. The general verdict of Churchmen of our
own times as to the state of the Church of England
in the eighteenth century is the reverse of flattering.
It would be easy, indeed, by treating the Anglican
Church in the eighteenth century as many Protestant writers—notably Robertson—have treated the
Church of the Middle Ages, to prove that that epoch
was as dark as any century of the Christian era.

And, in judging of any past age, it is necessary
to remember that evil is more conspicuous than

good; that one great criminal attracts more attention than thousands of men living quiet and virtuous lives. One year of war furnishes forth more food for the historian than a decade of peace. Moreover, it is necessary to remember the Dark Ages were a time when Roman Catholicism was dominant, while the writers who formed the existing tradition were mostly Protestant. It is hardly too much to say that modern literature, as a whole, is Protestant. For whatever reason, a species of intellectual sterility seems to have fallen upon Roman Catholics within the last two hundred years. For a century past Roman Catholicism has produced perhaps three literary men of the first rank—Lamennais, Dollinger, and Rosmini,—and of these, two were driven out of the Church, and the third, now dead, has been condemned by the present Pope.[1] To anyone, however, acquainted with ecclesiastical history, the wonder will be not that Catholicism has lost the creative power it possessed in mediæval times, but that it continues to exist at all. For a century past a series of hurricanes have swept upon the Latin Church, which have reduced her policy to a desperate struggle for very existence. Perhaps no Church since the days of the Roman Empire has endured —and survived—so tremendous a persecution as that to which the Gallican Church was subjected at the close of the eighteenth century. In Italy a strong anti-Catholic movement, engendered by the secret societies, has culminated in the absorption of the Temporal Power, and is now again developing into a legislative policy, which will still further weaken and hamper the Italian clergy. In Germany the Catholics are just emerging from the obligations

---

[1] The condemnation is, however, limited to some posthumous works of Rosmini. The great bulk of his writings were examined and approved by Pius IX. Rosmini is probably the most brilliant and gifted philosopher that the Church of Rome has produced since the Reformation.

of the Falk laws. Everywhere education has passed
out of the hands of the Church. The old universities
are either Protestant or secularized, the primary
schools are passing into the hands of the State.
So complete is the de-Catholization of Europe, that
at the Vatican Council—Rome's last appeal to
the nations—representatives of the Catholic States
were for the first time omitted from the Papal
invitations. As Cardinal Antonelli said in his
despatch to the Nuncio at Paris—" If the Holy See
has not thought fit to invite Catholic princes to the
Council, as it did on other occasions, everyone will
easily understand that this is chiefly to be attributed
to the changed circumstances of the times."

But it is not the Latin Church alone which is
threatened. Christianity itself is menaced. We
are face to face with a new phenomenon in the
intellectual history of Europe—a religion without a
God. Infidelity has developed into materialism, and
materialism propounds to the world a philosophy
which shall explain and solve the mysteries of the
past and the future, which shall guide the thoughts
and wills of men, but in which a Creator has no
place. Man, according to the new Gospel, is a
combination of chemical and physical atoms produced by evolution and dissolved by death. The
moral effects of such a creed, when once established
—and it is spreading daily—cannot but be disastrous.
For without God there is no morality and no
civilization, no joy in the past, no peace in the
present, no hope for the future. Let us eat and
drink, for to-morrow we die, and death is the end
of all things.

And this modern materialism comes upon us
not as other religious movements have done with
blare of trumpet and beat of drum, rather it
steals upon men's minds like some poisonous
malaria begotten of polluted river or unwholesome
marsh, asphyxiating the conscience and corroding
the intellect, so that men find that faith is dead

before they were conscious that it was in danger. Moreover, the germ of it is in every man's heart, from the theologian watching with perplexed spirit the perennial waves of human folly and misery, to the peasant sullenly gazing at his empty platter and fireless grate, and its spread is helped and furthered by the social and economic miseries of the times. More and more the great landlords and labour-lords are eating up the people as men eat bread, and grinding the faces of the poor. More and more the wealth of Europe, scanty in proportion to the needs and numbers of her population, is being garnered into the cellars of the banker and the safes of the usurer. More and more money is used not to satisfy the legitimate needs of humanity, but as coins in a vast system of public gambling, as bait for the unwary, as the minister of a luxury, upon which Caligula might have looked with envious eye.

The Dark Ages had their miseries, too. Since, the Garden of Eden was closed to our first parents, happiness has not been the lot of any considerable community for any considerable time. The corruption, seemingly incurable, of human nature and the malice of the unseen enemies of our race have always and everywhere proved too strong to be overcome by any creed or constitution. But, on the other hand, these ages had many advantages which we do not enjoy. They were ages in which Christian faith was what a recent writer has called a "vivid dynamic reality." Whatever may be thought of the Crusades—and more than one great authority has held that they resulted in great political advantage to Europe—they were one of the most splendid displays of faith and manhood that the world has ever witnessed, except, perhaps, the earlier developments of Mahommedanism. Christ must have been believed in in those days when half the manhood of Europe was willing to undergo indescribable hardship and peril to rescue only " the grave made with the rich," and there was far more theological

liberty. The Church was indeed a monarchy under
the headship of Rome, but the Papacy was not the
centralized authority into which Ultramontanism
has developed it—a Power claiming absolute and
immediate authority over the life and conscience of
every human being on the face of the earth, not to
mention the realms of Purgatory. The Episcopate
was still a living authority, with power and capacity
to rule and judge. The assembling of Provincial and
General Councils was an ordinary feature of ecclesiastical government. The great theological schools
were full of activity and intellectual life. It was
during the very ages which moderns call dark that
Christianity was formulated and systematized into
its present shape. St. Thomas of Aquin, whose
Summa has dominated the Latin Church for six
centuries, did but reap where the earlier scholastics
had sown. Moreover, the influence of the scholastics
is not confined to the Roman Communion. In so
far as Protestantism has a positive side, it owes it
to the scholastics. The reformers pruned away
much of mediæval Catholicism, but they added
nothing of their own except the doctrine of
justification by faith—one of the most dangerous
delusions that Christianity has seen. The funda-
mental dogmas of the Trinity and the Incarnation
of heaven and hell, of the immortality of the soul
and the resurrection of the body, are held by the
Reformed Churches in the same sense, almost in the
same terms, as by the Roman Church, and although
the later Jesuit writers have somewhat modernized
and developed the scholastic methods, the approved
theology in the Catholic Schools at the present day
is substantially the same as in the Dark Ages.
Rome is still moored to the Summa, which the
present Pope has once again publicly approved and
recommended to his clergy, and the Summa was
but the codification and systematization of the work
of the theological writers of the Dark Ages.

Nor were the early writers during these times so

ignorant as is commonly supposed. They knew
little of natural science, though an accurate theory
about the glacial period is of much less practical
importance than correct views of another period to
come of a higher temperature. No man who is
really grounded in the truths of Christianity can be
truly said to be ignorant, and the practical teaching
which the early writers of the Dark Ages obtained
from the pulpit and the confessional was of far
more real intellectual and moral value than the
farrago of scraps of grammar and elementary
arithmetic imparted to an unwilling generation in
Board Schools and such like. "This," said Christ,
"is life eternal to know Thee, the only true God,
and Jesus Christ, whom Thou hast sent" (John
xvii. 3), and this knowledge the men of the Dark
Ages had in a degree which we, who live in times
when the Church is traversing the vast desert which
separates the devout faith of the past from the
baptised science of the future, can hardly realize.
For the poison of unbelief has affected even the
Churches. Many of those who regard themselves
as orthodox do not really believe, do not get beyond
a nominal acceptance of Christian dogmas. The
spectacle which Europe has witnessed for a whole
generation of a Catholic people like the Italians,
living in avowed indifference to a succession of
Papal anathemas, would have been as impossible
in the Middle Ages as an interdict would be now.
Much of the so-called morality of the present day is
on a par with that of the estimable burglar who
never stole what he did not want. Among the
Reformed Churches, with the exception of the
Catholic party in the Church of England, the spirit
of asceticism is almost dead. Fasting, specifically
named by Christ as a means of sanctification, has
fallen into general disuse. It would perhaps savouf
too much of justification by works.

Lastly, the Dark Ages were distinguished for the
vigour and success with which the mission work or

the Church was carried on. During the ninth
century, Christianity, says Dean Milman (Lat. Chris.
Vol. III. c. viii.), "was gathering in nations of
converts." The Bulgarians were won to the Gospel
by Cyril and Methodius, and one of the first steps
taken by the new Church was to submit a list of no
less than 106 questions to Pope Nicholas I. Some
of the Papal decisions indicate that at Rome at least
the standard of morals was by no means a
barbarous one. No violence was to be used to
those who adhered to Paganism. Torture, with the
object of obtaining evidence, was strictly forbidden,
as was also polygamy. The same century witnessed
the conversion of Moravia and Bohemia, and the
despatch of missionaries to Scandinavia, where the
work of conversion begun by Anschar (who was
created Archbishop of Hamburg) was carried on for
a century and a half, until, in the reign of Canute,
who wore the English and Danish crowns, the task
was completed by a band of English missionaries
sent by the king. During the tenth, eleventh, and
twelfth centuries, the Normans, Magyars, and a
multitude of formidable tribes were won to Christianity, and the havoc wrought in Christendom by
the ravages of these pitiless invaders before their
conversion were repaired. Nor was this period
intellectually barren. "The Church," says Milman,
"did not entirely rely on fixing the infamy of
heretical doctrine upon the more daring reasoners.
She reasoned herself by her sons with equal vigour,
if with more submissiveness, sounded with her
antagonists the depths of metaphysical inquiry,
examined the inexhaustible processes of human
thought and language, till gradually the gigantic
bulwark of scholastic theology rose around the
Catholic doctrine." (Lat. Ch. Bk. VIII. c. v.)
And Milman was a writer who cannot be suspected
of any undue leaning towards Romanism.

It is much to be regretted that there are comparatively so few authentic records of the period

from 800 to 1200. There were no newspapers, no printed books, no Royal Commissions, or Parliamentary debates (if these last can be really regarded as sources of information). Men worked, and fought, and argued, and preached, and died, leaving no other record than a tombstone. Hence a large part of the criticism of the Dark Ages is too often mere generalization and declamation, representing rather the prejudice of the writer than the verdict of the scholar.

Perhaps the safest way to arrive at a just judgment of the Dark Ages will be to study some of the actual changes wrought in the condition of Europe during this epoch. Voltaire's traveller, wrecked, as he supposed, upon a desert island, was cheered by the sight of a gallows—to him a convincing proof that he was in a civilized country. In a less cynical spirit the student of history may see what actual modification of the condition of men was effected during the historic period under consideration. The age during which Westminster Abbey was built cannot have been architecturally blank. The men who built up the scholastic philosophy cannot have been wholly indifferent to learning and culture. The men who died in myriads on the plains of Syria to rescue the Holy Sepulchre can hardly have been devoid of love of Him who was laid there.

At the beginning of the ninth century the foundations of modern Europe had been laid. Three centuries earlier the Western Empire had perished before the incursions of the barbarians, and during the interval between the fall of the older Western Empire and its restoration under Charlemagne, the history of Europe had been an almost unbroken record of war, destruction, and ravage. The marvel is not that Christianity should have been wanting in enlightenment, but that the Christian Church survived those terrible centuries when Europe was thrown into the crucible. In the ninth century,

however, the storm of anarchy and ravage had
begun to abate. The genius of Charlemagne had
united under a single sceptre the whole Western
part of Continental Europe, including what is now
France, Germany, Northern Italy, and the Western
part of Austria. England, heretofore split up into
several small kingdoms, founded by the Angles and
Saxons, and for the most part engaged in constant
warfare, was united by Egbert in a single kingdom.
Here, as on the Continent, the ages preceding the
date which Maitland takes as the beginning of the
Dark Ages—A.D. 800—had been times of invasion,
ravage, and conquest. There can be no doubt that
the condition of England at the end of the eighth
century was far inferior in wealth and civilization to
the state in which it had been left at the withdrawal
of the Roman eagles. Almost every vestige of
civilization had perished under the attacks of the
Teutonic invaders. The work of founding a polity
and a civilization had to be recommenced, and this
is one of the salient facts to be borne in mind in
judging of the Dark Ages. The men of those ages
had to recreate the political and social world.
They had to rebuild almost from the foundation.
Not quite; for Christianity, the basis of European
civilization, had not only survived the storms of the
age of invasion, but had to a large extent converted
the barbarians themselves. In Spain, indeed, the
Moors were master from Gibraltar to the Pyrenees,
but, throughout the rest of Western Europe, Christianity was dominant. To take our own country.
When the Dark Ages began, the Heptarchy was
still standing ; when it closed, the conquest of
Ireland had begun. During the interval England
had been welded into a single kingdom, and the
main outlines of that Constitution, which has
survived in its chief features down to our own days,
had been formed. The Universities of Oxford and
Cambridge had been founded. A code of laws was
drawn up by Alfred the Great, and subsequently

revised by Edward the Confessor—the last English
king who obtained the honour of canonization. The
Irish schools had a high reputation for learning and
piety. These are only a few examples of the rapid
and solid progress of Christendom during the Dark
Ages.

Others will be found recorded in Maitland's work,
although the author's object may be said to be
critical rather than constructive, for Maitland was
one of those in whom the critical faculty existed
in its highest perfection, and his ecclesiastical
position enabled him to deal impartially with both
sides of his subject.

One of the points upon which there is a strong
contrast between our own times and the Dark Ages
is the greater degree of individualism in the latter.
We live in an age of machinery. Government is
carried on by Parliaments, ballots, caucuses—all
machinery. We travel by machinery and fight by
machinery. In the Dark Ages it was not so. It
was a time when men were governed by men. The
work that would nowadays be the platform of a
party was accomplished then by princes, such as
St. Louis of France, whom Hallam describes as
" perhaps the most eminent pattern of unswerving
probity and Christian strictness of conscience that
ever held the sceptre in any country." (" Middle
Ages," Vol. I., p. 40, 5th ed.) Whether the
majority of men were better off under personal rule
and simple civilization is a debatable question. It
is doubtful whether any more terrible example of
wide-spread suffering took place anywhere in the
Dark Ages than the Irish famine of 1848. It is
doubtful whether any population during the Dark
Ages lived in more bitter and hopeless misery than
do the sweated workers of East London. Civilization has done much for the few, but it is question-

able whether it has really benefited the many. Shelter, food, and clothing are the three great bodily wants of men, and the poorer classes in olden times were at least as well supplied with these in the Dark Ages as they are now. They had no votes, nor third class carriages, nor cheap newspapers, but they lived for the most part in the open country, not penned together like swine in huge cities. They had at least fresh air, and pure water, and healthful environment, which is more than can be said of the bulk of our city populations nowadays. Nor was their ignorance so deep as is commonly supposed. In those days faith was a vivid reality, and the confessional and the services of the Church in themselves constituted an education in that which is the most important of all knowledge—the knowledge how to live ;—and die.

On the whole, one is tempted to believe that the Dark Ages were not so very dark, nor our own times so very full of light as some of the authors criticized by Maitland would have us believe. Men lived simpler and rougher lives, but it does not follow that they led less happy ones. It is doubtful whether the influences of the nineteenth century do not tend to degrade men rather than to elevate them. "The individual withers, and the State is more and more." There is scant opportunity for prayer and repose in the restless, commonplace age in which we live. The whole atmosphere of the times is fatal to that spirit of faith which is the motive power of all real progress.

FREDERICK STOKES.

London, July 4, 1889.

PREFACE

FIRST EDITION.

NEARLY eight years have elapsed since the first of
the following essays was printed ; and they have all
been more than five years before the public.   I wish
the reader to be aware of this, not only because it
may account for some references to matters which
occurred during the period of their publication, but
because it will show that some things which may
wear that appearance, are not in reality allusions to
more recent occurrences.

My purpose in these essays, I stated very fully at
the outset ; and the collateral objects which I had in
view, I mentioned as occasion offered.   I need not,
therefore, here tell the reader over again what I
meant in writing them ; but I do not like that this
reprint should issue without a few words of distinct
statement as to what I did *not* mean.   It is *possible*
that I may have been misunderstood; though I
think that no one who fairly and candidly reads
these essays can imagine that I designed to hold
up to imitation what has, since I wrote them, been
much talked of as " the mediæval system."   As to
some superstitions and heresies, and a thousand
puerilities, which seem likely to creep into the
Church under that name, I do not feel it necessary
to say anything.   I have never, I hope, written a
line which the most ingenious perversion could

construe into a recommendation or even a toleration of them. But there is one great feature of the mediæval system of which I feel, and of which I have spoken, very differently, and in terms which may have been, though I can hardly think that they really have been, misunderstood.

It is quite impossible to touch the subject of MONASTICISM without rubbing off some of the dirt which has been heaped upon it. It is impossible to get even a superficial knowledge of the mediæval history of Europe, without seeing how greatly the world of that period was indebted to the Monastic Orders ; and feeling that, whether they were good or bad in other matters, Monasteries were beyond all price in those days of misrule and turbulence, as places where (it may be imperfectly, yet better than elsewhere) God was worshipped—as a quiet and religious refuge for helpless infancy and old age, a shelter of respectful sympathy for the orphan maiden and the desolate widow—as central points whence agriculture was to spread over bleak hills, and barren downs, and marshy plains, and deal bread to millions perishing with hunger and its pestilential train—as repositories of the learning which then was, and well-springs for the learning which was to be—as nurseries of art and science, giving the stimulus, the means, and the reward to invention, and aggregating around them every head that could devise, and every hand that could execute—as the nucleus of the city which in after-days of pride should crown its palaces and bulwarks with the towering cross of its cathedral.

This I think no man can deny. I believe it is true, and I love to think of it. I hope that I see the good hand of God in it, and the visible trace of His mercy that is over all His works. But if it is only a dream, however grateful, I shall be glad to be awakened from it ; not indeed by the yelling of illiterate agitators, but by a quiet and sober proof that I have misunderstood the matter. In the meantime, let me thankfully believe that thousands of the persons at whom Robertson, and Jortin, and other such very miserable second-hand writers, have sneered, were men of enlarged minds, purified affections, and holy lives—that they were justly reverenced by men—and, above all, favourably accepted by God, and distinguished by the highest honour which He vouchsafes to those whom He has called into existence, that of being the channels of His love and mercy to their fellow-creatures.

But admitting all this, does it form any reason why we should endeavour to revive the monastic system in the present day, and in this country? This is a thing which has been very seriously proposed, and for which much that is specious may be said, without any violation of truth or fairness. But is it a proposition which should be listened to? Is it, in fact, one that *can* be carried into effect? Many others have, I suppose, as well as myself, received a circular letter, bearing no name, but supposed to emanate from persons entitled to respect,[1] and headed " Revival of monastic and conventual institutions on a plan adapted to the exigencies of the reformed Catholic Church in England."

After a brief statement of what are considered as the objects, the means, and the constitution, the writer proceeds to say, ",It is hoped and earnestly requested that the friends of primitive piety, order, and simplicity, into whose hands this paper may

---

[1] [It certainly was on this supposition that I wrote the observations in the text. The truth is that a mistake arose from an erroneous judgment respecting the handwriting of a document. I do not mean to insinuate, for I really do not believe, that any deception was intended. Neither do I pretend to say from what quarter the letters did emanate. Having, however, been led by the mistake to say what I did, and seeing no reason for retracting it, I let the observations remain, not without an impression that some things which have happened since they were published, may have tended to manifest their truth.—*Note to Third Ed.*]

fall, will contribute their thoughts and endeavours towards expanding these hints, and devising some method of bringing them to a practical issue." No channel for the contribution of thoughts is, however, pointed out : but, for the reason which I have already stated, I wish to say something on the subject; and I will take the opportunity of offering some which have occurred to me; and I venture to hope, that, being fully convinced that the suggestion cannot be brought to any good " practical issue," I may be allowed to say so plainly, and without offence. I have no wish to dogmatize on the subject, but on the other hand, I know not how to speak of it with doubt or hesitation, and therefore wish to say, as decidedly as may be lawful, that the " monastic and conventual system" never can be adapted to meet the present exigencies of the Church of England ; and that any attempt to revive that system in this time and country, can only prove a sad and mischievous failure.

When I say this, I do not mean to dispute that it would be easy to make a plan and raise money for the building, and even for the endowment, of a monastery and to settle all the details on paper ; or to deny that a sufficient number of very good men might be found to inhabit it, on such terms as those who might have the settling of the matter would venture to propose. A few such institutions might, we may believe, be founded, and carried on for a longer or a shorter period. There is such variety in the minds and feelings of men, that such a scheme (indeed *any* scheme that had so much of both antiquity and novelty to recommend it) would immediately find supporters enough to keep it up for some little time, and a fresh supply of others to keep it up for some little time longer.

But even this must be done by " adaptation," as will be seen by the heading of the letter which I have quoted ; or according to the language used in the body of that document, the proposal is for the " Revival of the Monastic and Conventual System *in a form* suited to the genius, character, and exigencies of the Church of England." But really this is (to use plain terms, which I hope will not offend, for I know of no others to express my meaning) mere playing at monkery; if not quite like children playing at soldiers, yet something not much beyond the customary show and service of our rural militia. Anything like *real* monasticism, anything for which the use of such terms as " THE MONASTIC AND CONVENTUAL SYSTEM " is not a most unwarrantable and delusive usurpation, anything really calculated to produce its advantages, such as they were, or even such of them as are wanted or could be desired, in these days—an attempt to revive anything that can fairly be called the Monastic and Conventual System, on a scale of any magnitude and permanence, must, I think, fail, for want of one great thing—that thing on which, by the Divine appointment, it flourished, while it did flourish, as truly as man lives by the air he breathes—namely, that concurrence of men's minds which forming what is called the Spirit of the Age wants, desires, imagines, carries forward its own schemes, irresistibly bears down opposition, creates, protects, uses, and then, in its progress neglects, disowns, and tramples down its old institutions, and knows no use in their ruins but to furnish quarries or foundations for new ones.

It seems to me that we can no more revive the Monastic System than the Feudal System. We cannot recall the days of ancient republicanism, or mediæval chivalry. The French republic was tragic enough; but who does not feel,—who, except the lowest and weakest of the wretches whom it was meant to impose on, did not feel at the time,—that all its archaism was purely farcical ? Why could not the French have what Greece and Rome had had, if they liked ? Simply for the same reason that it could not be dealt with as a matter of solemn propriety, if the Duke of Wellington should go down to the house in complete armour, or if Julius Cæsar should tread the stage in a field-marshal's uniform.

And why cannot we have tournaments as our forefathers had ? Why was the attempt to hold one, a
few years ago, so laughed at that the experiment has
not been repeated ? Why is that ridiculous now,
which was honourable and almost sacred four
hundred years ago ? Why may not our nobles
amuse themselves as their ancestors did, without
being laughed at ? I am not expressing any wish
for the revival of such a pastime ; but merely asking
why the attempt to revive it is considered as actually
absurd, and whether it is because the thing itself is
so very much less dignified and worthy of great men,
and so very much more ridiculous in itself than a
horse-race, a fox-hunt, or a steeple-chase.

I shall be told that the state of society is so different.
I know it. It is just what I am saying. Why it
should differ, and differ in that particular way, are
questions not so easily answered. Nor is it my
present business to attempt any answer to them. It
is more to the purpose to offer one or two reasons
for believing, that the altered state of society renders
the revival of monasticism altogether impracticable.

Do what he may, no man can strip himself of the
circumstances, and concomitants, which it has pleased
God to place around him. He may say, "I will be a
monk;" and he may call himself, and get others to
call him by the name ; but if he says, "I will be a
monk of the *fourth* century," or "a monk of the
twelfth century," we can only assure him that he is
mistaken, that the thing is impossible, and that if he is
a monk at all nowadays, it must be of the *nineteenth*
century. I am not speaking of either one of those
centuries as better or worse than the others, but only
mean that whatever character he may assume, he
must take it in his own circumstances. They may
be friendly or hostile ; and, as it relates to the case
now under consideration, they may be in the Church
or in the world ; in Christians or infidels ; in others,
whoever and whatever they may be, or in himself,
such as he is naturally, or such as he has been made

by education and habit: and nothing can be more
clear than that any man, whether young or old,
whether lay or clerical, a nobleman or tradesman, a
soldier or sailor, a peasant or mechanic, a man rich
or poor, single or married, who is now living in
England, is, both as to externals, and as to the
modification of himself, in very different circumstances from those in which he could have been
placed, had he lived in the same character and station
in the fourth or in the twelfth century. And for the
English monk of the nineteenth century, there seem
to be some peculiar obstacles. They may exist, and
in some degree, more or less, they certainly do exist,
in some other parts of Christendom, but they are
particularly obvious and powerful in this country.

In the first place, consider how completely, and by
what means, the monastic system has been put down
in England. There is no need to enter into the
matter of motives or proofs. The fact, which is all
that we want, is, that popular indignation and hatred
of the bitterest kind was excited, and has been
studiously kept up, and that for centuries the
general notion in this country has been that a
monastery naturally, almost necessarily, is a place
dedicated to idleness, gluttony, lewdness, hypocrisy,
political intrigue, fraud, treachery, and blood; so
that, as a matter of course, a nun is to be supposed
something as bad as can be, and a monk no better.
Now, certainly, no candid man will deny, that before
the period of the Reformation, the monastic system
in the Western Church had got into a very bad
state. Too many monasteries were really societies
of dissolute men; and a vast many more had so far
departed from their bounden discipline that there
was nothing to restrain the vicious. That is, the
monks lived in them under scarcely, if any, more
control from vice than fellows of colleges do now.
That under these circumstances, in a dissolute age,
a great number of monks became profane and
debauched, and a great many more secular and

careless of religion, is not to be doubted; but that there ever was truth in the coarse and filthy abuse heaped upon the monastic order as a body by some who were forward in the business of the Reformation, is what I suppose never was believed by anyone who had a moderate knowledge of facts. The truth perhaps is, and it is such as should satisfy all but the infidel and profane, that if we take any period whatever in the history of Christianity, and compare the morals of the monks and clergy with those of the laity, we shall find that, however bad the former might be, the latter were worse. In fact, it appears to be the testimony of history, that the monks and clergy, whether bad or good in themselves, were in all times and places better than other people.

Be this as it may, however, the point with which we are concerned is, that this odium, just or unjust, does exist, and would form an obstacle to the revival of monastic institutions in this country. There are, perhaps, some lively young men who would reply, "We should like it all the better. We should enjoy being persecuted, especially as nobody would venture to harm us in life, or limb, or property, to burn us up as the Danes did, or sell us up as Henry VIII. did, or hang us up as Elizabeth did; and we should go about with shaved crowns and rope-girdles, and people would look at us, and come to hear us intone from our lecterns." Of this, one can only say, that in such hands the matter would soon be laughed out of countenance. But others, who deserve more respectful consideration, may tell us that we are not to truckle to the spirit of the age, but to do that which is right. That is plain enough, and I trust that no one will imagine that I am recommending a servile obsequiousness to popular notions and feelings. Of course we are not to shrink from duties, to compromise principles, to adopt or renounce doctrines or practices in mere compliment to the irreligious—but there is no need to repeat the string of truisms which are not only obvious to

common sense, and instinctively felt by common
honesty, but which must be familiar to most
readers, as being perpetually in the mouths of those
who are conscious that they are proposing or practising what the great body of the Church may deem
eccentric or absurd.

But these truisms are inapplicable to the matter
in hand, which involves no fulfilment or breach of
any law human or divine. And in such a case it is
a matter of wisdom and duty, and, practically
speaking, of absolute necessity, to take into account
the state of thought and feeling in which the great
body of the Church has been brought up and exists.
If any man is fully satisfied that there is a divine
command, or a human law, by which he is bound to
build a monastery and carry on monasticism, let
him pursue his convictions, without troubling himself about the consequences. Or if he thinks that,
though there may have been no command on the subject, yet, having developed itself, monasticism must
be an essential and permanent part of the divine dispensation, I should not wish to discuss what appears
to me so entirely unreasonable, and so incapable of
being even approached in argument without the
settlement of many previous questions. But those
who believe with me that different states of society
may render specific institutions, forming no part of
the Church, though more or less connected with it,
useful at one time, noxious at another, and incapable
of existence at a third, I would beg to consider one
or two features of the present time, as compared
with the middle ages.

In the first place, as it regards *vows* of any kind.
I do not know whether, among the advocates for
the revival of Monasticism, there are any who would
maintain them; but in the letter to which I have
alluded they are fairly abandoned. In the adapted
form there are to be " no vows; but a solemn
declaration and engagement of obedience to the
Superior, and of compliance with the rules of the

Institution during residence." But this seems to
be in fact giving up the whole thing. Surely no
one who has at all considered the system of Monasticism, can doubt that the vow of perpetual self-
dedication was the very root of the matter. The
reserved power of change, even if encumbered with
difficulties, would alter the whole thing. The
monastic vow necessarily operates in two ways.
First, in making all but the most thoughtless careful how they enter upon such a mode of life; and
secondly, by making those who have taken it con-
tented with a condition which they know to be
unalterable, and in which, whatever other schemes
of life may occur to their imagination as brighter
than their own, they remain peacefully and cheerfully, because that very circumstance of perpetual
obligation has given it somewhat the character of a
divine dispensation. It is very well for political
agitators, and makers of fancy tales, to tell us of
raging monks and pining nuns, gnawing the chains
of their spiritual bondage, because they were either
in love commonly so called, or in love with the
vanities of the world,—as if such persons, with very
few exceptions, would not fairly run away, vow or
no vow—but it is no part of human nature to be
rendered permanently unhappy by unalterable dispensations. Generally men and women are satisfied
with the sex, and the stature, assigned to them,
and do not think of making themselves miserable
about the circumstances of native country, parentage, or anything else which, they know, *cannot* be
altered.

But the matter may be illustrated by a case in
which a vow of perpetual obligation remains among
us in the present day. No one can doubt that it
would make a difference scarcely to be imagined if
the marriage vow, instead of being perpetual and
irrevocable, were only a " solemn declaration " that
the parties would conduct themselves properly so
long as they should see fit to continue man and

wife. I do not mean merely that many unhappy marriages would be dissolved, and many unequally-yoked persons set at liberty, for it would certainly operate something far beyond this, and of quite a different nature. Thousands who are now living happily together, and who, if they ever thought of such a thing as separation, would consider it one of the greatest evils that could happen to them, would become unsettled, would be led to speculate, and tempted to experiment; the *possibility* would be present to their own minds, or perpetually suggested by others; a cross word or an angry look would be followed by divorce, and a state of things would follow, plainly showing that if the name of marriage was retained, its nature was changed, and its chief benefits were lost. I am not saying that the monastic vow was a good thing, or that those who took it did right; but, that without it the system could not have existed; and also, that without it neither the system, nor anything really like it, can be now established.

But there are, moreover, two particulars in the character assumed by the vow in question, which are strongly against its revival in the present age. In the early days of monasticism, a person self-devoted by a vow to a life of celibacy was *on that account* looked up to with respect. But the *vow*, which was then in itself a ground of reverence, would in the present day expose any men or women who should be known to have taken it, to the suspicion, or the remonstrance, or the ridicule, not merely of the frivolous and thoughtless, but of nine out of ten of those whom they were brought up to love and honour, and to whom they were bound by every tie of affection and respect. And it must surely make some difference in the working of a system, whether those who adopt it become objects of esteem and veneration, or of contempt and suspicion. There may be those who would answer as before, that persecution from anybody would be delight-

ful ; but, beside other reasons for taking courage,
we may comfort ourselves with the hope that they
are not sufficiently numerous to fill more than one
or two monasteries at the utmost, and that only for
a very little while.

For let us just look at another point—the monastic vow was one of obedience ; and in the proposed
adaptation there are to be " no vows ; but a solemn
declaration and engagement of *obedience to the
Superior*, and of compliance with the rules of the
Institution during residence." But what are we to
understand by " obedience to the Superior " in this
revived monastic system ? Is it, for instance, to be
such as the Rule of St. Benedict required ? The
reader may see what that was in a following page.[2]

---

[2] See p. 190. No. 60.—The original of it is " Præceptis Abbatis
in omnibus obedire, etiam si ipse aliter (quod absit) agat memores
illud Dominicum præceptum, Quæ dicunt, facite : quæ autem
faciunt, facere nolite."—*Cap.* iv. There is, indeed, in this Rule
such a plain statement of the doctrine of passive obedience and
non-resistance as would appear perfectly ridiculous in the present
day. What would those who talk most about obedience say to
such passages as these : " Primus humilitatis gradus, est obedientia *sine mora*. Hæc convenit his, qui nihil sibi a Christo carius
aliquid existimant propter servitium sanctum quod professi sunt,
seu propter metum gehennæ, vel gloriam vitæ æternæ ; *mox ut
aliquid imperatum a majore fuerit, ac si divinitus imperetur, moram
pati nesciunt in faciendo*." . . . " Sed hæc ipsa obedientia tunc
acceptabilis erit Deo, et dulcis hominibus, si, quod jubetur, non
trepide, non tarde, non tepide, aut cum murmure, vel cum responso
nolentis efficiatur : quia *obedientia quæ majoribus præbetur, Deo
exhibetur.*"— *Cap.* v. And this was to extend, not merely to
things specifically mentioned in statutes or Acts of Parliament, nor
yet merely to things reasonable in themselves, but to such things
as were grievous, and even impossible. The LXVIII. chapter is
headed " Si fratri impossibilia injungantur ;" and it is as follows :
" Si cui fratri aliqua forte gravia aut impossibilia injunguntur ;
suscipiat quidem jubentis imperium, cum omni mansuetudine et
obedientia. Quod si omnino virium suarum mensuram viderit
pondus oneris excedere ; impossibilitatis suæ causas ei, qui sibi
præest, patienter et opportune suggerat, non superbiendo aut
resistendo vel contradicendo. Quod si post suggestionem suam
in sua sententia Prioris imperium perduraverit, sciat junior ita
sibi expedire, et ex caritate confidens de adjutorio Dei, OBEDIAT."
Nor was this obedience to be confined to the Abbot : " Obedientiæ

Nothing of that sort, I suppose, can be intended in this enlightened country; and I am led by the disputes which I have heard for many years past respecting canonical obedience to our Bishops, to doubt whether the talk of obedience has any real meaning. I am afraid that in the present day nothing will give such a Superior *power*, except law or money; and that only the latter will procure for him anything which can properly be called *obedience*. In the former of these cases, where power is given by law, the obedience will be rendered to the law, and in no sense whatever to the Superior. If he has an Act of Parliament hanging in his cell, constituting and appointing him Ruler over certain persons named in the schedule A annexed, according to certain regulations set out in schedule B annexed, those certain persons must obey (whether *him*, or the *law*, is perhaps of no great consequence) so far as the law goes; but beyond that the Superior has no power. On the other hand, something further may perhaps be procured for him in the way of obedience, by money. I do not mean what lawyers call " monies numbered," paid down in pence by the Superior to the monks for capping him, or doing what he bids; but money's worth, provided by the expense of money. There may be endowments such as will (according to the familiar phrase) make it worth men's while—worth the while of men nursed up in sensitive independ-

bonum non solum Abbati exhibendum est ab omnibus : sed etiam sibi invicem ita obediant fratres, scientes se per hanc obedientiæ viam ituros ad Deum. . . . Si quis autem Frater pro quavis minima causa ab Abbate, vel a quocumque Priore suo corripiatur quolibet modo ; vel si leviter senserit animum Prioris cujuscumque contra se iratum, vel commotum, quamvis modice ; *mox sine mora tamdiu prostratus in terra ante pedes ejus jaceat* satisfaciens, usque dum benedictione sanetur illa commotio."—*Cap.* lxxi. I do not know whether it is proposed to revive anything like this ; but without it, how could the monasteries of the dark ages have been what they were ? In fact, what did they become as this spirit of submission, now lost in that of jealous independence, was gradually subsiding ?

ence—to put up, at least for a time, with the
degradation and annoyance of submission; or it
may give a lift in society, smooth the way to holy
orders, or more probably to a sectarian ministry;
or it may hold out various other advantages which
it is easy to imagine. But whatever they may be,
the obedience thus purchased will be of little value,
and the mode by which it is obtained will considerably qualify the nature of the society. It must, I
suppose, consist chiefly of those to whom such
advantages are an object; perhaps entirely, for men
of higher motives may not like that sort of constant
association, and close fellowship, with the sordid and
scheming.

There is, I repeat, a want of power; a want
which it is in the present day impossible to meet by
any legitimate and reasonable means. How is it
attempted in the plan to which I have so repeatedly
alluded? The author of it seems to have been
conscious that the Superior would be in rather a
helpless predicament, and to have thought that as
he could not be magnified, he should be multiplied.
I am afraid I shall hardly be believed, when I say
that under the head of "VISITATION," we are told
that the proposed monasteries are to be visited,
"monthly by the Parochial Minister, quarterly by
the Rural Dean, half-yearly by the Archdeacon,
yearly by the Bishop." I fear there would be
"many masters." Will the reader be so good as
to imagine monasteries in the parish, rural deanery,
archdeaconry, and diocese, in which he lives and
some three or four others which he may happen to
know—to consider the probabilities—and charitably
keep them to himself?

But let us look at the matter on a broader scale.
It must be obvious to everyone who has reflected on
the subject, that the progress of modern society—
particularly English society—has been most decidedly against the possibility of reviving any institution in which men should live together in common.

The way of living in this country has long been receding more and more from anything like cœnobitic life; and has been characterized by an increasing tendency to independence, individualization, and (to use the words in a mild sense) the dissociation and disconnection of men. It will be remembered that I am not speaking of parties political or religious, or of joint-stock companies, but of the habits of domestic life. How will these prepare men for the *Refectory?* There is now no such thing as " the Meeting of Gallants at the Ordinarye," although such common tables " were long the universal resort of gentlemen;"[3] and indeed of all classes of society in England, as they still are in other countries of Europe. But the most striking illustration is furnished by the principal clubs which have been instituted in London within about twenty years. Most of them have some distinguishing character; the Athenæum, for instance, as a literary club, the Carlton a political one, and in some others the name is a sufficient indication, as the United Service, the Junior United Service, the Travellers', the United University, the Oxford and Cambridge, the Reform. We may in all these cases imagine some degree of sympathy and congruity among the members of each club. At least, we may safely say, what is still more to our purpose, than an immense majority of members have at some time or other been used to eat what are significantly called "commons," in the hall of a College, or an Inn of Court, or at a Naval or Military mess-table. And

---

[3] I borrow these words from Nares, who places the word Ordinary in his Glossary with some apology on account of its not having *quite* fallen into actual disuse. Perhaps every year since his book was published has given it a greater right to be included among the " words, phrases, and names " which, as his title page states, " have been thought to require illustration." It means, he tells us, " A public dinner, where each person pays his share. The word, in this sense, is certainly not obsolete; but it is here inserted for the sake of observing, that ordinaries were long the universal resort of gentlemen, particularly in the reign of James I."

yet I am informed that in only one of the institutions which I have mentioned is there anything in
the nature of a *table d'hôte* ; and that in that one it
is only a recent experiment, of which it still remains
to be seen whether it will succeed, or whether, like
similar attempts in other clubs, it must be abandoned.   So totally different is the usual course of
things, that half a dozen gentlemen, it may be, are
sitting together until the moment at which each
has put down his name to dine on a particular joint ;
when it is ready, they go into another room, separate
to six different tables, and the ambulatory joint
seeks them out in their independent establishments,
while each is not supposed to know of even the
existence of the other five.   Perhaps it would not
be too much to say that, in the clubs which I have
named, nearly a hundred thousand dinners (to say
nothing of other meals) are annually served ; and
to add, that though eaten (as it regards each club)
in the same room, and in company, yet nine out of
ten are single, not to say solitary meals.[4]

I am not finding fault with this.   I shall probably be told that it is much the best way ; that it
does not arise from any want of good feeling, but
that it is found to be, on the whole, much more
pleasant,—" you are more independent."   I really
do not mean to contradict this, or to argue about
the comparative merits of the present, and any
former, system.   I am only stating a fact, and that
only as an illustration ; but I say that such a fact,

---

[4] I do not know how far it might be right to consider the
details of any one of the Institutions which I have named, as forming a ground for precise calculation respecting the others.   But
nothing of that sort is here required ; and though (as I suspect)
the following statement may exhibit proportions in a trifling
degree more favourable to my argument, than would be furnished
from some of the clubs which I have named, yet I think it will
show the reader that I have not on the whole exaggerated.   In
the month of June, 1843, the number of dinners served at the
Athenæum was 1,457, of which all but 36 were single.   Of the
latter, 30 were served to two persons, five to three, and one to
four.

or its cause, whatever that may be, is something much in the way of any attempt to revive cœnobitic life. And if the habits in which the present generation have been educated, have drifted them so far away from the refectory, is it worth while to waste a word about the dormitory? I will, therefore, here only ask the reader to reflect on these two very important points, and to draw out, for his own consideration, the details respecting them; unless indeed he should feel that he cannot do that until he knows from what class of society, or whether from all classes indiscriminately, the monks are to be taken; and on this point I am not at present able to give him any satisfactory information, being extremely puzzled about it myself.

I hope I have convinced the reader that whether the revival of Monasticism be practicable or impracticable, good or bad, I am no advocate for it; and having said perhaps more than enough to vindicate myself from the suspicion of any such design in the following Essays, will he indulge me in the further egotism of saying a very few words about the Essays themselves? They were originally published in the "British Magazine," between the months of March, 1835, and February, 1838. They were written at the request of my most dear, and honoured, and deeply-lamented friend, the Rev. Hugh James Rose, who was then, as he had been from its beginning, the editor of that work. After receiving the first, he wrote to me that he should "fully rely on a perennial, or, rather, *permensal* supply." I mention this, because, under the impression which it created, I was anxious that, throughout the whole series, whenever a paper appeared, another should be sent in time for the next number. In fact, the first thirteen were printed with no intermission; and though of course I do not mean that I had each month to begin the collection of materials *de novo*, yet the arrangement of raw materials is a work which takes some time and trouble, generally more than one expects, and which if it is hurried is likely to be ill-done. Some of the papers were written under disadvantages from want of health and leisure, and all without the help which many books, not within my reach at Gloucester, would have afforded. But chiefly they were written under that great disadvantage of anxiety to furnish a certain quantity, and only a certain quantity, by a given time, and therefore feeling obliged to select, and abridge, and condense, and cut up, and piece together, and omit, and copy over again hastily, and, in short, do all the things which were likely to present unfavourably, materials which I was sure were interesting in themselves. Such circumstances impress an indelible character on a work, which no subsequent labour can remove; but the reader may view it with more indulgence if he considers it as belonging to essays written under the disadvantages which I have described, and published in the pages of a monthly periodical work. I need scarcely add that, though printed much more accurately than I could have expected, such a mode of publishing such materials, of a great part of which I had no opportunity of correcting the press, ensured many typographical errors. Some, I fear, must have escaped, but I hope that the greater part are corrected.

ADVERTISEMENT

TO THE

THIRD EDITION.

———

THESE Essays have been again reprinted with very slight alteration. The little additions made in the two more recent editions, in the form of Notes, may be had separately by those who have the First edition.

THE DARK AGES.

No. I.

"I know nothing of those ages which knew nothing."

I REALLY forget to which of two eminent wits this
saying belongs; but I have often thought that I
should have liked to ask him how he came to know
so curious and important a fact respecting ages of
which he knew nothing. Was it merely by hear-
say?

Everybody allows, however, that they were *dark*
ages. Certainly; but what do we mean by darkness? Is not the term, as it is generally used, comparative? Suppose I were to say that I am writing
"in a little *dark* room," would you understand me
to mean that I could not see the paper before me?
Or if I should say that I was writing "on a *dark*
day," would you think I meant that the sun had not
risen by noon? Well, then, let me beg you to
remember this, when you and I use the term, *dark*
ages. I am sorry to waste time about words; but
it is so important that people should fully understand one another, and the sooner the better, that I
must just notice another point. Do we always
clearly know what we should understand — or,
indeed, what we mean to express—when we hear or
talk of the *dark* ages? Do we mean ages which
were dark in themselves, and with respect to those
who lived in them? Or, do we mean that they are

dark to us, and that it is very difficult for us to form a clear idea of them? I suppose that we sometimes mean one and sometimes the other, and very frequently both—and, in fact, both are true; but it is better not to confound the two ideas, which are in themselves perfectly distinct.

Many causes—of some of which I hope to speak hereafter—have concurred to render those ages very dark to us; but, for the present, I feel it sufficient to remind the reader, that darkness is quite a different thing from shutting the eyes; and that we have no right to complain that we can see but little until we have used due diligence to see what we can.

As to the other point—that is, as to the degree of darkness in which those ages were really involved, and as to the mode and degree in which it affected those who lived in them, I must express my belief, that it has been a good deal exaggerated. There is no doubt that those who lived in what are generally called the "middle" or the "dark" ages, knew nothing of many things which are familiar to us, and which we deem essential to our comfort, and almost to our existence; but still I doubt whether, even in this point of view, they were so entirely dark as some would have us suppose. I dare say you have observed, that, in a certain state of twilight, as soon as you have lighted only a taper in your chamber, it seems quite dark out of doors. Yet, perhaps, you have only just come into the house out of that which, if not broad day-light, was nevertheless such good serviceable twilight as that, while you were in it, you never once thought of darkness, or of losing your way, or not being able to see what you were about; yet, I say, as soon as ever you lighted, were it only a rushlight, in your chamber, all the look-out was darkness. Were you ever so misled as to open the window, and tell the people in the road that they would certainly lose their way, and break their shins—nay, even to condole with, or triumph over, those inevitable consequences of their wandering about in pitch-darkness ? I very much doubt it; if you had attempted it, I feel quite confident that, if from being at a loss for an exordium, or for any other reason, you had been obliged to wait with your head out at window until your eyes had recovered from the glare of your own little candle, you would have seen that there was *some* light abroad—you would have begun to distinguish houses, and highways, and sober people going about their business in a way which showed that they could see enough for common purposes—and you would have held your tongue and drawn in your head, rather pleased that you had not exposed yourself.

Certain it is that we are lighted up, and every man who struts about in our gas light can see that it is dark out of doors ; and, to bring him to anything like a right understanding of the case—not to prove to him that it is as light out of doors as in, for I beg the reader not to suspect me of any such folly—to bring him, I say, to a right understanding of the case, he must put his head out, and keep it out for some time. "What then," says the reader, "are we to do ? Can he mean that one is to wade through all the stuff that was written in the middle ages?" Certainly not; for, in the first place, a good deal of it (and, I suspect, much of what would be most interesting) is not known to be in existence. I say *known*, because who can take upon himself to say what is extant ? A good deal has been printed ; and, as to MSS., we know that there are a good many unpublished in the British Museum, the Bodleian, and other libraries of our kingdom; and I suppose that everybody who has the privilege of using those collections, or the King of France's, and a thousand others, can find out specifically what manuscripts they contain. Some, I suppose, know what is in the Vatican, and in other of the less open libraries ; but who knows what may be lurking up and down Christendom? Who knows what was hastily swept together when the libraries of suppressed monasteries, in some of the less frequented parts of Europe, were accumulated in large collections, without, perhaps, a full investigation of some of their less obvious and intelligible contents? Perhaps I underrate the pains that may have been bestowed on them; but the idea has been strongly impressed on my mind since I was, some time ago, in the midst of a collection drawn from such sources, in which the manuscripts alone amounted to sixty thousand. I cannot help thinking that a more thorough investigation of such collections may one day bring to light much that is not supposed to exist. But I am running on too fast; and all that was necessary was to assure the reader that, so far from requiring him to read all the works which were written in those ages, I by no means require him to read one-half of such of them as have been printed since; but by putting your head into the darkness, good reader, I do mean that you must, in some degree, make yourself acquainted with the original writers of the period. I have heard of a traveller at an inn, who wished to look out and see if it was day; and who returned to bed with a very wrong judgment on the matter, owing to his being in the dark himself, whereby he was led to open the glass door of a cupboard, instead of a window; and I must say, that, in trusting to the representations of some popular writers, you will be doing much the same thing.

This is a strong assertion; and it is one which I would not make if I were not fully prepared to defend it by sufficient examples, which I hope to give in subsequent papers. And, now I think of it, the reader may, perhaps, desire some account of my plan: and I shall be very glad to take the opportunity of assuring him that I have no plan whatsoever—that I do most absolutely and entirely disclaim everything of the sort—and that I would

rather put this very pen into the fire, than undertake to draw out a plan and keep to it in such a
matter as this must needs be.   I wish this to be
understood at the outset, that the reader may not
charge me with digressing—a thing to which I am
exceedingly prone, whenever restriction makes it
practicable.   For, to say the truth, I have seldom
taken much trouble to find any one thing, that I was
not rewarded by finding at least two or three which
I was not looking for ; and I cannot help digressing
myself, and wishing to carry the reader along with
me, when anything turns up which interests me,
and which I think may amuse or instruct others.

But while I thus disclaim all *plan*, let me say,
that I do not write without *purpose;* and this
purpose I wish to be fully understood.   It is to
furnish some materials towards forming a right
judgment of the real state of learning, knowledge,
and literature during the dark ages.   The *period*
which I have more particularly in view is that
extending from A.D. 800 to A.D. 1200; and to this
period I wish the reader to apply any general statement or remark which I may offer respecting the
dark or middle ages.   At the same time, I do not
consider myself as restricted to that precise period,
or precluded from adducing proofs or illustrations
which may be somewhat more ancient or modern.
The subject I have endeavoured to state in terms as
comprehensive as possible, by saying, " learning,
knowledge, and literature;" for I did not know how
else to include the variety of miscellaneous matter
into which it is my purpose to inquire, or which,
having incidentally met with it in such inquiries,
has appeared to me worthy of notice.   It will not,
however, be understood that I am pretending to
write a literary history of that period.   All that I
propose in these papers is, to bring forward some
facts illustrative of the points already mentioned.
For this reason a great part of the inquiry will, of
course, turn on *books ;* and I consider nothing

relating to them as foreign to my purpose, which includes any notices that may throw light upon their number, value, and materials—the means employed by proprietors, librarians, and scribes for their multiplication, correction, embellishment, and preservation—any hints tending to show what books were most in request—any notices of the love of books, or of the sale, loan, or gift of them—of the means employed to qualify or cause people to read them—anything in the shape of catalogues of libraries, or collections of books, during that period.

This looks so fine now I have put it on paper, that I must again beg the reader to understand that I am as far as possible from pretending to give a full account of these matters ; but I think that by bringing together and offering to notice some hints which lie scattered in various writers of those times, I may—I do not say enable him to form, but—assist him in forming an estimate of the learning, know-ledge, and literature of the dark ages ; and on this point I will only add, that though he may probably find (and if so, I hope pardon) some errors and mistakes, yet he may rely on my never intention-ally copying a reference—that is, whenever I give a reference he will understand (unless the contrary is stated) that I copy immediately from the book to which I refer. Those who have had any practice in verifying quotations will know what I mean, and I believe that they will have found reason to join me in wishing that all authors, great and small, would do the same.

It must be obvious to everyone who has any acquaintance whatever with the subject, that the learning respecting which I inquire was chiefly sacred or ecclesiastical—this, I say, is obvious as a matter of fact; but I wish it to be distinctly under-stood, that it is particularly with a view to such learning that I now offer these desultory notices to the public. My object is to inquire what know-ledge, and what means of knowledge, the Christian

Church actually had during the dark ages, and what was, in fact, the real state of the Church on these points during that period. All which does not *directly* tend to this is purely incidental, and is admitted with a view to another object in which I feel deeply interested—the promotion of the study of ecclesiastical history.

There is no difficulty in knowing where to begin, for before we can think of building, we must clear away the rubbish—or, to recur to the figure which I have already used, before we can possibly look out of the window, we must open the shutters ; for, if we only go to " windows that exclude the light," we might as well keep our eyes shut. I feel it necessary to do this, because statements extremely false have been handed about from one popular writer to another, and it is quite impossible to form any correct opinion on the subject without knowing that they are false. At the same time I cannot persuade myself to begin the business without begging the reader not to consider me as the advocate of ignorance, superstition, and error—not to suppose that I wish to hold up the dark ages as golden ages—not to think that I undervalue the real improvements which have been made in learning and science. I do not want to maintain any such silly paradox ; but I do want to contradict falsehood, and to bate down exaggeration into at least something like truth. Indeed, I cannot help wishing that the reader who has formed his idea of the dark ages only from some modern popular writers—I do not mean those who have written professedly on the subject—could be at once fairly thrown back into the midst of them. I cannot help thinking that he would feel very much as I did the first time that I found myself in a foreign country. A thousand novelties attracted my attention ; many were strange, and some displeasing ; and there was more or less that seemed foreign in everything. For this I was prepared ; but I was not prepared

for another feeling which very soon, and quite unexpectedly, sprung up in my mind—"How much is
different, and, go where I may, for ever changing!
True; but how much is the same everywhere!"
It was almost a surprise to me to find that the sun
and moon went on much the same way as at home
—that there were roads, and rivers, and fields, and
woods, and towns, and cities, and streets, and
houses filled with people who might, perhaps, talk
some other language, and dress in some other
fashion from mine, but who had evidently much the
same notions as to the necessaries of life, and the
substantials of society; and, without losing all my
pride, or patriotism, or prejudice, I got a new idea
of the unity of nature.   I felt that He had "made
of one blood all nations of men for to dwell on all
the face of the earth"—it brought with it a kind
of home-feeling—a sense that, wherever I wandered,
I was but moving in the hollow of His hand among
my own brethren.

Well, and these old folks of the dark ages were
our grandfathers and grandmothers; and, in a good
many points, vastly like ourselves, though we may
not at first see the resemblance in the few smoky
family pictures which have come down to us; but
had they "not eyes?" had they "not hands,
organs, dimensions, senses, affections, passions—
fed with the same food, hurt with the same
weapons, subject to the same diseases, healed
by the same means, warmed and cooled by the
same winter and summer" as we are? "Yes;
but they knew nothing." Well, then, it is
strange to think how they could do and say so
much as they did without any knowledge. But
you do not mean quite *nothing*—you will allow
that they knew the *Pater-noster* and *Credo*, and that
is *something*—nay, a good deal, in itself, and the
pledge of a great deal more.

No. II.

" ' Amongst so many Bishops,' says Fleury, ' there was not one critic, who knew how to discern true from false Records '— Critic ! quoth he. It is well if there was one amongst them who could write his own name."—JORTIN.

I HAVE said, that the state of things during the dark ages has been misrepresented by some popular writers ; and also that, in making that charge, I did not mean to reflect on those who had professedly written on those times. Indeed, as far as I know, the opinions of men in general on the subject are less frequently formed from these writers, than from those who, having obtained popularity on some other grounds, treat incidentally of the subject, or here and there give a passing sneer to the dark ages. Few books have been more popular, or more generally read by thousands who never thought of asking for authorities, than Robertson's " History of Charles the Fifth ; " and, perhaps, I cannot do better than take some proofs and illustrations of what I have said from that work. Some remarks on his statements may not only tend to obviate those prejudices which have been raised by him, and by other writers, but may also furnish a sort of introduction absolutely required by those who have not given any attention to the subject.

In his " View of the Progress of Society," prefixed to his History, Robertson says :—

" Literature, science, taste, were words scarce in use during the ages we are contemplating ; or if they occur at any time, eminence in them is ascribed to persons and productions so contemptible that it appears their true import was little understood. Persons of the highest rank, and in the most eminent stations could not read or write. Many of the clergy did not understand the Breviary which they were obliged daily to recite ; some of them could scarce read it."—(Vol. i. p. 18.)

On this statement Robertson adds a note, containing "proofs and illustrations;" but, before I come to it, let me observe by the way, that he is professedly speaking of the period "from the *seventh* to the *eleventh* century;" and, that unless we understand him to mean "from the seventh" to quite the *end* of the "eleventh century," it is not wonderful that the clergy did not understand the "Breviary," or true that they were obliged to recite it; for it did not exist. The fact is, indeed, unimportant: because the question is, not whether there was, at that period, a book called the "Breviary," but whether, supposing there were such a book, the clergy could have read it, or anything else. I notice the matter, however, as one of the proofs which Robertson gives that he was not very familiar with a subject on which he ventured to speak in very broad and general terms, but evidently without scrupulous exactness. The note, however, begins in the following manner :—

"Innumerable proofs of this might be produced. Many charters granted by persons of the highest rank are preserved, from which it appears that they could not subscribe their name. It was usual for persons who could not write, to make the sign of the cross in confirmation of a charter. Several of these remain, where kings and persons of great eminence affix *signum crucis manu propria pro ignoratione literarum*. Du Cange, voc. Crux, vol. iii. p. 1191. From this is derived the phrase of signing instead of subscribing a paper. In the ninth century, Herbaud Comes Palatii, though supreme judge of the empire by virtue of his office, could not subscribe his name. Nouveau Traité de Diplomatique par deux Bénédictins, 4to. tom. ii. p. 422."—Note X. p. 232.

It is extremely difficult to meet broad general assertions which it is, in the nature of things, impossible to disprove; but we may reasonably call for evidence of their truth, and, if it is not produced, we may be allowed to doubt and to dispute them. If "*many* charters" are preserved in which "kings and persons of great eminence" avow their ignor-

ance, surely many might be, and, I think, would
have been, produced. The ignorance of the dark
ages has long been a matter of triumphant retro-
spect ; and such regal curiosities of literature or
illiterature, would have been highly interesting to
an enlightened public. Perhaps, indeed, " many "
instances have been adduced ; but I do not remember to have seen, or specifically heard of, more
than four. One of them is, I believe, less commonly
known ; but the other three have been repeatedly
paraded in declamations on this subject.

First—WITHRED, King of Kent, who reigned from
A.D. 671 to A.D. 725, and one of whose charters is
subscribed " Ego Withredus Rex Cantiæ omnia
supra scripta confirmavi, atque a me dictata propria
manu signum Sanctæ Crucis pro ignorantia litterarum expressi."

Secondly—TASSILO, Duke of Bavaria, in the eighth
century, subscribed a charter containing a grant to
Atto, abbot of Saltzburg, "quod manu propria, ut
potui, characteres chirographi inchoando depinxi
coram judicibus atque optimatibus meis. Signum
manus meæ propriæ Tassilonis," etc.

Thirdly—HERIBAUD, Comte du Palais under Lewis
II., subscribed a charter in A.D. 873, "Signum
Heribaldi Comitis Sacri Palatii, qui ibi fui et
propter ignorantiam litterarum, signum sanctæ
crucis feci."[1]

Fourthly—The authors of the " *Nouveau Traité
de Diplomatique*," after arguing against those who
considered such ignorance as incredible, say,
" L'usage d'avouer pareille ignorance est attesté

---

[1] These three instances were given by Mabillon (De Re Diplom.
p. 163, 544), and were thence transferred to vol. ii. (not iii.) of
the Benedictine edition of Du Cange. I write here with reference
to the statement of Robertson ; for the reader will observe, that
two out of the three cases are earlier than the period which I have
specified—that is, A.D. 800—1200.

par tant de traits historiques, que toutes les
chicanes de l'esprit humain ne pourront en obscurcir
l'éclat. Il suffira d'en rappeler quelques uns dans
les notes." In a note on this passage they exhibit
poor Withred "Roi de Cantorberi," and the
"Comte du Palais," already mentioned, and add
the case of GUI GUERRA, Count of Tuscany, who
was reduced to the same necessity, "quia scribere
nesciebat." "Il seroit superflu," say they, "d'ac-
cumuler un plus grand nombre de faits, pour vérifier
un usage, dont la certitude est démontrée."[2]

To me it appears that three or four instances, oc-
curring between the eighth and twelfth centuries,
are so far from demonstrating the certainty of a
custom, that they do not prove that anything which
can properly be called a custom existed; unless,
indeed, these writers meant (as perhaps their
language elsewhere might almost incline us to
believe) that these instances prove the *usage* of
kings and great men, when they could not write,
to state that fact on the face of the instrument.
There is, however, no need to pursue this point;
for, of course, I do not mean to deny that there
was, in those days, a much greater ignorance of
writing than in ours, and that men of rank were much
more frequently unable to write then than they are
now. But when Robertson talks of "*innumerable*
proofs," and tells us that "*many*" charters are preserved, from which "it *appears*" that such persons
could not sign their names, I feel it right to question
his statement. Had he seen the original charters?
I very much doubt it. If he had seen them, would
it have enabled him to decide the point? I am sure
that it would not; and I feel this certainty, not only
because I do not give him credit for so much
research *in re diplomatica* as that he should bring

---

[2] Tom. ii. p. 426.

forward " innumerable proofs " when Mabillon, and Toustain, and Tassin, gave only four between them, but from the very nature of the case. The fact that a man's name was subscribed to a document by another, was, in those days, no proof that he could not have done it himself ; and though, in the present day, we should hardly give anyone credit for being able to write if we found that he had only made his mark, yet we must not entirely judge of other ages by our own.

Mabillon has given and discussed four reasons why charters were frequently signed by proxy :— (1.) The inability of the parties to write ; which was, of course, a very common reason, and may well be supposed, upon the great scale, to have been the most frequent. Under this head he gives the well-known story of Theodoric, and the three cases first mentioned above.   (2.) Physical inability, arising from blindness, disease, or old age; as in the case of Eugenius, at the council of Constantinople, in the year 536, who subscribed by the hand of Paul, a deacon of his monastery, ὡς μὴ δυνάμενος διὰ τὸ γῆρας ;[3] of St. Omer, whose will was subscribed —" Hæc abocellis feci, et alius manum meam tenens scripsit et subscripsit ; " and of some others whom he mentions. (3.) An affectation of dignity, through which many high official persons chose that their names should be written by the notary.   (4.) What is most to our purpose, a custom growing out of this, and extending so far as that by the eleventh century it had become almost universal.   In imitation of their superiors, almost all persons—all at least who could pretend to any kind of distinction or title—preferred having their names written by the notary (who could say of them what it might have seemed ostentatious to say of themselves), and then adding, or sometimes omitting to add, their

[3] Conc. Tom. V. p. 136.

mark—that is, the sign of the cross made with their
own hands. It will be obvious, therefore, that it
does not " appear " in all cases, even from the
original document, whether the parties *could* write
their names. Indeed, if it did not suppose an
almost incredible degree of ignorance, one would
be tempted to think that Heribaud's affixing the
sign of the cross, " pro ignoratione litterarum,"
had led Robertson to infer, that all persons who
made the sign of the cross on such occasions did it
for the same reasons ; for he says, it was usual "*for
persons who could not write* to make the sign of the
cross in confirmation of a charter." No doubt; but
it was also usual for those who *could* write. The
sign of the cross was, in fact, " *the* confirmation and
the signature "[4] and the subscriber, in thus making

---

[4] Take, by way of specimen, the subscription to the will of
Hagano, Canon of St. Martin's at Tours in A.D. 819 :—" Hagano
diaconus cessionem a me factam sub signum Sanctæ Crucis confirmavi."—(*Martene, Thesaurus Novus Anecdotorum,* vol. i. p. 23.)
(And here let me say, by the way, that as I hope to make frequent
reference to this work, as well as to the " Veterum Scriptorum et
Monumentorum Amplissima Collectio," edited by *Martene and
Durand,* I shall be glad to be allowed, for brevity's sake, to refer
to the former as " *Mart.*," and the latter as " *M. & D.*") A
charter, too, of Robert, Abbot of St. Martin's in the same city,
and of the year 897, is subscribed " Robertus Comes et inclytæ
congregationis S. Martini Abbas, per hoc signum Sanctæ Crucis
subterfirmare studuit." (*Mart.* i. 57.) Or, to take a subscription
belonging to our own country, which may, at the same time, be a
specimen of notarial eloquence :—" Anno Incarnationis Dominicæ
nongentesimo sexagesimo sexto scripta est hujus privilegii syn-
grapha, his testibus consentientibus, quorum inferius nomina
ordinatim charaxantur ; " and then follow the subscriptions—
" Ego, EDGAR, divina largiente gratia, Anglorum Basileus, hoc
privilegii donum nostro largiens Redemptori locoque ejus sanctissimo, primus omnium regum, monachorum inibi collegium constituens, *manu propria signum hagiæ crucis imprimens confirmavi*—
Ego, DUNSTAN, Dorobernensis ecclesiæ archiepiscopus, largifluam
benevoli Regis donationem venerans, *crucis signaculo corroboravi*—
Ego, EADMUND, clytos legitimus præfati filius, *crucis signaculum,*
infantuli florens ætate, *propria indidi manu*—Ego EDWARD, eodem
rege clyto procreatus, præfatam patris munificentiam *crucis signo*

the sign of his holy religion, was considered as
taking an oath. He was, in fact, said *manu jurare ;*[5]
and, for greater solemnity, the cross was sometimes
made with the consecrated wine.[6] The subscriber's
adding his name was no essential part of the confirmation, but simply a declaration and notification
that the person, whose name was there written, was
he who had thus bound himself by his *signature.* If he
was unable, or if he did not choose, to do the *writing*
for himself, it was done for him by the notary.

I beg the reader not to suppose that I wish
to do more than to moderate the extravagance
of Robertson's statement, and to show that he
made it without sufficient grounds. Does he not, in
fact, show this himself when he proceeds to say —

" So late as the fourteenth century, Du Guesclin, Constable of
France, the greatest man in the state, and one of the greatest
men of his age, could neither read nor write.   St. Palaye Mémoires
sur l'ancienne Chevalerie, t. ii. p. 82."

Well, then surely two instances in the eighth
century, one in the ninth, and one in the twelfth, of
men of rank who could not *write*—it does not appear,
and really does not follow, that they could not *read*
—form too slender a ground for such broad assertions as Robertson has ventured to make respecting
the state of letters.

---

consolidavi—Ego ÆLFTHRYTH, legitima præfati regis conjux, mea
legatione monachos eodem loco rege annuente constituens, *crucem
impressi*—Ego EADGIFA prædicti regis ava hoc opus egregium
crucis thaumate consolidavi ; " and Athelwold, Bishop of Winchester, says, " *crucis signaculo benedixi."* (Conc. tom. ix. 673.)

[5] " Comes Tolosanus hanc eandem donationem ibi deveniens
rogatu nostro corroboravit, firmavit, *manuque propria juravit,* id
est, subscriptione crucis."—(*Du Cange in v.* Crux.)

[6] " Interdum quo solemnius ac firmius esset pactum, quod
scribebatur, cruces ipsæ exarabantur calamo in pretioso Christi
sanguine intincto." (*Du Cange, ibid.*) See also Odo Aribertus
(cited by Baluze in his notes on Agobard, p. 129), who says,
" Pace itaque cum sanguine eucharistico separatim per Regem et
Comitem firmata et obsignata," etc.

Having, however, disposed of the laity, he proceeds :—

" Nor was this ignorance confined to laymen ; the *greater part* of the clergy was not many degrees superior to them in science. *Many* dignified ecclesiastics could not subscribe the canons of those councils in which they sat as members. Nouv. Traité de Diplom., tom. ii. p. 424."

If the reader turns to the authority cited, he will find some general statements respecting the ignorance of the *laity* as to writing (with no specific instances, however, except those already named), but no mention of ecclesiastics. It is true, that, in the succeeding pages, the bishops and other ecclesiastical persons are mentioned, and several are named in a note at page 426 ; but Robertson should have observed, what is there so plainly stated, " *Tous ces exemples sont antérieurs au VIIe Siècle.*" I do not say that later instances might not be produced ; but I do not remember to have seen any. He proceeds :—

" One of the questions appointed by the canons to be put to persons who were candidates for orders was this, ' Whether they could read the Gospels and Epistles, and explain the sense of them, at least literally ? ' Regino Prumiensis ap. Bruck. Hist. Philos. v. iii. p. 631."

I am sorry to say that I have not the Abbot of Prum's book ; and I must, therefore, answer as well as I can without it ; and perhaps some reader who has it, or who is so happy as to have access to a public library, will be kind enough to give me an extract, or some information as to the specific canon to which Robertson (or rather Brucker) refers. In the meantime I must observe —

First, that supposing all which Robertson meant to convey to the reader were true, still such a canon would show that, bad as things were, there was some attempt to mend them. Granting that up to about the year 900, when Regino wrote, all

bishops, priests, and deacons had been entirely
ignorant and illiterate—granting that these very
canons were written by those who could not write,
for the use of those who could not read, still they
would be a standing proof that the heads of the
church did, at that time, require even from candidates for orders, what Robertson would lead us to
consider as rather an unusual accomplishment in a
bishop.

Secondly, though I have not Regino's book, I
have Brucker's, from whence Robertson professes
to borrow the quotation; but, on turning to it, I
find a very important difference. The reader will
observe that the question, even as Robertson gives
it, is, in fact, whether the candidate could read
Latin publicly, and explain the meaning; but,
beside this, the inquiry was really essentially
different. It was not whether the candidate had
learned to read, nor even whether he could *read
Latin;* but whether he could read Latin *well*. The
words, as quoted by Brucker, are—" Si Evangelium et Epistolam *bene* legere possit, atque saltim
ad literam sensus ejus manifestare. Item, si
sermonem S. Athanasii de fide SS. Trinitatis
memoriter teneat, et sensum ejus intelligat, et
verbis communibus enuntiare sciat." Surely there
was no proof of brutal ignorance in inquiring
whether a candidate for holy orders could read
Latin well in public—could repeat, understand, and
explain the Athanasian Creed, and preach the doctrine contained in it, in the vernacular tongue.
The question did not imply the slightest doubt
whether the man could read; but only directed an
inquiry whether he could do that which many a
man of the present day, who has chuckled over the
ignorance of the dark ages, could not do.

Thirdly, if my object were merely to answer
Robertson, I should think that I had said enough
on this point; but having a farther and more

important design, let me, without at present entering very fully into the subject, give a few extracts
from "the canons," and one or two writers of the
dark ages, or at least of the period to which
Robertson refers.

Isidore, Archbishop of Seville, who lived until
the year 636, in his work on Ecclesiastical Offices,
has a chapter of rules for the clergy, in which he
says, that they should be "continually occupied
in teaching, in reading, in psalms, and hymns, and
spiritual songs;"[7] which seems to imply, at least,
that in his time it was no uncommon thing for the
clergy to be able to read.

At the eighth council of Toledo, held in A.D. 653,
regret was expressed that persons had been admitted into holy orders who were altogether incompetent to the discharge of clerical duties ; and
it was expressly provided, that no one should be
admitted to any degree of ecclesiastical dignity
unless he knew the whole Psalter, the hymns of
the church, and the office for baptism; and that
those who had been admitted without such necessary knowledge should forthwith set to work to
acquire it, or be made to do so by their superiors.
"For," says the canon, "it is absurd that they
who are ignorant of the law of God, and not at
least moderately learned, should be promoted to
any degree of orders, or ecclesiastical office, in
which it is their business to teach simple and lay
persons, to whom they ought to be mirrors of life
and discipline. Let no one, then, who is unlearned,
approach to meddle with the holy mysteries of
God[8] . . . none who is blinded by the darkness
of ignorance ; but let him only come who is adorned
with innocence of life and splendour of learning.
Otherwise the vengeance of God, and of His church,

---

[7] Bib. Pat. x. 203.
[8] There is apparently some hiatus in the MSS.

will hereafter fall on both the ordainers and the ordained." [9]

Whether the council of Nantes, to which the following canon belongs, was held in the year 658, or more than two centuries after, has been disputed ; but, either way, it falls within Robertson's period, and is in itself worth notice :—" When a bishop purposes to hold an ordination, all those who are candidates for holy orders are to be cited to the city on the Wednesday preceding, together with the archpresbyters, who are to present them. And then the bishop is to appoint priests and other prudent men, skilled in the divine law, and conversant with the ecclesiastical sanctions, who shall diligently inquire as to the life, family, country, age, and education of the candidates ; and as to the place where they were educated, whether they have made good progress in learning (*si sint bene literati*), and are instructed in the law of the Lord. Above all things, whether they firmly hold the catholic faith, and are able to set it forth in plain language. Those, however, to whom this is entrusted must take care that they do not depart from the faith, either from favour or for interest, so as to present to the bishop any unworthy or unfit person to receive holy orders ; for should they do this, he who has unworthily approached the altar shall be removed from it ; and they who have attempted to sell the gift of the Holy Ghost, being already condemned in the sight of God, shall be deprived of their ecclesiastical dignity. They shall, therefore, be diligently examined during three following days, and then those who are approved shall be presented to the bishop on the Saturday." [1]

To come to our own country, it was decreed by the sixth canon of the council held at Cliffe, or Cloveshou, near Rochester, in the year 747, " that

---

[9] Conc. vi. 406.　　　[1] Conc. ix. 471.

the bishops shall ordain no man, either of clerks or monks, to the holy degree of priesthood without public inquiry as to his previous life, and his present purity of morals, and knowledge of the faith. For how can he preach to others the whole faith, minister the word of knowledge, and appoint to sinners the measure of penance, unless he first, with studious care, according to the measure of his capacity, takes pains to learn, so that, according to the apostle, he may be able to 'exhort according to sound doctrine?'" The seventh canon directs, "that bishops, abbots, and abbesses . . . shall study and provide, with diligent care, that the custom of continual reading may be practised in their societies, and may become more common, to the benefit of souls and the praise of the eternal King. For it is a lamentable thing to say that, in these times, very few are to be found who are carried away by a thoroughly hearty love of holy learning (*qui ex intimo corde sacræ scientiæ rapiantur amore*), and they are scarcely willing to take much pains to learn anything; but rather from their youth they are occupied with divers vanities, and lusts of vain glory; and, with wandering minds, they seek after the unstable things of this world rather than the unchangeable things of holy scripture. Let them, therefore, be compelled; and let the children in the schools be brought up to the love of sacred learning, that, by these means, well-educated persons may be found for every kind of service in the Church of God. Nor let their earthly rulers be so tenacious of their services as that the House of God should fall into contempt, being destitute of all spiritual ornament." [2]

This brings us to the time of Charlemagne, of whose exertions in the cause of literature I hope to say more hereafter; but, in the mean time, I must

_____

[2] Conc. vi. 1575.

just notice his Capitulary of Aix-la-Chapelle, addressed to the ecclesiastical authorities in A.D. 789.
He says, " We beseech your piety, that the ministers
of God's altar may adorn their ministry by good
morals—whether, as canons, by the observance of
their order, or, as monks, by the performance of
their vow—we entreat that they may maintain a
good and laudable life and conversation, as our
Lord in the gospel commands, ' Let your light so
shine before men, that they may see your good
works, and glorify your Father which is in heaven ; '
so that, by their good conversation, many may be
drawn to God. And let them collect and keep
under their care (*adgregent sibique socient*), not only
children of servile condition, but those belonging to
persons of better rank ; and let there be schools of
reading boys. In all monasteries and dioceses, let
them learn the Psalms, the musical notes, the chants,
the calendar,[3] and grammar. But let them have
catholic books well corrected ; because frequently,
when they desire to pray for anything very properly, they ask amiss, by reason of incorrect books.
And do not suffer your boys to spoil the books, by
either their reading and writing ; and if you want a
gospel or a missal to be written, let it be done by
men of mature age, with all diligence."[4] Again, in
the *Capitula data Presbyteris*, in the year 804, he

---

[3] " Chants and calendar " is not a very satisfactory translation
of " cantus et compotus." To call the latter (as I have seen it
called) " the compost " would not be very intelligible to the English reader. Still calendar does not express the thing, which was
rather that learning, that *compotus*, or *computus*, which would enable
a *computista*, or *artis computatoriæ magister*, to make a calendar, or
computorium ; and some of which (enough to show its nature) the
reader may find in the beginning of his Prayer Book. I may,
however, perhaps, be allowed at present to pass over some words
without explanation, of which I hope to speak more fully hereafter.
What is implied in knowing the cantus, compotus, grammatica, and
penitential, will then more fully appear.

[4] Capit. Reg. Fr. edit. Baluz., tom. i. 237.

says, "I would admonish you, my brethren and
sons, to give attention to these few capitula which
follow:—first, that a priest of God should be
learned in holy scripture, and rightly believe, and
teach to others, the faith of the Trinity, and be able
properly to fulfil his office. Secondly, that he
should have the whole Psalter by heart. Thirdly,
that he should know by heart the Creed and the
office for Baptism. Fourthly, that he should be
learned in the Canons, and well know his Penitential. Fifthly, that he should know the Chants and
the Calendar." [5] More might be quoted from this
source, but perhaps it is not necessary for my present purpose,—which is, to show that it was pretty
commonly taken for granted that a clerk could read.

But, in case any reader should have thought that
I lay undue stress on the word *bene*, and should
suppose (as it is charitable to hope that Robertson
did when he left it out), that it was a mere ex-
pletive, I will here give an extract from a writer of
this period, from which it will appear that the
inquiry as to reading *well* was one actually and particularly made. Rabanus Maurus, who was afterwards Archbishop of Mentz, and who wrote his
book *De Institutione Clericorum* in the year 819,
says, "The canons and the decrees of Pope Zosimus
have decided, that a clerk proceeding to holy orders
shall continue five years among the readers, or
exorcists; and, after that, shall be an acolyte, or
subdeacon, four years. That he shall not be admitted to deacon's orders before he is twenty-five
years of age; and that if, during five years, he
ministers irreproachably, he may be promoted to
priest's orders; but on no account before he is thirty
years of age, even though he should be peculiarly
qualified, for our Lord himself did not begin to
preach until he had attained that age." [6] Now, as

---

[5] Ibid. p. 417.   [6] Lib. i. c. xiii. ap. Bib. Pat. tom. x. 572.

Rabanus had just before remarked, " *Lectores* " are so-called " *a legendo;* " and if a man was to fill that office for five years before he became even a sub-deacon, we may reasonably suppose that, when he came to be examined for, what the Romish church calls, " greater Orders," it might be taken for granted that he had learned to read ; but as to reading *well* (I hope no offence to modern times), it certainly was then quite another question, and one to which some attention was paid. " He," says Rabanus, " who would rightly and properly perform the duty of a Reader, must be imbued with learn-ing, and conversant with books, and instructed in the meaning of words, and the knowledge of words themselves ; so that he may understand the divisions of sentences, where a clause ends, where the sense is carried on, and where the sentence closes. Being thus prepared, he will obtain such a power of read-ing as that, by various modes of delivery—now simply narrating, now lamenting, now angry, now rebuking, exhorting, pitying, inquiring, and the like, according to circumstances—he will affect the understanding and feelings of all his hearers. For there are many things in the scriptures, which, if they are not properly pronounced, give a wrong sense ; as that of the apostle—' Who shall lay any-thing to the charge of God's elect ? God who justifieth.'—Now if, instead of pronouncing this properly, it were to be delivered confirmatively, it would create great error. It is, therefore, to be so pronounced as that the first clause may be a *percon-tation,* and the second an *interrogation.* Between a percontation and interrogation, the ancients made this distinction—that the former admitted a variety of answers, while the latter must be replied to by ' yes ' or ' no.' It must, therefore, be so read that, after the percontation—' Who shall lay anything to the charge of God's elect ? '—that which follows be pronounced in an interrogatory manner—' God that justifieth?'—that there may be a tacit answer, 'no.' And again we have the percontation—'Who is he that condemneth?' and again we interrogate— 'Christ that died? or rather that is risen again? who is at the right hand of God? who also maketh intercession for us?' At each of which there is a tacit answer in the negative. But in that passage where he says, 'What shall we then say? that the Gentiles, which followed not after righteousness, have attained to righteousness,' unless after the percontation—'What shall we say then?'— the answer were added—'that the Gentiles which followed not after righteousness have attained to righteousness,' the connexion with what follows would be destroyed. And there are many other parts which, in like manner, require to be distinguished by the manner of pronouncing them. Beside this, a reader ought to understand the force of the accents, that he may know what syllables he is to lengthen; for there are many words which can only be prevented from conveying a wrong meaning by being pronounced with the proper accent. But these things he must learn from the grammarians. Moreover the voice of a reader should be pure and clear, and adapted to every style of speaking, full of manly strength, and free from all that is rude or countrified. Not low, nor yet too high; not broken, not weak, and by no means feminine; not with inflated or gasping articulation, or words mouthed about in his jaws, or echoing through his empty mouth; not harsh from his grinding his teeth; not projected from a wide-open mouth,—but distinctly, equally, mildly pronounced; so that each letter shall have its proper sound, and each word its proper quantity, and that the matter be not spoiled by any affectation." [7]

It is true that Rabanus Maurus has taken the

---

[7] Lib. ii. c. lii. Bib. Pat. x. 616.

substance of this from Isidore of Seville,[8] who wrote
more than two hundred years before, though he has
improved it; but if it was good, why should it not
be repeated? So thought Ivo, Bishop of Chartres,
who gave it again in his discourses *De Rebus Ecclesiasticis*,[9] nearly three hundred years after
Rabanus wrote—and I cannot help suspecting that
if Robertson had gone to the Archbishop of Seville
in the seventh century, the Archbishop of Mayence
in the ninth, or the Bishop of Chartres in the
eleventh, for holy orders, he would have found the
examination rather more than he expected. If I
have failed to convince the reader of this, by the
extracts already given, I shall hope to do so hereafter; but I think that what has been said must be
sufficient to show that it was not a very uncommon
thing, even in the dark ages, for the clergy to be
able to read and write.

---

[8] De Eccles. Office., lib. ii. c. xi., Bib. Pat. x. 209.
[9] Serm. ii. ap. Bib. Pat. x. 774.

No. III.

"—— nil dulcius est, bene quam munita tenere
Edita doctrina sapientum templa serena ;
Despicere unde queas alios, passimque videre
Errare, atque viam palanteis quærere vitæ."—LUCRETIUS.

" Rivers of waters run down mine eyes, because they keep not
thy law."—Ps. cxix.

WHEN I began the preceding paper, I had no idea
of replying to Robertson's character of the clergy
during the dark ages at such length ; and meant
only to notice, very briefly, such parts of his statement as are absolutely untrue. I intended, until I
should have thus gone through his remarks, to say
little or nothing on matters which may be more conveniently, intelligibly, and convincingly, discussed
after untruths have been exposed, and the prejudices created and fostered by them removed ; and
also, after a variety of facts have been adduced,
which may be referred to for proof or illustration.
Perhaps enough has been already said to show that
the clergy of the period to which Robertson refers
were not so universally, or even so entirely, ignorant
as might be supposed from his language ; yet, having said so much, and considering that it all tends
to the elucidation of our subject in more than one
way, I feel desirous (without professing here to
enter fully into the matter) to add one or two more
extracts, which are not, I think, in themselves uninteresting.

From the Constitutions of Reculfus, who became
Bishop of Soissons in A.D. 879, and who is supposed
to have issued these instructions to his clergy ten
years afterwards, it appears as if he took it for
granted that they could, not only read, but write.
The fourth, fifth, and sixth sections are as follows :
—" Know, therefore, that this is addressed to you,

' Be ye clean, ye that bear the vessels of the Lord ; ' [1]
which you must not suppose to refer only to the
cleansing of the chalice and paten, wherein the body
and blood of Christ is consecrated, but also to personal cleanliness and mental purity. For, as St.
Gregory says, in treating of the parable of the ten
virgins, ' Our vessels are our hearts, wherein we
bear about with us all our thoughts.' [2]   We have,
therefore, a frail vessel, that is, our body, which we
ought always to keep clean, with the most scrupulous
care ; so that, while we offer ' pure offerings,' we
also ourselves may be acceptable sacrifices before
his holy altar.   Also we admonish that each one of
you should endeavour to have by heart, truly and
correctly, the Psalms, the Discourse on the Catholic
Faith which begins ' Quicumque vult,' etc., and the
Canon of the Mass, and the Chants, and the
Calendar.   The office for Baptism (both for male
and female children, and also singular and plural),
as well as the offices for consecrating fonts, water
to be sprinkled in houses, the commendation of the
soul, and the prayers at the burial of the dead, you
are to have distinctly and correctly written out ;
and, by frequent study, you are to qualify yourselves
to perform them correctly and unblameably for
both men and women.   As to the aforesaid office
for the baptism of infants, we would that you
should write it out in a fourfold manner ; that is to
say, the singular masculine and the singular
feminine ; the plural masculine and the plural
feminine ; as we, if Christ permit, will furnish you
with a copy.   Also we admonish that each one of
you should be careful to have a Missal, Lectionary,
a Book of the Gospels, a Martyrology, an Antipho-
nary, Psalter, and a Book of Forty Homilies of St.

---

[1] " Mundamini qui fertis vasa Domini."   Isaiah lii. 11.   I give
the words of our translation ; and wish to mention that I do so
wherever there is not any material variation.

[2] Hom. in Evan. XII., t. ii. p. 357.

Gregory, corrected and pointed by our copies which
we use in the holy mother church. And, also, fail
not to have as many sacred and ecclesiastical books
as you can get; for from them you shall receive
food and condiment for your souls, our Lord himself having declared, 'Man doth not live by bread
alone; but by every word that proceedeth out of
the mouth of God.' If, however, any one of you is
not able to obtain all the books of the Old Testament, at least let him diligently take pains to transcribe for himself correctly the first book of the
whole sacred history, that is, Genesis; by reading
which he may come to understand the creation of
the world." [3]

This, as I have observed, seems to imply that the
priests in the diocese of Soissons, in the ninth
century, could both read and write; and, indeed,
from the sixteenth section, it appears that the
secular clergy in that diocese kept schools; and so
not only read and wrote themselves, but were the
causes of reading and writing in others. But this
is anticipating; for what reader of Robertson is
prepared to believe that the schoolmaster was
abroad in the ninth century? I will, therefore,
only here add one more extract on this subject, and
that shall be from the history of our own country.
The Canons of Ælfric, whether we owe them to the
archbishop or the grammarian, or whether they
were one and the same person, were written between the years 950 and 1000. They were addressed to Wulfin, Bishop of Sherborn; and written
in such a form as that he might communicate them
to his clergy as a kind of episcopal charge. The
twenty-first canon orders—"Every priest, also,
before he is ordained, must have the arms belonging
to his spiritual work; that is, the holy books—
namely, the Psalter, the Book of Epistles, and the
Book of Gospels, the Missal, the Book of Hymns,

---

[3] Conc. ix. p. 418.

the Manual, the Calendar,[4] the Passional, the Pœnitential, and the Lectionary. These books a priest requires, and cannot do without, if he would properly fulfil his office, and desires to teach the law to the people belonging to him. And let him carefully see that they are well written."

The passage of Regino, quoted by Robertson—of which, in this long reply, I am afraid the reader has almost lost sight—tempts me to add the twenty-third canon—" The mass-priest shall, on Sundays and on mass-days, explain the Gospel in English to the people ; and, by the Lord's Prayer and the Creed, he shall, as often as he can, stir them up to faith and the maintenance of Christianity. Let the teacher be warned to avoid that which the prophet has said—' *Canes muti non possunt latrare* '—' Dumb dogs, they cannot bark.' We ought to bark and preach to the laity, lest perchance we should cause them to perish for lack of knowledge. Christ saith in his Gospel of ignorant teachers, 'if the blind lead the blind, both fall into the ditch.' Blind is the teacher if he is illiterate, and deceives the laity by his ignorance. Beware of this, as your office requires."[5]

---

[4] The Latin translation in Wilkins's Councils has *numerale ;* that in Labbe's preserves the original Anglo-Saxon *gerim ;* and I translate it *calendar*, because I have no doubt that it means the *compotus*, which I have before (somewhat improperly) so translated. It occurs in a "Calendarium seu Menologium Poeticum," given by Hickes, *Thes. Ling. Vett. Sept.*, tom. i. p. 203, from a MS. in the Cottonian Library, at the 18th line " Ianuaрɪuᵹ ᵹeрɪm," where it is translated " Januarium Calendarii ; " and in a note on it, at p. 209, he says, " Sic enim ᵹeрɪm, ut ríɪꝛ apud veteres *calendarium, fastos, ephemerida* denotat." Considering the purpose for which I write, it may be worth while to state that Collier, in his *Ecclesiastical History*, vol. i. p. 207, gives this canon, thus :—" By the one-and-twentieth, ' Every priest, before his ordination, was obliged to be furnished with church books, that is, with a Psalter ; a Book of Epistles and Gospels ; a Missale ; a Book of Church Hymns ; a Penitentiale, and a Lectionarie, or Ræding Boc,' " etc., thus leaving out the Gerim, Manual, and Passional ; a convenient way of quoting.

[5] Wilkins's Conc., i. 250.

To proceed, however, with Robertson :—

"Alfred the Great complained that, from the Humber to the Thames, there was not a priest who understood the liturgy in his mother tongue, or who could translate the easiest piece of Latin ; and that, from the Thames to the sea, the ecclesiastics were still more ignorant. Asserus de rebus gestis Alfredi, ap. Camdeni. Anglica, &c., p. 25. The ignorance of the clergy is quaintly described by an author of the dark ages. ' Potius dediti gulæ quam Glossæ ; potius colligunt libras quam legunt libros ; libentius intuentur Martham quam Marcum ; malunt legere in Salmone quam in Solomone.' Alanas de art. Prædicat. ap. Lebeuf. Dissert. tom. ii. p. 21."—p. 233.

I will not here run into what must necessarily be a long discourse about Alfred, and which would anticipate what I may more properly say when some facts shall have come under notice which may enable us to form a better judgment of the state of things in England during the reign of that monarch, as well as before and after it. Here I only observe that, supposing Robertson's statement to be quite correct,[6] it only shows that the Anglo-Saxons were at that period behind their neighbours on the continent of Europe ; which nobody would think of disputing. Let us, therefore, with Robertson, leap over about *three centuries,* and into Flanders, to see how quaintly " the ignorance of the clergy " was described by Alanus. Are we to take this as the character of " the clergy " generally in all places during the dark ages ? or only of " the clergy " in the time and neighbourhood of Alanus ? And is it by jumping over time and space in this manner, to pick out parts of sentences, that we can hope to understand the matter aright ?

Though, after taking and giving some trouble, I

---

[6] Which, by the way, it is not. Alfred said " very few," which is quite a different thing, if I may trust the Latin translation of Wise (p. 87*)—*" paucissimi ;" and Mr. Sharon Turner's English translation, " very few," in his History of the Anglo-Saxons, vol. ii. p. 277.

am not at present able to say whether this passage
has been correctly and fairly quoted either by or
from Lebeuf, yet I feel authorized by what I have
seen of Alanus to suspect that he did not speak in
these terms of "the clergy" in general. Of this,
however, one cannot judge without seeing what is
to agree with "dediti;" and, indeed, the whole
connexion of the sentence. Yet it matters little:
the words may be there; and whether they are or
not, and whether they meant all that Robertson
pretends, is of no consequence. It is of more
importance to observe the taste and the spirit which
are manifested in the citation of such ribaldry. I
notice it the rather, because I have remarked that
so many moderns seem disposed to speak and write
with self-satisfied glee of their dark ancestors; and
to be much amused with the quaint humour which
describes and exaggerates their ignorance, barbarism, and vice. I believe the feeling is natural to
man—it was avowed with infernal candour by the
heathen whose hackneyed lines I have placed at the
head of this paper—but it is one which we might
expect to find disavowed with abhorrence by every
man pretending to be a Christian. That men were
wandering in error, and seeking in vain "the way
of life," with such guides as Alanus has "quaintly
described," can be no subject of mirth to a Christian mind. Superstition may put on a ridiculous
form, and ignorance may commit ludicrous blunders
—we *may* laugh, for, by the law of our nature, we
must laugh at some of these things—but to find
amusement in the brutal and degraded state of the
ministers of religion at any time, and, indeed, I may
say of any religion, must, I think, be peculiar to
bad men.

It is, however, very important, and very much
to our present purpose, to add a few words on this
subject; because I apprehend that, for the want of
a little consideration, many persons have been led
into a mistaken view of the case. There were in

the dark ages (as well as at other times) two sets
of persons, from whose writings it is easy to cull
passages describing " the clergy " as less learned
and religious than they were bound to be ; and each
set tempted to detail, and perhaps to exaggerate,
the vices of ecclesiastics.

First, there were those who hated the religion
which the clergy maintained, and who envied the
property, privileges, and influence which they enjoyed ; and which (whatever the personal character
of some of them might be) they generally employed
to check the licentiousness of others. Among these
there have perhaps always been facetious persons
who have considered religion and its ministers as
fit subjects for their drollery; and who have
delighted to represent the clergy as a vile race of
knaves and fools, characterized only by pride,
sensuality, avarice, and ambition, except where all
these, and all that was better, was kept under by
idiot superstition. Yet, as far as I know, there
was but little of this ribaldry during the period of
which Robertson writes. He talks of the *seventh
to the eleventh* century ; but for the single instance
which he gives (and I cannot but doubt whether it
properly belongs to this class) he goes to, at least, the
middle of the twelfth century. Without entering
into the dispute about the precise period, or the
identity of Alanus, this is the earliest date that can
be assigned to him; and, in fact, it is to the
thirteenth, and yet more to the fourteenth and
fifteenth, century that we must go for quaint
descriptions of the corrupted church. I should
like very much to bring forward some of these,
with the remarks of some modern writers on them ;
but I am afraid that, notwithstanding all I have
said, such a proceeding really would be a digres-
sion ; and, therefore, it may suffice, for the present,
to say that what we know of the incapacity or vices
of the clergy or the monks during the period in
question, we derive principally from their own

confession; or, at least, from their own statements.

The second set of writers to whom I have alluded,
are those who either under pretence, or with the
real object, of producing reformation, have been
vigilant to spy out, and forward to publish, the
vices of churchmen. If there were but few of the
former class of writers during the period more
immediately under our consideration, there were
some (I hope to be able to show ground for believing that there were many) virtuous, pious, and
comparatively enlightened persons[7] who belonged
to this class; and who, when their lot was cast
among ecclesiastics who disgraced their profession
by ignorance and vice, did seriously desire (and
were joined or imitated by others who pretended to
desire) a reformation of such evils. But I need not
say that the zeal of reformers, whether real or pretended, has often exaggerated the evils which it
desired to redress; sometimes by describing them
as greater, and oftener by representing them as
more general, than they really were.

From both these sets of writers very strong
statements may be extracted; and the testimony
which they apparently give will seem, to the young
student of ecclesiastical history, to be confirmed by
the proceedings of Councils, and the tenor of their
canons, as well as by a good deal of what he will
find in the works of secular historians, even supposing that he does go to original sources. He must,
however, remember that sin, in some shape or other,
is the great staple of history, and the sole object of
law; and he must expect, from both the historian
and the legislator, to hear more of one turbulent
prelate, or one set of factious or licentious monks,

---

[7] I use this qualification in deference to the popular view of the
subject; for I cannot tell why, in things pertaining to the kingdom of God, and on which man can be enlightened only by the
word and Spirit of God, they might not be as truly, and even as
fully enlightened as any of mankind before or after their time.

than of a hundred societies, or a thousand scattered clergy, living in the quiet decency suited to their profession. Yet even of such societies, passing through the year, and the century, in orderly obscurity, annals are not wanting—" but they are generally written in very shocking Latin"—very true.

However, to illustrate what I have said, let me recur to the canons of Ælfric, of which I have already spoken. One might find words in his address to Wulfin, from which it would seem as if he meant to testify, that the wickedness of the clergy was such, as that they had completely destroyed the church. "You ought," he says, " frequently to talk to your clergy, and to rebuke their negligence ; for, by their perverseness, the laws, religion, and learning of the church are almost destroyed. Therefore deliver your soul ; and tell them what are the duties of priests and ministers of Christ, lest you likewise perish, being counted as a dumb dog. We have written this epistle which follows in English, as if spoken by you, and you had addressed it to the clergy of your diocese, beginning thus :—' I myself tell you priests, that I will not put up with your negligence in your ministry ; but, in truth, I will tell you what is the law concerning your order,' " etc. Fuller illustration I hope to give hereafter ;[8] in the meantime I wish to get

---

[8] To pursue this point here would lead us into what is, perhaps, a much wider field than some readers may suppose—the subject of *church reform* in the middle ages. To me it has appeared extremely interesting, and I hope to give some extracts, which may lead us to believe that, bad as things were, there were always some who were trying to mend them. Conceive a bishop of the tenth century writing to two archbishops in such terms as these :—
" Relicto penitus eo qui nos proposuit mundo, relicto omni præter nomen officio, ipsi ita specialius deservimus ceteris mundo, ut dum ceteri Deo quæ Dei, mundo quæ mundi sunt contendunt reddere, nos e contra mundo quœ Dei, id est omnigenum amorem et cultum ; Deoque quæ debuerant mundo reddi, reddamus, id est omnigenum despectum et contemtum, et ut ipsi alligemur arctius, ne quando scilicet, dum ab eo non recognoscimur, despiciamur,

through Robertson's statement.   He goes on to say —

"To the obvious causes of such universal ignorance arising from the state of government and manners, from the seventh to the eleventh century, we may add the scarcity of books, and the difficulty of rendering them more common during that period. The Romans wrote their books either on parchment or on paper made of the Egyptian papyrus; the latter, being the cheapest, was of course the most commonly used. But after the Saracens conquered Egypt, in the seventh century, the communication between that country and the people settled in Italy, or in other parts of Europe, was almost entirely broke off, and the papyrus

---

relicto ritu cultu, habitu quoque nostro, ipsius mundi consuetudine atque studiis, amictibus etiam in tantum utimur, ut solo, ut ita eloquar, barbirasio et corona, et quod non a nobis ut ab eis ducuntur uxores, qualescumque etiam, quas Domino ore tantummodo, et hoc rarissime, reddere videmur, laudes, in nullo alio sæcularibus videamur dissimiles ; ita ut de nobis, proh nefas ! dictum prophetiæ possit credi quod continent tempora præsentis ævi: ' Et erit sicut populus, sic sacerdos,' " etc.   And he presently afterwards relates an anecdote which I must translate, though for the other matter I wished the reader to have the bishop's own words.   A certain priest who saw his bishop playing at dice, shook his head in a scornful manner.   The prelate perceiving it, was very angry (justly enough, says the bishop who relates it, if his anger had been directed against the right person), and told the priest, that if he did not show him that what he was doing was forbidden by the canon law, he would immediately send him to gaol.   The priest, with an aspect of horror, fell at his feet, and said, "Pardon me, my lord, I am so overwhelmed with fear that I could not repeat even the first verse of the first psalm " (the very alphabet of a priest in those days), " nor any one decree from the canons ; but I beseech you, most pious prelate, that you would recal to my mind what in my terror I have quite lost."   On this the bishop, and the rest of the company, began to laugh and jest ; but, the priest being still urgent, the Bishop yielded to his entreaties, and repeated a couple of verses :—" Blessed is the man that walketh not in the counsel of the ungodly, nor standeth in the way of sinners, nor sitteth in the seat of the scornful ; but his delight is in the law of the Lord ; and in his law doth he meditate day and night."—" Very right, most holy father," cried the priest, " and then the rest of your time you may play at dice."

As to the zealous bishop, who relates this story, are we to take his words respecting the state of the church as a plain statement of facts, and set them down as cold-blooded history ? or do the very act and circumstances of his writing them constrain us to receive them with some qualification ?

was no longer in use among them. They were obliged, on that account, to write all their books upon parchment, and as the price of that was high, books became extremely rare, and of great value. We may judge of the scarcity of the materials for writing them from one circumstance. There still remain several manuscripts of the eighth, ninth, and following centuries, wrote on parchment, from which some former writing had been erased, in order to substitute a new composition in its place. In this manner, it is probable, that several works of the ancients perished. A book of Livy, or of Tacitus, might be erased to make room for the legendary tale of a saint, or the superstitious prayers of a missal. Murat. Anti. Ital. v. iii., p. 833. P. de Montfaucon affirms, that the greater part of the manuscripts on parchment which he had seen, those of an ancient date excepted, are written on parchment from which some former treatise had been erased. Mém. de l'Acad. des inscript. tom. ix., p. 325. As the want of materials for writing is one reason why so many of the works of the ancients have perished, it accounts likewise for the small number of manuscripts, of any kind, previous to the eleventh century, when they began to multiply, from a cause which shall be mentioned. Hist. Liter. de France, tom. vi., p. 6.''

Much of the foregoing, which relates to the materials, value, and scarcity of books during the period in question, would lead us into multifarious discussion ; yet it is so interwoven with the specific statements with which it is my object at present to deal, that I know not how to convince the reader that I am acting fairly, or even to make the matter intelligible, except by thus quoting the whole passage. I do not know whether there ever was a time when readers looked out the passages referred to, or granted the writer's request that they would, " see," " compare," etc., such-and-such things, which for brevity's sake he would not transcribe : but if readers ever did this, I am morally certain that they have long since ceased to do it ; and, therefore, where I feel it necessary that the reader should know what has been said, I dare not content myself with merely referring even to so common a book as Robertson's.

As to the specific statements, allow me to say— but perhaps the reader would be offended at my saying all that I might be inclined to say on the subject—it brings us on rather tender ground, and he may think that I am as bad as the monks ; and, besides, one is really ashamed to say, in the nineteenth century, what they might have been allowed to say a thousand years ago. Let me rather suppose some monk, of the period to which Robertson refers, to rise in defence of his order. He may say what he pleases ; and if he should talk nonsense, the enlightened reader will smile and forgive him. Let him be as absurd and wretched a creature as modern taste can conceive—such as, from his own description, we may suppose the historian Ditmar to have been [9], or the Prior of Grandmont, whose

> " Frequens genuflexio nasum oblicavit,
> Genibus et manibus callum concreavit."

Let us suppose such a person brought to light, and blinking in our sunshine, and at length made to understand the nature of the charge preferred against him and his brethren. He might, perhaps, answer—" Truly, Dr. Robertson, you are rather hard upon us. To be sure, some part of what you say cannot be denied—a book of Tacitus or Livy *may* have been erased to make room for a legend, or a missal—it is, as you say, a peradventure ; but it *may* have been so ; and, if it was, people could do better without books of Tacitus and Livy than without prayer-books. Nay, you who go on to tell us that in those days ' even monasteries of considerable note had only one missal,'—you who profess yourself to be a Christian minister (which many of us were not), ought to applaud us for spoiling the Egyptians, and serving ourselves of the heathen. We *may* have destroyed a book of Tacitus or Livy, to preserve a legend, or make a missal ; or it *may*

---

[9] " Agnosce, lector, proceritatem, et videbis in me parvum homuncionem, maxilla deformem leva, et latere eodem, quia hinc olim erupit semper turgescens fistula. Nasus in pueritia fractus ridiculum me facit, idque totum nil questus essem, si interius aliquid splendiscerem."—*Lib.* IV. *ap. Leibn. Scr. Bruns. Tom.* I. *p.* 364.

have been the other way. We *may* have saved the youth of Christendom from some heathen obscenity, and preserved a valuable treatise of Jerome, Ambrose, or Augustine—or, if these names only provoke a sneer, we *may* have thus preserved some of those Annals to which you modern historians are indebted (not immediately, I fear, in most cases) for whatever is true in your works; and which, in grateful return, some of you love to describe as dull, stupid, barbarous, musty, old records, with which you have condescended to defile yourselves for the public good. But then, as to our substituting the *legendary tales* of the saints—under favour, doctor, I cannot help thinking, from the way in which you write, that you have not quite a correct idea of the time when what are commonly known to Protestants as the legends of the Roman Church were principally written. We, who lived between the seventh and eleventh centuries, had comparatively little to do with the matter. We plead guilty to great ignorance, bad Latin, and blunders ; to much nonsense, some lies, and a good deal that was, in fact, legendary—but as to what your readers would understand by legendary tales of saints, you must look to a later period,—you must go forward to the times when (as that so good inquisitor and bishop, Bernard Guido, says) ' Frater Jacobus de Voragine Lombardus, postmodum Archiepiscopus Januensis, suam conflavit compilationem *more suo* in *vitis* sanctorum *novis,* sicut et de aliis sanctis fecit, prout ibiden patet.' [1] You must talk to writers of the thirteenth century ; you may go on, and talk to the Council of Trent, and the Congregation of the Index, and ask them why they never expurgated the Golden Legend, why they never even weeded out its barbarous blunders, to say nothing of its lies. Yes, to the horrible disgrace of our church, you may ask why they never stretched out the hand

---

[1] Libellus de Magist. Ord. Prædic. *M. & D.* VI., 405.

of correction, or restriction—never even directed
the slightest breath of censure—towards it, and the
thousand and one lying books that began to be
made, and circulated, and devoured, as soon as what
you are pleased to call the revival of letters had set
men to read the monstrous figments, the foul and
scandalous obscenities of the pagan poets. Then
you may go on with Ribadaneira, and a host of
moderns,—but do not accuse *us*,—look for yourself,
and see what we *did* write ; and I am persuaded
that, though you may sometimes see a legendary
tale of a saint, and sometimes a superstitious prayer
of a missal, you will find comparatively little for
which it would have been so very sinful to scrape a
parchment, which might, or might not, contain a
book of Tacitus or Livy.

"Moreover, in case we should not come to anything like an agreement as to relative value, let me
add, that as we are not the people principally concerned in concocting the legends, so we are not the
people who were most addicted to scraping parch-
ments. I do not mean to deny that what you say
is true as to the letter, and that 'there still remain
several manuscripts of the eighth, ninth, and *following* centuries,' which have been so treated. There
are, I confess, *several* such specimens ; but you
know, though you slur over (not to say misrepre-
sent) his words, by saying ' of ancient date,' that
Montfaucon expressly limits his statement to manuscripts written *since* the *twelfth* century ; [2] and

---

[2] Not having it in my power to verify the citation of Montfaucon, I applied to a learned friend who has access to a public
library. He replied, " This reference is wrong --there is nothing,
in the volume referred to, by Montfaucon, nor any mention of him
in the page given above. I therefore looked to the index, where,
under Montfaucon's name, I got a reference to a paper of his, vol.
vi. p. 592, entitled, ' Dissertation sur la plante appellée Papyrus,
sur le papier d'Egypte, sur le papier de coton, et sur celuy dont
on se sert aujourd'huy.' In p. 606 is the following passage,
which, I presume, gave rise to Robertson's statement. After
having mentioned the fact, that ' depuis le xiie Siècle,' ancient

therefore I put it to your own conscience, whether
it is not probable that we were more sinned against
than sinning in this matter—whether those who
wanted writing materials were likely to prefer
parchment which was older than our time, to that
which we had used—and whether our works were
not more exposed to erasure than those of earlier
writers ? I have said that you know this—for I
cannot affect to suppose that you did not see the
words which you have omitted or altered—but I
doubt whether you do know, that a great part of
the scraping of manuscripts was not owing to our
writing legends or missals, but was perpetrated in
order to carry on the ungodly quarrels, or worldly
business, of secular men ; so that as late as the
fourteenth and fifteenth centuries notaries were restricted from practising, until they had taken an
oath to use none but new parchment."

I do not mean to make myself responsible for all
that a monk under such circumstances might say ;
but yet I cannot suppress my opinion, that if any of
that fraternity had so addressed Robertson, his
most prudent and popular course would have been
to turn short round on the opposite tact, and to
reply—" Ah ! you sensual, ignorant, lazy monks ;
you could not read or write—potius dediti gulæ
quam glossæ," etc.

---

writings were erased to make way for books of the church—and
thus that Polybius, Dio, Diodorus, etc. were converted into
Triodions, Pentecostaries, Homilies, etc. he says, ' Après une
exacte recherche, je puis assurer que des livres écrits sur du
parchemin *depuis le xii Siècle*, j'en ay plus trouvé dont on avoit
raclé l'ancienne écriture, que d'autres.' "

No. IV.

Bibliothekar. Haben sie des *Muratorius* seine Werke nicht
                gelesen ?
P. Priszilian. In meinem Leben nicht; ich kenne sie gar nicht.
                                                    DIE HEILIGEN.

I HAVE already observed that there is often great
difficulty in meeting broad general assertions, even
when one is sure that they are untrue ; and I may
add that it is as difficult—perhaps it is impossible—
to prevent, or remove, the erroneous impressions
likely to arise from statements which though really
false are *verbally* true. My meaning will be
illustrated by considering the statement with which
Robertson follows those already discussed.

" Many circumstances prove the scarcity of books during these
ages. Private persons seldom possessed any books whatever. Even
monasteries of considerable note had only one missal. Murat.
Antiq. v. ix. p. 789."

Certainly there needs no proof that books were
scarce during the middle ages. No doubt the
scarcity, as compared with the plenty, and even
surfeit, of the present day, was great indeed. Yet,
great as it was, I cannot help suspecting that it has
been exaggerated ; and I think we shall find ground
to doubt the truth of the assertion that " private
persons seldom possessed any books whatever " —
or if, by assigning a lax, and comparative, meaning
to " seldom," the statement should be turned into
a notorious truth not worth uttering, we shall see
reason for believing that the impression which it
was calculated to convey, and probably has conveyed
to most readers, is erroneous.
To come, however, to the specific statement,

backed by the authority of Muratori—for my
present business is chiefly with it—" even monasteries of considerable note had only one missal."
In the first place, will anybody tell me what they
wanted with more? " Monasteries of considerable
note " had but one church, or chapel, and not more
inmates than that one building would contain ; and
might not mass be said every hour of every day all
the year round, out of *one* missal, as well as if there
had been fifty? " Yes," it may be said " but one is
accustomed to look on monasteries as having been,
in some small and comparative degree, places where
there was *some* learning, and some appearance at
least of religion ; and one is surprised to hear of
their being so ill provided with books." I know it
—I know that no man who has any tolerable
acquaintance with history, sacred or secular, can
help having some idea—perhaps a very vague and
discouraged idea—that, in those ages, the monastery
was the refuge of want and weakness, the nursery
of art, the depository of learning, and the sanctuary
of religion. This, I say, every man who is moderately acquainted with history must know ; even
though he should not be aware of the less obvious,
but not less certain influence of monastic institutions on agriculture, commerce, and those comforts
and pleasures of social life from which their inmates
were themselves excluded. Something like this, I
repeat, every tolerably educated man does feel ; but
a strange sort of vague contradiction is thrown over
it by such foolish statements as that which I have
quoted from Robertson. Half the readers of his
History of Charles V. do not know what a Missal is,
or why the monks wanted any, or what they did
with that single one which they are admitted to
have had ; but yet, from the way in which it is
stated, they take it for granted that it was a
horrible delinquency in " monasteries of considerable note," to have only one missal—and if *they*
were so wretchedly off, in what state were the thou-

sands of monasteries which were of inconsiderable note, or of no note at all?

But, to say the truth, all this, though not I hope untrue or entirely useless, is not to our present purpose; as the reader will find if he refers to Muratori, or favours me with his attention to a brief statement of the grounds on which Robertson ventured to make his assertion.

The Abbot Bonus appears to have been born about the year 990; and though the place of his birth is not certainly known, it seems probable that he was a native of Pisa.   At all events we are informed that he became a monk at Nonantula, and that he, and his uncle Peter, came from thence in the year 1018, to Pisa, where they laid the foundation of the monastery of St. Michael, which certainly was afterwards " of considerable note." Bonus presided over it for thirty years; after which period some dispute or dissension (it does not clearly appear of what nature, but it seems not to have been any quarrel with his monks) caused him to quit his monastery, and set off for Corsica, where some property had been bequeathed to him, and where he proposed to live as a private person. Stopping, however, on his voyage at the island of Gorgona, where there was a monastery, he found the monks greatly distressed by the recent loss of their Abbot.   They unanimously called on Bonus to take his place.   He resisted for some time; but overcome by their importunity, he consented; requesting only leave to return to Pisa, in order to bid farewell to his old associates, and to exhort them with respect to the choice of a successor. Having obtained permission, and executed his purpose, he returned to Gorgona, and undertook the office of abbot there, which he held until his death in the year 1070.   On quitting the monastery at Pisa, however, he wrote a statement of what he had done in the matter of founding and maintaining it; and it is to this " Breve Recordationis," printed by

Muratori, in the fourth volume (not the ninth, for there are but six), of his *Antiquitates Italicæ medii ævi* that Robertson refers.[1]

I by no means suppose that the Abbot did, or could foresee what inferences would be drawn from a fact which he relates ; but really, if he had, he could hardly have told his story in terms more adapted to preclude the possibility of such perversion. The monastery " of considerable note " (that is, as the Abbot says, in the pride of his heart many years afterwards, " que *nunc* est cœnobium ") was *then* no monastery at all, but a chapel near Pisa (*capella, que tunc temporis detinebatur a presbyteris*), which was in a most deplorable and destitute condition, when " Senior Stephanus," I presume the principal authority in Pisa, procured this poor monk to come and perform divine service. Not only does Bonus call it simply a chapel, but he tells us that when he came there he found *neither monk nor abbot*, nor any decent dwelling place, and in fact nothing but a hut. (*Neque monachun, neque abbatem ibidem inveni ; et non casam neque mansionem sed tantummodo unum tugurium, ubi cepi habitare cum avunculo meo.*) He then proceeds to detail the destitute state of the place as to service-books, vestments, bells, and all the requisites for the performance of divine service; and, having given a lamentable picture, he breaks out, with honest pride—may I not hope with real and pious gratitude ?—" Now hear, and understand, how that place is improved by the help of Almighty God, and by mine, and by that of my monks, and that of the good Christians

---

[1] It was, I believe, first printed by Mabillon ; then by Grandius (an abbot of St. Michael's, who, after seven centuries, erected a statue in honour of his predecessor, Bonus) ; by Muratori, to whom Robertson refers ; and, fourthly, by Mitarelli and Costadoni, in their " Annales Camaldulenses." This latter work contains, I believe, the fullest account of the abbot, and to it I am indebted for the facts and extracts which I here give. [The " Breve Recordationis " at full length will be found at the end of this paper.]

of our city." After five years he set to work on
the church, and went to Rome, where he bought
columns for it; and then made a belfry, which he
furnished with two bells. Fifteen years afterwards,
this belfry gave place to one much handsomer, containing seven bells, the largest of which weighed
twelve hundred pounds. The vestments, by the
time when the Abbot wrote, had not only increased
in number, but some of them were so costly that, as
he tells us, the bishop of the diocese might have
said mass in them on Easter Sunday, "cum honore"
—the single tin cup had been exchanged for four
chalices, one of gold and three of silver—the single
hut had expanded into a monastery, with all suitable
offices and appendages, and a considerable estate in
land; and, what is more to our purpose, instead of
the " single missal," the monks of the monastery of
St. Michael rejoiced in a library consisting of thirty-
four volumes. But this requires more specific
notice, for it is the ground of Robertson's statement.

In describing the destitute state of the chapel as
he originally found it, the Abbot tells us, " in ipsa
ecclesia non inveni aliud nisi unum missale;" and
afterwards he repeats, "quando veni in ipsum
locum non legebatur in ipsa ecclesia, per totum fere
annum, nisi epistole et evangelia quia non habebatur
nisi unum missale."

Now, the first thing to observe is, that there is
no pretence for calling the place a " Monastery" at
all at the time when it had only one missal.

Secondly, that in speaking thus of " one missal,"
Robertson obviously misunderstands the drift of
the Abbot's complaint, which was not that the
chapel had *only one* missal, but that it had no other
service-book *but* a missal; and that, therefore, only
that service could be performed which was contained
in the Missals. *Unus*, in writers of that period,
whether Italian, French, or German, no more implies
definite singularity than the corresponding word in

either of those languages now does. We alone, I believe, have discarded it, or turned it into "a," and are apt to smile when our foreign friends very naturally say, "Here is one book," etc.

Thirdly, be it observed, that as soon as this place did become a monastery it began to have books. And this seems to me the more creditable, because, during a great part of the time, the monks were in want of the comforts, and even perhaps of the necessaries, of life; and what they got was principally obtained by begging. The great and ruling passion of the poor Abbot seems to have been to form a monastery, and provide it with everything needful; and, as to himself, he tells us, that for the first two years he had only a single shirt per annum, and used to lie in bed while it was washed; and that during the whole thirty years he was never possessed of two suits of clothes, or a horse.

As to the books, however, I must give the list in his own words, grammar, and spelling :—

Sermonum liber unus quem ego scripsi solus cum Priore meo, sicut habetur domui Sancte Marie, valde optimus.

Liber Historiarum unus, ubi continetur quidquid in sancta ecclesia pertinet ad legendum per totum annum.

Textum Evangeliorum unum, valde optime scriptum, cum tabule de argento valde bone.

Passionarium unum novum, ubi sunt omnes passiones ecclesiastice.

Tractatum super Genesis, Sancti Augustini liber unus.

Dialogorum, liber unus.

Moralium Job, liber unus.

Summum bonum, liber unus.

Diadema, liber unus.

Paradisi, liber unus.

Glossarum, liber unus.

Canones, liber unus.

Sancti Benedicti Regula, liber unus.

Pastorale, liber unus.

Antiphonarii VIII.

Quinque Diurnales.

Tres Nocturnales.

Liber Bibliothece[2] novum quod est comparatum libras decem.

Missales quinque; unum missale valde optimum, quod semper in arca manebit, valentem solidos C.

Super Ezechiel, liber unus.

Libri Psalmorum valde optimi V.

---

[2] I hope to give some catalogues relating to the period with which we are engaged, which will offer a fitter opportunity for saying something of these and other books; but I am apprehen-

I am aware that this catalogue may provoke a smile from those who are conversant with modern collections; but I am not ashamed to say that I honour the man who, under such circumstances, had the spirit, and found the means, to rebuild or enlarge his church, to provide all things necessary for the honourable performance of divine service, to annex a monastery, and make a beginning for a school of learning. Let me also (partly to illustrate what I have said in the preceding number, and partly to prepare the way for what I hope more fully to show) request the reader to observe the nature of the books in this little list—are they legendary tales of saints? mere lies and rubbish? But more of this, I hope, hereafter.

Having said so much of the Abbot Bonus, I am anxious to proceed to the account which Robertson gives of the Abbot Lupus; but I wish first to add a few words respecting the canons and the Abbot Regino. In the second number I stated that I had not got the original work of the Abbot, but since that number was printed, the kindness of a learned friend has furnished me with the book, and I am desirous to give the passage as it really stands. Besides, I am induced to recur to the subject because, after I had written the preceding part of this paper, I happened to take up a "History of Switzerland, designed for young persons," published by Harvey and Darton in 1825, which tells the rising generation that, "so small were the qualifications thought requisite for the priesthood before the Reformation, that candidates were admitted to holy orders if they could only read and tolerably understand what they read," p. 237. This, I

---

sive that some readers may not know that *Bibliotheca* was, in those days, the latin, or at least the name, for a Bible. Will the protestant reader give the abbot and his monks any credit for buying it, in so early a period of their monastery, at so great a price? and, honestly (but quite between ourselves), would he have expected to find *that* book in the list?

presume, is taken from Robertson's statement, that " one of the questions appointed to be put to candidates for orders, was this, ' Whether they could read the Gospels and Epistles, and explain the sense of them, at least, literally.' " It may be said (and is very likely to be said by anybody who may take the trouble to read such a paper as this) that though this history of Switzerland costs six shillings, it is only a child's book, that they never heard of it, and that it is not worth notice. To this I answer, first, that children's books are not read by children only, and it was not in the hands of a child that I found this book; and also that, in my opinion, even children should not be set to read lies ; secondly, I confess that I never saw the book until this very day, but I do hold it to be very well worth notice as an instance of the way in which the errors of popular writers are copied and disseminated, and dribbled down in minor publications.

To come, however, to the point, the inquiry does not at all respect candidates for orders, but is one which a bishop is directed to make in all the cures in his diocese. I may have to recur to it, but for the present it is enough to say that it is entitled, " Inquisitio de his quæ Episcopus vel ejus ministri in suo districtu vel territorio inquirere debeant per vicos, pagos, atque parrœchias suæ dioceseos." It suggests ninety-five points of inquiry, of which the first fifteen relate to the church, its state of repair, and the requisites for the performance of divine service. No. 16—73, concern the life and conversation of the priest. No. 74—80, respect points on which the priest was to be personally questioned ; that is, as to his parentage, place of birth, by what bishop he was ordained, etc. No. 81—95, relate to his ministry (Posthæc de ministerio sibi commisso inquirendum est) and it is that part of the 83rd and 85th which I mark by italics that is quoted by Brucker,[3] but I must extract the two which precede :—" Si expositionem symboli atque orationis dominicæ juxta traditionem orthodoxorum patrum penes se scriptam habeat, et eam pleniter intellegat, et inde prædicando populum sibi commissum sedulo instruat. 82. Si orationes Missarum, præfationem quoque canonis, et eundem canonem bene intellegat, et memoriter ac distincte proferre valeat. 83. *Si epistolam et evangelium bene legere possit atque saltem ad litteram ejus sensum manifestare.* 84. Si psalmorum verba et distinctiones regulariter ex corde cum canticis consuetudinariis pronuntiare sciat. 85. *Si sermonem Athanasii Episcopi de fide Sanctæ Trinitatis* cujus initium est ' Quicunque vult salvus esse ' *memoriter teneat, et sensum illius intellegat, et verbis communibus enuntiare sciat.*" The remaining ten questions inquire minutely as to his capability to perform different parts of the service, and the 94th inquires, " Si habeat quadraginta homilias Gregorii et eos studiose legat atque intellegat." To say nothing of the erroneous application of this document to the examination of candidates for orders, is it not most extraordinary that it should have been brought forward to prove that the clergy could not read ?

Let us, however, proceed to another case. Robertson goes on to say :—

" Lupus, Abbot of Ferrieres, in a letter to the Pope, A.D. 855, beseeches him to lend him a copy of Cicero de Oratore, and Quintilian's Institutions. ' For,' says he, ' although we have parts of those books, there is no complete copy of them in all France.' Murat. Antiq. v. iii. p. 835.' '

The plain matter of fact is, that two monks, named Adulphus and Acaricus, having resolved on

---

[3] Of this, indeed, Robertson ought to have been aware, for Brucker introduces it as a formula inquisitionis . . . "secundum quam inquirere debebat Episcopus per vicos, etc. . . . In ea enim *inter alia* circa *presbyteros* jubetur inquiri, ' Si,' " etc.

a pilgrimage, the Abbot took the opportunity of
sending to Rome what was in fact a letter of introduction as it respected them, a tender of his own
humble service to the Pope, and a request that his
Holiness would lend him some books, in order that
he might have them copied for the library of his
monastery. From the part of the letter which
relates to this latter point,[4] it appears, in the first
place, that Lupus says nothing about " all France ;"
though here, I confess, that Robertson seems to
have been misled by Muratori, who, after quoting
a part of the letter, says, "Hæc Lupus, in cujus
verbis non solum animadvertere possumus codicum
raritatem, quum supra memoratos *universa Gallia*
suppeditare Lupo non posset, iique *in tam remota
regione* quærendi essent, sed, etc." Lupus, however, only says, of certain works of Cicero and
Quintilian, " *we* have parts, but desire through you
to obtain the whole ;" and by " we," he obviously
meant his own monastery. Why Robertson did not
mention that the request included Donatus on
Terence, I do not know ; but what he says of " all
France "—though obviously a very exaggerated
translation of *nostris regionibus*, considering the
state of things in those days—applies *not* to the

---

[4] " Cæterum quia parentes thesaurizare debent filiis, ut doctor
gentium manifestat, nosque vobis obsequentissimi filii   esse
cupimus, commentarios beati Hieronymi in Hieremiam, post
sextum librum usque in finem prædicti prophetæ per eosdem
fratres nobis mitti deposcimus in codice reverendæ veritatis, vestræ
sanctitati, si id obtinuerimus, postquam celeriter exscriptus fuerit
sine dubio remittendos.   Nam in nostris regionibus nusquam ullus
post sextum commentarium potuit inveniri ; et optamus in vobis
recuperare quicquid parvitati nostræ deesse sentimus.   Petimus
etiam Tullium de Oratore et xii libros Institutionum Oratoriarum
Quintiliani, qui uno, nec ingenti, volumine continentur : quorum
utriusque auctorum partes habemus, verum plenitudinem per vos
desideramus obtinere.   Pari intentione Donati Commentum in
Terentium flagitamus.   Quæ auctorum opera si vestra liberalitas
nobis largita fuerit, Deo annuente, cum memorato Sancti Hieronymi
codice, fideliter omnino restituenda curabimus."—*Ep.* 103, *edit.
Baluz.*, p. 155.

books which Robertson mentions, but to the Commentaries of Jerome on Jeremiah, from the sixth
book to the end.

Now as to the Abbot's not having a complete copy
of these books of Cicero and Quintilian, and his pre-
ferring, as he had so good an opportunity, to borrow
a volume of no great bulk which he knew to contain
all that he wanted *from Rome,* to sending about in
his own country, even if that had been equally
easy, or even practicable ; and indeed, generally, as
to the sort of half-contraband trade which was
carried on about the classics by the more learned
ecclesiastics of those days—as to this point, which
is not uninteresting when viewed in connexion with
our subject, I hope to speak more fully elsewhere ;
here it is only worth while to notice that, according
to the Abbot Lupus, the commentaries of Jerome
on Jeremiah, from the sixth book to the end, were
not to be found " in regionibus nostris;" and
whether we interpret this to mean what a modern
reader would understand by " all France," or
restrict it to more reasonable limits, it was still a
very broad assertion. Might not the Abbot be mistaken as to the fact ? With all due respect for the
Abbot of Ferrieres, and on some grounds he
deserved not a little, are we bound to believe that
he knew of *all* the books " in regionibus nostris,"
whatever we may suppose that phrase to mean ?
Robertson elsewhere says :—

" Many proofs occur in history of the little intercourse between
nations during the middle ages ;" [and it is rather a singular
coincidence, that he states in proof of this,] " Even so late as the
beginning of the twelfth century, the monks of *Ferrieres,* in the
diocese of Sens, did not know that there was such a city as
Tournay in Flanders ; and the monks of St. Martin, of Tournay,
were equally unacquainted with the situation of Ferrieres. A
transaction in which they were both concerned made it necessary
for them to have some intercourse. The mutual interest of both
monasteries prompted each to find out the situation of the other.
After a long search, which is particularly described, the dis-
covery was made by accident. Herimannus Abbas de Res-

tauratione St. Martini Tornacensis ap. Dach. Spicel. vol. xii.,
p. 400."[5]

I am induced to make this extract, not only
because it states what is, under proper and reasonable limitations, an acknowledged truth, and one
which it is very necessary to bear in mind, but
because it incidentally furnishes another instance of
what I hope it is true, as well as charitable, to call
the extreme carelessness with which Robertson
quoted. No doubt monks situated at places as far
distant, and as little connected, as Ferrieres and
Tournay were not likely to know much about each
other ; but the view which Robertson gives of the
matter is quite erroneous. It would occupy too
much space to show this in detail ; but I must just
observe, that so far from its appearing that the
monks of Ferrieres did not know that there was
such a city as Tournay—which is indeed a supposition altogether absurd, especially as the conversation
between the two monks which brought about an
understanding and intercourse between the monasteries took place at Courtray, and he of Ferrieres
must have passed comparatively near to Tournay to
get there, as anybody may see by the map—it is
perfectly clear, from Heriman's account, that they
did know of the existence of Tournay and where to
find it ; and that the place which they did *not* know,
and could *not* find, was a certain monastery of St.
Martin, said to be at Tournay. They had in their
possession old documents relating to it, but of the
place itself as existing they could learn nothing—
and why? simply because, though there had been
such a place, it had ceased to exist for some centuries, insomuch that some, perhaps most people,
disputed whether it had ever existed at all. The
monks of Ferrieres had no " interest " (but rather

---

[5] See note [FF.] No. XIX., p. 325.

the contrary) in finding out the place, but they had
some curiosity on the subject; and when one of
them being at Courtray accidentally met with a
monk, who told him that he belonged to the monastery of St. Martin, at Tournay, he was surprised,
and asked him where in the world it was, for they
had never been able to find it.   It did not probably
appear strange to the monk of Tournay (and it will
not seem strange to any reflecting person) that the
monks of Ferrieres should not have heard how
Master Odo and his clerks had revived this monastery of St. Martin—that is, had settled down on the
old foundation (like Bonus and his uncle at Pisa),
and dragged on about twenty years of miserable
poverty and obscurity, in restoring, or rather re-
founding, what in after ages became most eminently
a "monastery of considerable note."   He answered
(truly, we may believe, as far as he knew) that it
was quite a recent foundation ; and he seems not to
have known, or not to have cared, about its claim
to antiquity, or to have made any farther inquiries
when the monk of Ferrieres told him that they had
documents relating to its former existence.   When,
however, he returned to his monastery at Tournay,
and related to his brethren what he had heard, they
lost no time in sending to Courtray for farther information ; but the monk of Ferrieres was gone,
and it is true that they did not know how to follow
him.   How Heriman hunted for the Abbot of
Ferrieres, and found him at the Council of Rheims,
and how he followed him, by his direction, to
Ferrieres, and found that by that time he had
changed his mind as to parting with the documents,
or giving information on the subject, from fear, as
it seemed, of giving offence to one or more of his
neighbours, by setting on foot a claim to property
which was supposed to belong to St. Martin's, at
Tournay, but which had got into other hands ;
these, and many curious and interesting particulars,

the reader may find in Heriman's own account of
the matter to which Robertson refers, but they
would be out of place here.

I quote the statement, as I have already said, not
to question so notorious a fact as that intercourse
between distant places was comparatively small at
that period, and attended with difficulties unknown
in these days, but to show the carelessness with
which Robertson quoted,—and moreover the in-
consistency with which he argued, for if the monks
of Ferrieres in the twelfth century did not know
that there was such a city as Tournay, could we
suppose that an Abbot of Ferrieres, more than
two centuries and a half before, was competent to
say that any given book was not to be found " in
all France ?"

My own feelings with regard to this letter of
Lupus are much like those expressed by Fleury
respecting another of his epistles. After having
said, that " Dans une autre lettre il prie un ami de
lui apporter les guerres de Catilina et le Jugurtha
de Salluste, et les Verrines de Ciceron," he adds,
" C'est la curiosité de ces sàvans abbez, et le travail
de leur moines, qui nous ont conservé les livres de la
bonne antiquité ecclesiastique et prophane."[6]   Indeed, when Robertson had Muratori before him, and
adopted that part of his remarks on Lupus which I
have already extracted, I wish he had also attended
to what Muratori proceeded to say. After remark-
ing on the scarcity of books, in the terms which I
have quoted, and on the assurance of the abbot in
asking that such treasures should be exposed to the
perils of such a journey, Muratori says, " *Potius
tamen hinc discendum nobis*, quamplurimas iis
ipsis monachis habendas esse gratias, quum ferme
eorum tantummodo cura, quidquid librorum veterum
superest, nos habeamus; et majores quidem nostros

---

[6] Tom. x. p. 609.

excusatione dignos, si plura in literis excolendis non
præstitere; nos vero indignos, qui in tanta librorum
copia adhuc desides et indocti esse pergimus." ⁷

---

⁷ I hope I may be forgiven if there is any vanity mixed with the
feelings which induce me to retain the note which my dear and
partial friend the Editor annexed to this paper when it was first
printed in the " British Magazine " for June, 1835 :—[" The
following passages from the letters of Gerbert, afterwards created
pope in A.D. 998, by the name of Silvester II., may afford some
confirmation and illustration to the very interesting and valuable
paper in the text. He was abbot of Bobbio during part of the
time when they were written. In his 130th letter, to Rainald, a
monk, written long before his elevation, he says, 'I entreat you to
render me one service, which you can do without danger or injury
to yourself, and which will bind me most closely to you. *You know
with what zeal I seek for copies of books from all quarters; and you
know how many writers there are everywhere, both in the cities and
the country parts of Italy.* I entreat you then, that, *without any
other persons knowing it,* and at your own cost, transcripts be made
for me of M. Manilius de Astrologia, Victorinus de Rhetorica,
Demosthenes Ophthalmicus.' (This is explained by another
letter.) ' I promise you most faithfully that this kind service shall
be kept in sacred secrecy, and that whatever you lay out I will pay
you to the full, according to your accounts, and whenever you
require it.' In letter 123 he writes to Thietmar of Mayence, for a
part of one of the works of Boetius, which was wanting in his copy.
In letter 9, to the Abbot Giselbert, he writes respecting deficiencies
at the end of his MS. of the oration of Cicero, ' Pro Rege Dejotaro,'
and at the beginning of a treatise of Demosthenes the Philosopher,
called ' *Ophthalmicus.*' In letter 8, to the Archbishop of Rheims,
he requests that prelate to borrow for him, from Azo, an Abbot, a
copy of Cæsar. In return, he promises to communicate whatever
literary treasures he had, especially eight volumes of Boetius on
astrology, some very beautiful geometrical figures, and other things
not less to be admired. In letter 7, he requests a friend (Airard)
to attend to other business of the same kind—the correction, as it
would seem, of a MS. of Pliny (*Plinius emendetur*), and the transcribing MSS. (not named) which were kept at two different
places. Again, in letter 44, to Egbert, the Abbot of Tours, he
mentions his own diligent study of philosophy, and of the arts of
eloquence, and states, that with a view to them, he had been very
busy in collecting a library; that he had been paying, for a long
time, transcribers at Rome, and other parts of Italy, in Germany
and Belgium, and buying copies of authors at great expense, by
the aid of friends in his own country. He then goes on to beg the

abbot to assist him in the same pursuit in *his* country ; adding, that he gives a list, at the end of his letter, of the works which he wishes transcribed (unfortunately lost, or not printed), and will supply parchment, and other necessary costs, at the abbot's demand. In many other letters he mentions his own works on rhetoric, arithmetic, and his completion of a sphere. But if in the tenth century we find the work of transcribing so common, that there were writers everywhere, in the cities and country places in Italy, and, as it would seem from other letters, no difficulty in finding them elsewhere, if the collection of a library was so great a matter, that many were ready to assist, surely matters were far different from our common notions.—ED."]

THE "BREVE RECORDATIONIS" OF THE ABBOT BONUS.

Referred to p. 64.

This document would have been too long for insertion in a magazine; but I hope it is not out of place here; and I cannot resist the temptation to give it entire, not only because it seems to be the fairest way of dealing in the matter, but also because it is really a curious document, both as to facts and style. No translation would do it justice. The good abbot does indeed

" From settled rules with brave disorder part,
And snatch a grace beyond the reach of art."

The dignified, though unpretending, simplicity with which he breaks his way through the little restraints of grammar, and gratefully uses the first case or tense that comes to hand, will probably be new to most readers, and will, I trust, convince those who are suspicious, that I am not upholding the pure latinity of the Dark Ages.

" In nomine Domini nostri Jesu Christi Dei eterni. Breve recordationis facio ego Bonus Abbas, qualiter ab initio inchoavi conversari in Ecclesia Sancti Michaelis, *que nunc est cenobium.* Fecit me venire Senior Stephanus de Nonantulis, cum avunculo meo Petro, et investivit me de *ista capella,* que tunc temporis detinebatur a presbyteris, et *neque monachum, neque Abbatem ibidem inveni;* et non casam, neque mansionem, sed tantummodo unum tugurium, ubi cepi habitare cum avunculo meo. Et operabatur tunc temporis in turre ipsius ecclesiæ, et quod habebam, et habere potui dedi in restaurationem ipsius turris ad magistros et ad manuales, et ad quod necesse erat. Et cessavit ipse Stefanus laborare in ecclesia post unum mensem quam ego cepi habitare in ipso loco, et non levavit in altitudinem ipsam turrem nisi tantummodo unum passum super ipsam ecclesiam. Et post hec finitus est annus quod ipsa ecclesia fuit offerta ad honorem Dei et Sancti Michaelis, et ad officium Sancti Benedicti, et ad ipsius regulam monachis ibidem in perpetuum conversandis. Et hoc vobis notum sit, quia *in ipsa ecclesia non inveni aliud nisi unum missale*, et unum calicem de stagno, et unum camisum cum amicto, et unam stolam de lino, et unam planetulam, que nunc superest.[8] . . . quia non inveni in ipso loco neque squillam, neque campanam, sed tantummodo unam tabulam et cum ipsa tabula . . . ipsa ecclesia quatuor . . . nunc audite et intelligite qualiter melioratus est locus ipse cum auxilio Omnipotentis Dei, et meo, et de meis monachis, et de bonis christianis nostre civitatis. Post quinque annos cepi laborare in ipsam turrim quam nunc videtis de helemosina bonorum hominum que nobis dabatur, et edificavi in ipsa turre ecclesiam que nunc videtur ab omnibus et perrexi ad Romam per columnas ipsius ecclesiæ, et comparavi, et feci eas venire in navim per mare, de nostro pretio ; et post hoc edificavi super ipsam ecclesiam campanilem. Cum autem consummatum fuisset ipsum campanilem cum turris et ecclesia, ambulavi per civitatem nostram cum Burello quondam bone memorie, et cum Landulfo parente ipsius et cum tribus aliis religiosis hominibus, et acquisivimus ipsa die centum solidos, quos dedi pro pretio ad magistros, et posui in ipsum campanile duas campanas. Et post quindecim annos videbatur mihi et fratribus meis ipsum campanilem parvum et rusticior, et everti eum a fundamentis, et feci fabricare illum quomodo videtis valde pulchrior, et posui in ipsum campanas septem, quos omnes de helemosinis fecit Domnus Dominicus meus Prior,[9] quem ego enutrivi, et nunc

---

[8] I give the document as I find it, presuming that such marks here and elsewhere indicate an hiatus in the MS.

[9] The authors of the Annales Camaldulenses combat what they suppose to be the mistake of thinking that the Prior cast the bells himself ; but I confess I so understand the Abbot, and am rather jealous of any attempt to rob the Prior of the credit due to him for this work of art. Who else was so likely to be able to do it ? Of an Archdeacon of Verona, nearly two hundred years before, we are told :

> " Quicquid auro, vel argento, et metallis ceteris,
> Quicquid lignis ex diversis, et marmore candido,
> Nullus unquam sic peritus in tantis operibus ; "

and plenty of such instances will occur to those who have paid any attention to the subject; but I notice it because I do not like to pass an opportunity of telling the march-of-intellect gentlemen, how much they are indebted to the monks for even what they are pleased to call " useful knowledge " in contradistinction to that knowledge which, to be sure, is of no more *use* to them than Alnwick or Chatsworth is to me. Of the same Archdeacon I read, " Horologium nocturnum nullus ante viderat "—but I hope to say more of him another time.

est Abbas Monasterii Sancti Zenonis : et omnes facte sunt de
helemosinis, que nobis facte sunt, et de missis, quas ego et
monachi mei decantaverunt. . . . Et habent in se ipse campane
libras metallorum tantas. Una campana major est ponderis
M.CC. . . . alia quingentarum, tertia trecentarum, quarta ducen-
tarum, quinta centum, sexta et septima quinquagintarum. Quando
veni in ipsum locum, non inveni, sicut superius memoravimus,
nisi unum camisum cum planetula et stola sua linea. Nunc autem
habemus in istum locum sanctum camisi XIII cum amictis suis. Et
tres camisi sunt tam perfecti et optimi ut Episcopus Opizus [1]
domui Sancte Marie possit cum honore cantare missas in die
Pasche. Et tres planetas, duo de pallio, una valentes solidos
centum, alia valentes solidos xxx, tertia de castanea, et tres stolas
optimas cum manipulis suis, due de purpure, et alia de pallio et
tres corporales de pallio valde optimo. Unum corporale de ipsis
tribus est de brusco deaurato valente solidos xx quem fecit Leo
Papa quarto Romanus, et habet in se depicta imago Salvatoris
nostri de brusco, et ex una parte imago Sancti Petri Apostoli, et
ex alia parte Sancti Johannis Evangeliste, et unum pluviale de
purpura, et alium de pallio valde bonum. *Quando veni in ipsum
locum non legebatur in ipsa ecclesia per totum fere annum nisi
epistole et evangelia quia non habebatur nisi unum missale.* Nunc
autem scitote quod melioratus est de libris ipsum locum.
  [Here follows the list of books already given at p. 66.]
  " Quot sunt insuper totum numeris XXXIV. Quando veni in
ipsa ecclesia non inveni nisi unum calicem de stagno. Modo,
autem, cum auxilio Domini, habentur ibi calices IIII. Unum
de auro, valde bonus, et habet uncias XI. Alius de argento
major, et habet libras III et mediam. Alii duo habentes in se
libram unam de argento per unamquemque. Quando veni in
ipsum locum non inveni nisi unum parvam domum, et postquam
cepi commorari cum meis monachis, feci levare mansiones ibidem
novas, et post decem annos disrumpebantur ipse mansiones quas
feci, quoniam erant de ligno de mala generatione, hoc est fuere de
cerro. Et dejeci ipse mansiones a fundamentis. Et hedificavi alias
mansiones de lignis castanietis quas venire feci per mare de Luni.
Et non post multum tempus comparavi da Erigo filio Eritii terram,
ubi nunc ipsum monasterium consistit, et dedi in ipsa terra libras
XLII, et post hec hedificavi ipsam domum a petra et calcina, ubi
sunt omnes officines, sicut abbatia habere debet ; et est tam perfecta
domus, ut in tota Marcha melior non est, cum columnas, quas de
Insula Ilba et de Luni adduci feci. Et hoc sciatis, quia quando
veni in ipsum locum non dedit amplius terre Stefanus in offersio-
nem in ipsa ecclesia, nisi stariorum sex in loco Sejo de valde mala,
et stariorum XXIIII ad Tramarice et similiter mala. Nunc audite

---

[1] He was Bishop of Pisa in A.D. 1044. See Ughelli, Italia
Sacra, tom. iii. p. 407.

qualiter, adjuvante Domino, amplificatus est locus ipse de bona
terra. Habet Monasterium Sancti Michaelis modo DC stariorum de
terra. Dedimus nos pretium in ipsa terra, quod nobis Dominus
dedit magnam partem, videlicet libras C valde modice minus, et de
alie terre cantavimus et promissimus ad ipsos parentes, que in
ipsum locum dari fecerunt in manibus nostris, multe misse decan-
tari. Cui mille, cui quingente, cui trescente, cui centum, et adjuto-
rium et consilium habuimus in aliquantulum de nostris senioribus.
Et dedit Albertus de Acuto in ipsum locum curtem unam in
Corsica, propter amorem et servitium quod fecit Johannes nepoti
meo ad predicto Alberto; et promisi dare predicto Johanni
servitium x libr. ut me adjuvaret, et non tulit mihi propter meum
amorem nisi solid. xx et fecit mihi dare hanc curtem, et detinet
ipsam curtem, inter montes et colles et planities et agros sis-
tariorum innumerabiles. Hoc est malum quod ego feci cum
monachis meis per annos xxx in ipsum locum; et non vobis
abscondam verecundiam meam, quoniam quando inchoavi habitare
in eodem loco, tam pauper erat locus, in duobus annis non habui
nisi unam stamineam per annum, et tempore estatis in meridie,
quando dormire pergebam, ipsam stamineam ad lavandum dabam :
et quando surgebam, predicta lota staminea induebar. Et nunquam habui equum, sicut ceteri abbates habent, et etiam viles
monachi. Sed si necesse erat in silva ambulare, aut in aliquo loco,
pedibus meis ambulabam ; et non duplicia vestimenta desideravi,
sed quando novum induebar, neque per Pascha neque per Natalem,
alium mutavi usque dum scinderetur, quia consideravi paupertatem
loci, ut cum debito non maneret. Et multa alia feci, que com-
memorare longum est . . . argenteum et alium ereum, quando
elongavi ecclesiam Sancti Michaelis expendi in ipsa ecclesia solidos
mille sine pane, et sine vino, et sine carne, et sine pisces. Omnia
ista expensaria in breve habentur scripta." p. 123.

No. V.

" Sed quis pejerat hoc ?   Non Muratorius hercle
Maffejusve, et Averanius, non qui Calepinum
Restituit nuper."—L. SECTANUS.

" Scientia fere omnis exolevit : et ubique locorum non mediocris
ignorantia successit.   Quod cum aio, non est mihi animus
significandi, Italiam in Lapponiam tum fuisse conversam, liter-
asque adeo sublatas, ut neque legere neque scribere quisquam
nosset.   Aut delirantis, aut infantissimi plane hominis hæc
opinio foret."—MURATORIUS.

PROCEEDING with his proofs and illustrations of the
extreme darkness of the middle ages, Robertson
tells us —

" The price of books became so high, that persons of a moderate
fortune could not afford to purchase them.   The Countess of Anjou
paid for a copy of the Homilies of Haimon, Bishop of Halberstadt,
two hundred sheep, five quarters of wheat, and the same quantity
of rye and millet.   Histoire Literaire de France, par des Religieux
Bénédictins, tom. vii. p. 3."

Of course we are to understand that this was
somewhere about the market price of a volume of
homilies ; and a price arising out of the scarcity of
the article, and the consequent difficulty of procuring it ; and, if this was the case, it is quite clear
that in those days most people must either have
made homilies for themselves, or gone without
them.   The story is, however, so very good that
one would be tempted, at first sight, to suspect it
of not being true.   Let us see what the price stated
by Robertson actually was, for it is fortunately
given in terms more intelligible—at least in such a

way as that we are more likely to come at a true notion of value—than if it had been stated in terms of money. The scribe, it is said, received two hundred sheep, and fifteen quarters (that is, thirty sacks) of grain. It may reasonably be presumed that the sheep were alive, and likely to increase; that they had wool, which was worth something; or, at any rate, two hundred skins, which would, of themselves, be a little fortune to a man who lived upon parchment. But waiving all this, and considering the sheep as mere mutton, the scribe would be furnished with almost half a sheep, and more than half a bushel of grain, per week for four years. Was there nobody who would transcribe a few homilies on more reasonable terms? Surely, from that time forth, every man in Anjou, and everywhere else, who heard of the transaction, set about learning the art of penmanship, which must have been, beyond all comparison, the most lucrative which had ever been practised, and which might fairly vie with alchemy itself.

Let us, however, look at the authorities. Robertson refers to "the Histoire Literaire de France," where the story is thus told :—" Un trait que l'histoire nous a conservé touchant le prix excessif des livres en ce temps là, nous doit faire juger de leur rareté. Encore s'agit-il d'un auteur ecclésiastique, le recueil des homilies d'Haimon d'Halberstadt. Grécie Comtesse d'Anjou, l'acheta deux cents brebis, un muid de froment, un autre de seigle, un troisième de millet, et un certain nombre de peaux de martres. Il falloit être riche pour former de nombreuses bibliothèques au même prix." Perhaps nobody will dispute the inference which these historians draw from the story; but some will be surprised that Robertson omitted the " certain nombre de peaux de martres." This certain (that is, of course, uncertain) number may be supposed to stand for any quantity of rich and costly furs, and increases the price and the wonder greatly.[1]

But let us retrograde another step, and look at the authority to which the authors of the " Histoire Literaire " refer. Mabillon, having occasion, in his " Benedictine Annals," to mention the Countess Grecia as a subscribing witness to a charter of about the year 1056, by which Geoffry Martel, Count of Anjou, granted certain privileges to the monks of St. Nicholas at Angers, adds, that she was the second wife of that Count, and married to him after his divorce from his first Countess, Agnes of Burgundy. He farther says, that the divorce is mentioned in a letter from a monk to the Abbot Oderic, who had asked him about a certain homilary of Haymo; and remarks, that though not very important in itself, the monk's letter is worth transcribing, because it shows both the high price of books and the estimation in which these homilies were held at that period. He then gives the letter, which is as follows :—

" To his Lord the Abbot O. brother R. offers his prayers in Christ. Most dear father, I would have you to know that the Countess bought the book of which you have heard, for a great price, of Martin, who is now a bishop. On one occasion she gave him a hundred sheep on account of that book ; at another time, on

---

[1] It is a happy thing that some failings and vices carry with them to a certain extent, and so far as regards the general mischief which they are calculated to produce, their own antidote or mitigation. Certainly the same carelessness which gives rise to a great part of the mistakes and misquotations of popular writers prevents them from making the best of a good story when they have got one. Mr. James Petit Andrews, F.A.S., in his " History of Great Britain connected with the Chronology of Europe "—" an undertaking which had probably been blighted in the bud if he had foreseen the toil that would attend it "—tells us that it was " a large parcel of rich furs," p. 87; but unaccountably (unless he suspected a blunder which he did not know how to correct) says nothing of the wheat, rye, and millet. He professes to quote from Henault —that is, I suppose, from the English translation of Henault, in which, if I remember right, the French *muid* stands untranslated.

account of that same book, a *modius* of wheat, another of rye, and a third of millet. Again, on the same account, a hundred sheep ; at another time, some marten skins. And when she separated herself from the Count he received from her four pounds to buy sheep. But afterwards, when she asked him for the change, he began to complain about the book. She immediately gave up to him what he owed her."[2]

On this letter I would observe —

1. If there is really any reference to the divorce, it seems obvious that it must have been Agnes (who separated herself), and not Grecia (her successor), who purchased the book. I cannot help doubting, however, whether there is any such reference ;

---

[2] Mabillon's words are—" De hoc divortio fit mentio in quadam epistola cujusdam monachi ad Odericum Abbatem qui monachum illum de homilario Haimonis percontatus fuerat. Hæc epistola, tametsi in speciem non magni momenti, hic referenda videtur, ex qua nimirum intelligitur, quanti tunc temporis constarent libri, quantique hoc homilarium haberetur. Sic autem habet illa Epistola.

" Domno suo Abbati O., frater R. orationes in Christo. Pater carissime, scire vos volumus, quod codicem, de quo audivisti, pretio magno a Martino, qui est modo præsul, Comitissa emit. Una vice libri causa centum oves illi dedit : altera vice causa ipsius libri unum modium frumenti, et alterum sigalis, et tertium de milio. Iterum hac eadem causa centum oves : altera vice causa quasdam pelles martirinas. Cumque separavit se a Comite, quatuor libratas, ovium emendi causa, ab illa accepit. Postquam autem requisivit denarios, ille conqueri cœpit de libro. Illa statim dimisit illi quod sibi debebat."

Mabillon proceeds to say—" Martinus ille præsul, capellanus fuerat Gaufridi Comitis et Agnetis, postmodum Episcopus Trecorensis, ut superius vidimus ex quadam charta eorundem quam scripsit Martinus tunc Capellanus, postea Treguerensis Episcopus." *Lib. LXI. No.* 6, *p.* 528.

Mabillon gives no authority, that I see, for the letter, and may therefore be presumed to quote from the original. It will be observed that the letter itself mentions neither *homilary* nor *Haymo*. Mabillon says both ; I should like to know why he says that the codex contained the homilies of *Haymon ;* for I cannot help thinking that the CODEX might be that service-book which was then more properly and strictly, and commonly too (if not exclusively) called a Homilary ; and, if it was a book got up for the church service, in any such way as some which will be described presently, the price is not so remarkable.

though I have so far deferred to Mabillon as to
translate *separavit se*, by "*she* separated," and
accepit, by "*he* received." We learn, from the
subscription to another charter, that Martin had
been the Count's chaplain; and, from this letter,
that he had ceased to be so; and I cannot but
think that the "*separavit se*" may mean when he
quitted the Count's service.

2. It is more to our present purpose to observe,
that this book of homilies was a peculiar volume,
which was the subject of particular inquiry. The
Abbot was asking about it, and the monk, who
knew its history, describes it as the volume
which the Countess bought at "a great price."
So that what she gave was *then* considered extraordinary.

3. The price was paid at different times, and in so
strange a manner, that it looks rather as if the
chaplain was some skilful artist who was honoured
on account of his talents, and took advantage of
them to work on the liberality of his patroness.

4. As to the quantity of grain—I suffer *modius*
to stand, because, if I were to translate it, I should
be inclined to say "one bushel" instead of "five
quarters," which would, of course, divide Robertson's quantity by *forty*. I do not mean to say that
the English bushel is the exact representative of the
modius here spoken of, for what that was precisely I
really do not know; and whoever looks into the
subject of weights and measures will perceive that
it is not very easy to determine; but I am inclined
to think that I should be giving very good measure.

Now let me appeal to every rational and reflecting
person, whether it is from such cases that we can
judge of the price of books in general, or of the
comparative ease or difficulty of procuring them?
Are we to form our ideas from the sums paid or
given by royal and noble patrons and patronesses
to artists, whose skill in writing, illuminating, and

embellishing manuscripts, enabled them to ask what they pleased, and get what everthey asked ? [3]

Suppose, however, that there was no fine writing in the case, it is still very possible that, on other grounds, the book might have been worth twice, or twenty times, as much as the Countess gave for it, without proving that books in general were so outrageously scarce and dear. From such cases, indeed, we cannot, as I have already said, prove anything. Will it not be quite as fair for some writer a few centuries hence to bring forward the enormous and absurd prices which have been paid by some modern collectors for single volumes, as an evidence of the price of books in our age? May he not tell his gaping readers (at a time, too, when the march of intellect has got past the age of cumbersome and expensive penny magazines, and is revelling in farthing cyclopædias) that in the year 1812, one of our nobility gave £2,260, and another, £1,060 10s. for a single volume? and that the next year, a Johnson's Dictionary was sold by public auction, to a plebeian purchaser, for £200? A few such facts would quite set up some future Robertson, whose readers would never dream that we could get better reading, and plenty of it, much cheaper at that very time. The simple fact is, that there has always been such a thing as bibliomania since there have been books in the world ; and no member of the

---

[3] Look at the state of things in countries which are now similarly circumstanced. "The art of printing," says Morier, "is unknown in Persia, and beautiful writing, therefore, is considered a high accomplishment. It is carefully taught in the schools, and those who excel in it are almost classed with literary men. They are employed to copy books, and some have attained to such eminence in this art, that a few lines written by one of these celebrated penmen are often sold for a considerable sum." (*History of Persia*, vol. ii., p. 582.) He adds in a note, " I have known *seven pounds* given for *four lines* written by Dervish Musjeed, a celebrated penman, who has been dead some time, and whose beautiful specimens of writing are now scarce."

Roxburgh Club has yet equalled the Elector of
Bavaria, who gave a town for a single manuscript—
unless, indeed, it be argued that it was a more pure,
disinterested, and brilliant display of the ruling
passion, a more devoted and heroic sacrifice of
property and respect, to give £2,000 for an unique
specimen of obscene trash, than to part with a
German town for a copy of the New Testament.
Intrinsic value of this description, however, does
not enter into the question, though another species
of it does, and it is necessary to say a few words
about it, which I hope to do presently. In the
meantime let me ask, does not Robertson proceed
to state in his very next sentence what might, by
itself, show his readers that the transaction which he
had just recorded was not peculiarly characteristic
of the age in which it occurred. He goes on to
say :—

" Even so late as the year 1471, when Louis XI. borrowed the
works of Rasis, the Arabian Physician, from the Faculty of
Medicine in Paris, he not only deposited as a pledge a considerable
quantity of plate, but was obliged to procure a nobleman to join
with him as surety in a deed, binding himself under a great
forfeiture to restore it. Gabr. Naudè Addit. à l'histoire de Louys
XI. par Comines. edit. de Fresnoy, tom. iv. p. 281. Many
curious circumstances with respect to the extravagant price of
books in the middle ages, are collected by that industrious com-
piler, to whom I refer such of my readers as deem this small
branch of literary history an object of curiosity."

Might I not add, that " even so late as " two
centuries after the occurrence mentioned by Robertson, when Selden wished to borrow a MS. from the
Bodleian Library, he was required to give a bond
for A THOUSAND POUNDS ? but does it follow that in
that dark age he could not have got as much good
reading on easier terms ?
I have said, however, that there was frequently
an intrinsic value in books independent of that
which might arise from their subject; and I mean
that which was inseparable from the nature of the

costly materials of which they were composed, as
well as from the art and labour bestowed in making
them. This value was often, I apprehend, much
greater than many of Robertson's readers would
imagine ; and if they think of a book as nothing
but a thing to read, and (looking back to the dark
ages) as only a cramped illegible scrawl on dirty
parchment, they will form a very erroneous opinion
on the whole matter. Books, and especially those
used in the church service (of which, by the way,
general readers are most likely to hear, and to
which class, I suspect, as I have said, that this
Homilary belonged), were frequently written with
great care and pains, illuminated and gilded with
almost incredible industry, bound in, or covered
with, plates of gold, silver, or carved ivory, adorned
with gems, and even enriched with relics. Missals
of a later date than the period with which we are
at present concerned were, some years ago, the
objects of eager competition among collectors, and
some of them must always be admired for the
exquisite beauty of their embellishments. I am
not going to compare the graphic performances of
the ninth and tenth centuries with those of the
thirteenth and fourteenth ; in this point of view it
may suffice to say, that they were the finest
specimens of art which those who purchased them
had ever seen, and in all matters of taste and
fancy this is saying a good deal. As to the value
of books, however, which arose from the costly
materials of which they were made, or the labour,
industry, and taste, with which they were
embellished, I hope I shall find a more proper
place to speak. For our present purpose this
general reference to the subject is quite sufficient.

But there was another species of value attaching
to some books in those ages which does not present
itself to our minds so obviously or forcibly. The
multiplication of books, by printing, has not only

rendered them much cheaper by reducing the labour required for the production of a large number of copies, but it has provided that each one of that large number should be a fac-simile of all the rest. He who sees one copy of an edition sees all : that edition is dispersed among those who can best judge of its value; it receives from their suffrages a certain character ; and from that time forth, if we see the title-page, we know what are the contents or the errors of every other page in the book. Among those who are likely to want it, it is sufficient to mention the time and place of its publication, and if we admire the correctness and readableness of our own edition of a Father or a Classic, we recommend our friends to get it, well knowing that as there is one there are many ; or that, at least, our own copy is not likely to be *unique,* or we should infallibly have heard of it from our bookseller. Now, in those days *every* copy was unique —every one, if I may so speak, stood upon its own individual character; and the correctness of a particular manuscript was no pledge for even those which were copied immediately from it. In fact, the correctness of every single copy could only be ascertained by minute and laborious collation, and by the same sort of tedious and wearisome process which is now required from the editor who, with infinitely more ease and better helps, revises the text of an ancient writer. We may, therefore, naturally suppose that if a manuscript was known to be the work of a good and careful scribe—it it came out of the Scriptorium of some well-respected monastery—if it had passed through learned hands, and had been found, by the scrutiny which it was then necessary to give to each individual copy, to be an accurate work which might be safely trusted as a copy for future transcripts—if all this was known and attested, it would form another and a very good reason why a book should fetch an extraordinary price.

But to return to Robertson —

"When any person made a present of a book to a church or a monastery, in which were the only libraries during these ages, it was deemed a donative of such value, that he offered it on the altar *pro remedio animæ suæ*, in order to obtain the forgiveness of his sins. Murat. vol. iii. p. 836. Hist. Liter. de France, t. vi. p. 6. Nouv. Trait. du Diplomat. par deux Bénédictins, 4to. tom. i. p. 481."

Now really if a book was to cost two hundred sheep and fifteen quarters of grain (to say nothing of the furs and money), I do not see anything very absurd in its being treated as a donative of value; at least, I wish that people would make gifts of the same value to churches nowadays, and I believe they would find that they were not considered quite contemptible. I think I have seen in a parish church a board (whether gilt or not, I do not remember) informing the world that Esquire somebody had given "forty shillings a year for ever to the poor of the parish—viz., to the vicar, five shillings," for preaching an annual sermon to commemorate his bounty, and so forth.

But let me say a few words, first, as to the authorities, and then as to the fact.

First, then, as to the authorities, which it will be most convenient to notice in an inverted order. In the part of the Nouv. Traité du Diplom. referred to, I cannot find anything to the purpose, and I can only suppose that there is some mistake in the reference. To the Histoire Literaire de France, I have not at present access;[4] but the passage of

---

[4] Since this was published I have referred to the passage, which is as follows :—

"D'autres ne croïoient pas faire aux eglises et aux monasteres de plus excellens dons, que de leur offrir des livres. [How could they get such an idea in the dark ages?] Et pour mieux marquer le cas qu'ils en faisoient, ils les déposoient ordinairement sur l'Autel, comme une chose sacrée. L'usage de les offrir de la

Muratori referred to is as follows :—"Rari ergo
quum olim forent, multoque ære redimerentur
codices MSti, hinc intelligimus, cur tanti fieret
eorum donatio, ut si quando vel ipsi Romani Ponti-
fices ejusmodi munera sacris templis offerebant, ad
eorum gloriam de iis mentio in historia haberetur.
Stephanus V. Papa, ut est in ejus Vita, tom. iii.
pag. 272, Rer. Italicar. circiter annum Christi
DCCCLXXXVI. præter alios libros ibi commemoratos
'pro animæ suæ remedio contulit ecclesiæ Sancti
Pauli cantharam exauratam unam (fortasse, can-
tharum) Lib. Comment. I. Prophetarum, Lib. I.
Gestarum Rerum Lib. II.' "

Here it will be obvious that the drift of Muratori's
remark, which has been misapprehended by Robertson, is, not that the books given to churches were
offered on the altar,. or that they were offered *pro
remedio animæ*, though the instance which he quotes
happens to contain the words "*pro remedio animæ
suæ*," to which he undoubtedly attached no importance, as well knowing, and expecting everybody to
understand, that this was, in all such cases, implied,

sorte devint assés commun en ce siecle.[a] On ne trouve des vestiges
à la tête d'un recueil manuscrit des Conciles généraux et des
Décretales des Papes, où se lit une inscription qui porte, que ce
livre fut offert à l'Autel de Nôtre-Dame du Puy par Adalard qui
en étoit Eveque en 919.[b] S. Maieul, Abbé de Cluny, aïant fait
copier le Commentaire de S. Ambroise sur S. Luc, et celui de
Raban Maur sur Jéremie, les offrit de même à son Monastere, en les
mettant sur l'Autel de S. Pierre.[c] Letald nous apprend la même
chose de Pierre, sçavant Moine de Mici son contemporain, qui y
donna divers recueils d'histoire après les avoir déposés sur l'Autel
de S. Etienne le jour du Jeudi saint."

I give the passage, to show what it is ; it is not perhaps worth
while to add any remark. It will be observed that the second of
these authorities (which is in fact to the *Itinerar. Burgund.*) I had
myself noticed, and quoted in the next paragraph with rather a
different view.

[a] Gall. chr. nov. t. 2. p. 693.   [b] Mab. opusc. t. 2. p. 22.
[c] Act. B. t. I. p. 598. n. 3.

if not expressed ; but that, when given even by popes,
it was thought worth while to record the donation
in history, that is, in their lives.   Even this remark,
however, surprises me as coming from a writer who
must have known that the gifts of some of the
popes to various churches and monasteries were
scrupulously registered, and have been unmercifully
detailed by their biographers ; and, indeed, some of
the books which occur in such lists might well be
considered " donatives " of great value, even by
those who could not read.   For instance, when Leo
III., in the beginning of the ninth century, gave
a copy of the Gospels so ornamented with gold
and precious stones that it weighed seventeen
pounds, four ounces ;[5] or, when Benedict III.
gave one to the church of St. Calistus, adorned
with gold and silver of nearly the same weight.[6]
Surely when such books, or even books of less
value, were given, it was as natural to record
the donation as that of a silver chalice, or a
silk vestment.   We may also believe that when books
—especially such books—were formally presented
to churches, they were offered on the altar, though
I have met with very few instances of it ;[7] and,

---

[5] " Hic fecit B. Petro apostolo fautori suo, Evangelia aurea cum
gemmis prasinis atque hyacinthinis et albis miræ magnitudinis in
circuitu ornata, pensantia libras decem et septem et uncias quatuor."   See a list of his donations to various churches, occupying
nearly twelve of the large close printed, double-columned pages of
Labbe's Councils, tom. vii. c. 1090.

[6] " Ad laudem et gloriam ipsius Ecclesiæ fecit Evangelium argento
auroque perfusum unum pensans libras quindecim . . . et in
ecclesia beatæ Balbinæ Martyris obtulit evangelium ex argento
purissimo . . . et in titulo beati Cyriaci Martyris obtulit evangelium unum ex argento purissimo ad laudem et gloriam ipsius
ecclesiæ."—*Ibid.*, tom. viii. p. 230.

[7] Mabillon thought it worth while to mention that he found in
the library at Cluny a copy of St. Ambrose on Luke, at the end
of which was written, " Liber oblatus ad Altare S. Petri Clunien-
sis Cœnobii ex voto Domni atque Reverentissimi Maioli Abbatis."
And he remarks upon it, " Sic libros offerebant veteres ad altare, et
ad sepulcra sanctorum, quemadmodum de Mammone S. Augendi

indeed, with scarcely any charter or deed of gift conveying such things as books at all. The reason is plain, for churches and monasteries not merely (as Robertson observes very truly, if not taken strictly) had the only libraries, but they were the great and almost the only manufactories of books. Still books might be, and sometimes were, presented; and, on such occasions, were likely to be offered on the altar, though neither because they were books, nor because they were peculiarly rare or costly, but for another reason which is worthy of notice.

The false view which Robertson gives, and which I wish to expose and remove, arises from appropriating to a particular case what was in principle, and as far as could be in practice, general and universal. Robertson would have spoken more correctly, though not to his purpose, if, instead of saying, " When any person made a present of *a book*," he had said, " When any person made a present of *anything* to a church," he offered it on the altar, etc. That he offered it *pro remedio animæ suæ*, or for the spiritual benefit of some other person, was always understood, though not always expressed ;[8] and that he should offer it on the altar

---

præposito superius vidimus." In this he refers to a book which he had mentioned as being in the Boherian Library at Dijon, and of which he had said, " Hic codex voto bonæ memoriæ Mammonis, ad sepulchrum Sancti Augendi oblatus est regnante Carolo Calvo, uti et Epistolæ Paschales, quæ ibidem habentur pluresque alii codices, quos in varias Bibliothecas dispersos deprehendimus."—*Itinerar. Burgund.*, p. 9, 22. That of which such a man as Mabillon thus spoke, could scarcely have been at any period a general and notorious custom in the church.

[8] This is not, however, to be understood as having exclusive reference to purgatory. Pommeraye has very well observed :— " Le motif plus ordinaire qu'apportoient dans leurs chartres les bien-faiteurs, étoit afin que l'aumosne qu'ils faisoient servist au soulagement de leurs ames et de celles de leurs parens et amis : c'étoit aussi quelquefois pour estre associez aux prières et aux bonnes œuvres des monastères, dont les seigneurs et les personnes de piété recherchoient très soigneusement la participation."—*Hist. de l'Abbaye de S. Catharine du mont de Rouen*, p. 84.

was perfectly natural when we consider to whom
the donation was made. We, indeed, commonly
say that a man 'gave property " to the monastery of
St. Bertin," or " the monks of St. Martin," or
" the canons of Lille," and a donor then might say
so in his deed of gift for brevity's sake; for, as we
have heard often enough, and I pretend not to deny,
parchment was expensive in those days. Many
charters run in that form—as Hildebert, Bishop of
Avignon, in 1006, " donamus monachis qui in
Cœnobio S. Andreæ et S. Martini . . . . . modo
famulantur Deo,"[9] etc.; but, in fact, the donation
was not made to the church or the monastery—the
canons or monks had no property in it, and nothing
to do with it, except as servants and stewards to
provide for its safe keeping.   The gift was to God
and the patron saint ; and, therefore, it was laid on
the altar erected in honour of both.   Nothing could
be more natural or reasonable as it respects Him
who, though He dwelleth not in temples made with
hands, was once pleased to dwell between the
cherubim, and who, of all that He has framed for
man, or given him skill to fashion, reserves only the
altar for Himself, and sets it over against His
mercy-seat as the symbol of that glory which He
will not give to another.
     Beside this, the superstition of the age supposed
the glorified saint to know what was going on in
the world, and to feel a deep interest and possess a
considerable power in the church militant on earth.
I believe that they who thought so were altogether
mistaken, and I lament and abhor, and am amazed
at the superstitions, blasphemies, and idolatries
which have grown out of that opinion ; but as to
the notion itself, I do not know that it was wicked,
and I almost envy those whose credulous simplicity
so realized the communion of saints, and anticipated
the period when " the whole family in heaven and

---

[9] Dach. Spic., iii. 384.

earth " shall be gathered together in one. Be this
as it may, however, they did in fact conceive of the
saint as a being still conversant among mortals—
hearing their prayers, assisting them in their need,
acknowledging their gifts by intercession and protection, and not unfrequently making his presence
known, and even visible, among them—and his
altar was naturally the place where all business
relating to his property in this world, or his patronage in another, was transacted.

The form of such deeds of gift naturally varied
at different times and in different places ; and even
according to the taste of individual scribes and
notaries. I have already said that the gift was
sometimes described as made to the monks,—sometimes, but I think comparatively seldom, to the
monastery,—more frequently to God, and the patron
saint, and the abbot,—as frequently the abbot was
omitted, and still more frequently, perhaps, the
saint only was mentioned, and he was sometimes
actually addressed as a party to the conveyance.[1]

---

[1] It may illustrate what I have here said, and perhaps amuse
some readers, if I throw together a few specimens of the different
forms taken at random from the various charters, the dates of
which are indicated by the numbers in parenthesis :—" Dono ad
monasterium sancti Bonifacii " (759).—*Schannat., Trad. Fuld.*, p.
8. " Trado ad sanctum Bonifatium et ad monasterium quod dicitur
Fulda " (759).—*Ibid.* " Tradidit Deo et sanctissimo martiri ejus
Bonifacio, necnon et venerando Abbati Eggeberto ceterisque fratribus sanctæ Fuldensis Ecclesiæ " (1058).—*Ibid.*, p. 255. In these
cases the trusteeship was fully understood ; but sometimes it was
expressed, as by Poncius, Count of Gervaudan and Forez, in a
charter to the church of Brioude (1010). After saying—" Reddo
Creatori omnium Domino Regi Regum, et Domino dominantium,
necnon et cedo gloriosissimo Martyri Juliano," etc., he describes the
property, and adds—" Omnipotenti Deo reddo, Sanctoque Juliano,
ut, a die præsenti et deinceps, omnes res suprascriptas sub tuitione
ac potestate sanctissimi martyris Juliani, et Canonicorum ibidem
Christo militantium, sint omni tempore," etc.—*Dach. Spicil.*, iii.
385.—And an early form from the same Chartulary (945) runs,
" totum et ad integrum reddo Creatori omnium Domino, et sub
dominatione et potestate libenti animo committo beati Juliani,
Canonicorumque suorum."—*Ibid.*, 373. More frequently, however,

It was very natural that what was thus given to the
saint should be offered on his altar, for how else was
the donor to present it? It was, I say, *general*,
not meaning that every trivial donation was there

---

as I have said, it was to God and the patron saint, as in the donation of Amalric, to the schools of St. Martin's, at Tours (cir.
843)—" Offero Creatori Deo, necnon Sancto Martino Domino meo
gloriosissimo quem toto affectu diligo," etc.—*Mart.* i. 33 ; or, as
Gulfrad, the deacon to the same church (cir. 930) —" Offero,
dono, trado atque confirmo Omnipotenti Deo necnon Sancto Martino
Confessori suo egregio," etc.—*Ibid.*, 68. Or, the saint only, as—
" In Dei nomine. Ego Theothart trado in elemosinam meam ad
sanctum Bonifatium Mancipia IIII. id est uxorem Altrati cum
tribus filiis et cum omni substantia sua " (824).—*Schannat.*, p.
150. Of this, innumerable instances might be given ; but sometimes the matter was put in a still more business-like form by
addressing the saint as a party to the conveyance, as—" Domno
sancto et apostolico Patri Bonifatio Episcopo ego Adalberdus ;
constat me nulli cogentis imperio, sed proprio voluntatis arbitrio
vobis vendidisse et ita vendidi vineam unam," etc. (754).—
Schannat., p. 1. The emperor, in the year 962, began a diploma
thus—" Ego Otto Dei gratia Imperator Augustus, una cum Ottone
glorioso rege filio nostro, spondemus atque promittimus per hoc
pactum confirmationis nostræ tibi beato Petro principi Aposto-
lorum et clavigero regni cœlorum, et per te vicario tuo Domno
Joanni summo Pontifici," etc.—*Conc.* ix. 643. Again, in 1014—
" Ego Henricus Dei gratia Imperator Augustus spondeo atque
promitto per hoc pactum confirmationis nostræ, tibi beato Petro,"
etc.—*Ibid.*, 813. Leo IX., about 1050, began a diploma by which
he granted a tenth of the oblations made at the altar of St. Peter,
to the saint himself (or, as we should say, set apart that proportion
for the repairs of the church) with the following words—" Beate
Petre Apostole, ego Leo Episcopus servus tuus et omnium ser-
vorum Dei, de tuis donis aliquam tibi offero particulam," etc.—
Ibid., 985. In fact, numberless examples of various forms of
speech might be given ; and, without them—at least, without some
familiarity with the modes of expression which were perpetually
used—it is impossible to form an idea of the real spirit and character
of the times. With this view, I venture to add to this long note
one or two phrases from the charters of the Abbey of St. Peter, at
Condom—" Ego Amalbinus . . . . facio chartam de una pecia de
vinea . . . . ad opus sancti Petri."—*Dach. Sp.*, ii. 591. " In alio
loco possidet sanctus Petrus aliam vineam "—" in villa quæ
dicitur Inzlota habet beatus Petrus casalem unum."—*Ibid.*, p. 596.
" Quædam nobilissima fœmina . . . . suprascriptam ecclesiam
violenter beato arripuit Petro."—*Ibid.*, 585. " Molendinum quod
construxit familia beati Petri."—*Ibid.*, 596.

offered, but that, when property of any considerable value was given, this was the common course of proceeding. If that property consisted of moveable chattels, such as money, plate, etc., it was actually placed on the altar; or, if this could not be conveniently or decently done, they came as near to it as they could. For instance, the rule of St. Benedict directed that when a novice had passed through the prescribed trials, and was to be received, he should present a written petition, containing the promise which he had already made; and that, at the time of his actual reception, he should lay it on the altar—" De qua promissione sua faciat petitionem ad nomen sanctorum, quorum reliquiæ ibi sunt, et abbatis præsentis. Quam petitionem manu sua scribat : aut certe si non scit literas, alter ab eo rogatus scribat : et ille novitius signum faciat, et manu sua eam *super altare* ponat." (c. 58.) It was, in fact, offering himself ; and, as he did it, he began the 116th verse of the 119th Psalm—" Uphold me (suscipe) according unto thy word, that I may live; and let me not be ashamed of my hope." To this the congregation thrice responded by repeating the verse and adding the *Gloria Patri.* If a child was to be received, his hand was wrapped in the hanging of the altar, " and thus," says the rule of St. Benedict, " let them offer him." The words are—" Si quis forte de nobilibus offert filium suum Deo in monasterio, si ipse puer minore ætate est, parentes ejus faciant petitionem quam supra diximus. Et cum oblatione, ipsam petitionem et manum pueri involvant *in palla altaris,* et sic eum offerant."[2] (c. 59). Thus the idea of offering at the altar was kept up; and, indeed, though I know of no rule for it, nor that it was a usual practice, yet I apprehend that sometimes the matter was carried still farther. The

---

[2] See an "Antiqua Formula Oblationis Puerorum in Monasteriis," IX. M. &. D., p. 158.

Abbot Heriman (of whom I have already had
occasion to speak in connexion with the Abbot
Lupus[3]) tells us that, in the year 1055, his mother
took him and his brothers to the monastery of
which he was afterwards abbot—" She went to St.
Martin's, and delivered over her sons to God,
placing the little one in his cradle upon the altar,
amidst the tears of many bystanders." At the
same time, she placed on the altar two hundred
marks of silver, and gave to the monastery two
mills and the rest of her property.

Thus the offering on the altar was performed, in
most cases, as literally as could be ; and even when
the property was immoveable, as houses or lands—
or impalpable, as rights of toll or tithe, or market—it
was sometimes spoken of as if really laid on the
altar. Thus, in a charter of about A.D. 1120, Hugh
de Belmont says, " Ego ipse Hugo *dexteræ manus
meæ juramento* firmavi [I quote these words as con-
firming my statement at p. 35, that he who made
the sign of the cross was considered *manu jurare*],
et insuper ne successorum aliqua redeat in futurum
calumnia, Deo et Sancto Petro, et Fratribus
Besuensis ecclesiæ quicquid est, vel erat, quod
meum jus juste aut injuste possederat de hoc
mercato, *totum super altare posui,* et ipsum mer-
catum dono donavi."[4] Gertrude also, with her
daughter and son-in-law, " obtulerunt Deo et sancto
Petro Besuensis ecclesiæ, *super altare* in Vetus vineis
villa," a moiety of a house, six acres of land, and two
serfs named Tetbert and Oltrude.[5] In such cases, I
need not say, the property was not really placed on
the altar ; but it is probable, and, indeed, almost certain, that either the deed of gift or some other symbol
was actually so placed. Du Cange alone supplies an
immense number and variety of examples ; from

---

[3] See p. 72, 74.
[4] Chron. Besuen. ap. Dach. Spicil., tom. ii. p. 452.
[5] *Ibid.*, p. 441.

which I will extract a few scraps by way of farther
illustrating this matter.[6] Very commonly, especially in cases of land, a turf or a twig, or a bough of
a tree, was laid on the altar (obtulit super altare
B. Petri per cespitem—propriis manibus prædictam
oblationem ramo et cespite posuerunt super altare
beatissimæ Mariæ). Sometimes by a knife (ipsi tres
eumdem cultellum super altare Dominicum S. Nicolai
portaverunt) ; and very frequently, either that it
might be preserved from being stolen or from getting
into common use by being, in fact, rendered useless,
or, perhaps also, that the act might be remembered,
the knife was bent before the witnesses (posuit super
altare per cultellum in hujus rei memoriam plicatum
—posito super altare præscripti Confessoris cultello
incurvato), and, in some cases, it seems to have been
broken, as Fulk, Count of Anjou, in A.D. 1096, in a
charter giving a forest, says, "Super altare Sancti
Nicolai ipsam chartam pono, et cum cultello Roberti
Monachi quem ante ipsum altare frango, cum eadem
charta donum supradictæ forestæ concedens pono."[7]
Very commonly a book, either merely because books
were at hand, or perhaps also because the books belonging to the altar might be supposed to give a
greater degree of solemnity to the act (has omnes
elemosynas . . . cum libro super altare posuerunt—
cum libro missali eam super altare ibidem obtulerunt
—de hoc dono revestivit Quirmarhocus et duo filii
ejus, Gradelonem Monachum S. Nicholai in ecclesia
S. Petri Namnetensis, et osculati sunt eum de hac
donatione per fidem, librum quoque quo revestierunt
monachum posuerunt pro signo super altare S. Petri).
It was not, however, necessary that it should be one
of the service books ; for I find in a charter giving to
the church of Beze, already repeatedly mentioned,
" quinque homines, tres mares, et duas fœminas,"

---

[6] Those examples which are in parenthesis may be found under
the word *Investitura*.

[7] Brevic. S. Nic. Andeg., p. 30.

that the donor " propria manu donum roboravit
super altare per librum qui vocatur Regula S. Benedicti, coram multis testibus."[8]   In short, it might be
by anything—by a glove, or a girdle, or a candle-
stick, or a purse, or a spoon, or whatever came to
hand,—per wantonem, per wasonem, super altare
posui—candelabro pro more illius temporis (12
sæc.) super altare posito—super altare ipsius ecclesiæ
per eleemosynariam [a beautiful name for a purse]
meam, lapidem berillum intus habentem, propria
manu imposui—donum decimæ quam habebat apud
Atheiam posuit super altare per cochlear de turibulo
—accipiens in manibus particulam marmorei lapidis,
quæ ibi forte reperta est, venit cum ea ante altare
et tenentes omnes simul . . . obtulerunt eam super
altare.

Surely these instances are sufficient to show the
absurdity of making it a wonder that books should be
sometimes offered on the altar of churches to which
they were presented, as if other things were not so
offered, and as if it arose from their great rarity, and
the mere circumstance that they were books ; while
the simple fact is, that the church and the cloister
were, in all ages, the places where books were kept,
and made, and copied, and from whence they were
issued to the rest of the world ; as, indeed, Robertson had just admitted in terms which would scarcely
allow his readers to believe it possible that anybody,
out of a church or monastery, should have any book
to present.

---

[8] II. Dach. Spicil. p. 442.

No. VI.

"Assem para, et accipe *auream* fabulam : fabulas immo, nam me priorum nova admonuit."—PLINIUS.

ONCE upon a time there was a certain king who took it into his head to have a throne, or a chair, or a saddle, of some peculiar pattern, which, as far as I know, has never been described;[1] but whatever it might be, he could find no artificer who would undertake to execute his conceptions.

Now it so happened that shortly before this time a young artist had come to the place where the king held his court. He had been brought up, and for some years employed, by an eminent goldsmith,

---

[1] " Sella aurea "—but the learned are not farther agreed than that it was something to sit on. Fleury and Ceillier say, " un *siége* magnifique ; " and Butler, " a magnificent chair of state." Pommeraye, with more caution, calls it, " un ouvrage," and adds in the margin, " Sella aurea, qui se peut entendre, d'une selle de cheval selon l'opinion commun, ou d'un trône royale selon l'explication de M. de Montigni en ses annotations," etc. I am inclined to vote for the saddle, because I think that agrees best with a subsequent part of the story, which seems to imply something more portable, and producible, and concealable than a throne or a magnificent chair of state. I do not know how much of the saddle was made of gold, for, indeed, I am not very well acquainted with the history and use of such things ; but, without wishing tediously to detain the reader on a subject which I never get upon without extreme reluctance, I must add that Du Cange quotes a passage which mentions, " equos cum sellis aureis " (*in v.* Sella). That is, indeed, from a period considerably later than the king mentioned in my story ; but I find it mentioned elsewhere that when a rogue, named Winegard, robbed a bishop, who was almost a contemporary of the king, of the " ministerium ecclesiasticum aureum," which he carried with him on his missionary excursions, " de calice et patena fecit sibi fieri *sellam auream ;*" which I presume was a saddle.

who was master of the mint in what might then be
called another country.   I do not find any reason
assigned for this migration of the young workman,
who perhaps only went (like the mechanics of a
great part of Europe even now) on a *wanderschaft*
to acquire more perfect knowledge of his art.   He
seems, however, to have left home with a good
character, as one who was loved and respected by
those among whom he lived, not only for extraordinary skill as a workman, but for the simplicity
of his manners, and his strict and regular piety.
Whether he owed it to his professional skill, or to
his character, or to some introduction which is not
recorded, I do not know.   But in a few days after
his arrival at the place where the court was, he was
taken under the patronage of the king's treasurer,
under whose protection he set to work at his business, and soon made friends of all around him.
The treasurer was naturally consulted by his royal
master on the golden project which filled his mind,
and he, as naturally, thought of the young stranger.
He conferred with him, and reported to the king
that he had found an artist who would undertake
the business.

The king was delighted, and gave an order to the
treasurer for an ample quantity of gold, which he
faithfully delivered to the goldsmith, who immediately set to work.   He wrought with great
diligence, and with such ingenuity and honesty
that, from the materials which he received for one
saddle he made two.   This, though apparently
impossible, he was able to do, because he not only
used the materials very skilfully, but abstained from
the common practice of cheating under pretence of
waste occasioned by cutting, filing, and melting.
When he had completed them, he took one of the
saddles to the king, who was filled with admiration.
He praised the elegance of the work, and ordered a
suitable reward to be given to the artist; who thereupon brought forth the other saddle, and told his

majesty that he had thought it better to make up
what was over in that manner than to waste it.
The king was astonished, and, at first, incredulous;
but, finding that he had really made both saddles
from the materials delivered to him for one, he not
only praised his skill, but assured him that he
should from thenceforth consider him worthy of
confidence in greater matters.   In fact, this was
the first step of his advancement at court; and,
from that time forward, he not only rose to the
highest eminence in his art, but increased in favour
with the king and his nobles.   In a word, he seems
to have been in much the same circumstances as
those of George Heriot at the court of our James,
and to have enjoyed the same personal favour, or
perhaps I should say, royal friendship.

It appears to have been soon after this, and it
was probably on occasion of his being appointed
to some confidential situation, or employed in some
business of state, that he was required to take an
oath on the relics of the saints in the presence of his
sovereign.   " I do not know how it happened," says
his friend and biographer, " that I was present at
the time; but it may be naturally supposed that I
was likely to be there in the way of my duty, for I
was brought up in my childhood at that king's
court;" and he proceeds to relate that the goldsmith
respectfully, but firmly, refused to comply with the
requisition.[2]   His majesty was urgent; and the

---

[2] " Divinum intuitum verens," says his biographer.   I really do
not understand it; or know how far a modern writer may be correct
in saying that his reluctance arose from the fear of taking what he
considered as an *unnecessary* oath.   Indeed, I can hardly suppose
that to have been the case; and still less that his reluctance
proceeded (as has been suggested) from a superstitious dread of
meddling with relics.   To this, I presume, his business must have
accustomed him; but I notice the matter because I have been led,
by other circumstances, to suppose that there have been persons in
every age who doubted of the lawfulness of oaths in general; and
it seems not improbable that he may have been one of them.

poor goldsmith, seeing no alternative but to disobey
either God or the king (and each was considered a
sin in those days), burst into tears. The king had
the good sense to give way—to speak to him in a
kind and soothing manner—and to dismiss him with
a cheerful countenance, and an assurance that he
should feel more confidence in him than if he had
sworn all sorts of oaths—" pollicens se plus eum ex
hoc jam crediturum quam si multimoda tunc de-
disset juramenta."

Shortly after this, he seems to have entered on a
more strictly religious life, which he commenced by
a general confession of his sins, and a course of
great austerity. " Having arrived," says his
biographer, " at the age of full maturity, he desired
to manifest himself as a vessel sanctified for the service of God;" and he adds, that " he began stoutly
to resist the striving of the flesh by the fervour of
the Spirit," that is, according to the apostle, in
labours, in watchings, in fastings, in chastity, in
much patience, and in charity unfeigned ; for in
opposition to the present desires of the flesh, he set
before him the fires of future punishment, and the
consideration of the fire of hell kept out the heat of
concupiscence. He prayed without ceasing for
heavenly gifts, and offered his supplications to
God by day and by night, frequently repeating
from the book of Job—" I would seek unto God,
and unto God would I commit my cause, which
doeth great things and unsearchable ; marvellous
things without number . . . . to set up on high
those that be low ; that those which mourn may
be exalted to safety."[3] He restricted himself from fulness of bread that he might gain

---

[3] Job v. 8.—Ego deprecabor Dominum, et ad Deum ponam
eloquium meum : Qui facit magna et inscrutabilia, et mirabilia
absque numero. Qui ponit humiles in sublime, et mœrentes erigit
sospitate.

the bread of heaven. His face, indeed, was pale
with fasting, his body dry and withered; but his
mind glowed with ever-increasing love of his
heavenly country. The consideration of more heavy
evils made him bear light afflictions with patience;
for, habitually looking forward to the end of his
present life, he feared the future sentence of God,
and His tremendous judgment, knowing that it is
written, "Happy is the man that feareth alway,"
(Prov. xxviii. 14), and that of the apostle, "Work
out your own salvation with fear and trembling."
(Philip. ii. 12.) Also that saying of Job, "For I
have alway feared God like as the waves swelling
over me." (c. xxxi. 23[4].) By night he would lie
at the feet of his Lord, smiting his breast with his
hands, and watering his cheeks with tears; and
with eyes uplifted and suppressed sighs did he look
to Him whom he feared to have offended—and
many a time did he repeat, "Against thee only
have I sinned"—"have mercy upon me according
to thy lovingkindness" (Ps. li. 4, 1); and that of
Job, "O remember that my life is wind" (viii. 7),
and "let me alone, for my days are vanity" (17);
and, being as it were out of himself, he pictured to
his own mind that which eye hath not seen, nor ear
heard, nor hath entered into the heart of man, but
which God hath prepared for those who love
Him.

Whatever may be my motive for running into
this story, it certainly is not to set up the goldsmith
as a perfect model of doctrine and practice. If the
reader should think him foolish, or pharisaical, or
heterodox, it is no fault of mine—at least if I succeed in what is really my wish, and faithfully repeat
an old story. I do not want to conceal that the
goldsmith's religion—for I cannot help thinking

---

[4] "Semper enim quasi tumentes super me fluctus timui Dominum."

that he had some—was mixed with superstition. He had relics hanging up in his chamber, and he saw and smelt, or said (and I really believe thought) that he saw and smelt, a fragrant balsam distilling from them; and he took this to be an answer to the earnest and fervent prayer which he had poured forth beneath them, that God would vouchsafe to give him some sign that his repentance was accepted. "Remembering his prayer," says his biographer, "and utterly astonished at the goodness of the divine bounty, with deep groaning from his inmost soul, he blessed Christ the faithful rewarder, who hath never forsaken those who have trusted in Him. This, therefore, was the beginning of his goodness, or rather of Almighty God's, from whom all derive power for all things"—hoc ergo fuit initium virtutum ejus, imo omnipotentis Dei, per quem omnes omnia possunt.

The reader is not, however, to suppose that the artist, and the man of business and active benevolence, was lost in the ascetic. The goldsmith, it is true, came to have a very monkish appearance, and was commonly to be seen in very mean clothes, with a rope for his girdle. His biographer confesses that when he first came to court, he did, indeed, somewhat ruffle it in the bravery of silk, and gold, and gems; but even then, adds this bosom friend, who was in all his secrets, and who was, as I have said, brought up at the court—who was, in fact, a little scion of nobility, and induced by his admiration of the goldsmith to embrace a religious life, and who, with his brother, became, as he tells us, one heart and one soul with him—even then, says his biographer, his finery concealed a hair shirt. Still, however, though his finery was laid aside, and his dress and manners approached to the monastic, he was not less diligent in business than fervent in spirit. He wrought incessantly with his own hands at his trade, with a book open before him, having, it seems, constructed for this purpose a sort of revolving desk, by means of which he could bring before him a number of books in succession ;[5] and moreover, though a working man, and a reading man, and a man high in office and in court favour, he appears to have been always ready for, and constantly engaged in, works of active benevolence.

It is not my present business to enter into all the details of the goldsmith's life ; or to tell how the favour and confidence of his first royal master was continued by his son and successor. I pass over the accounts which his biographer gives of the favours which his sovereign heaped upon him, and which he so freely bestowed in acts of charity, that, if a stranger inquired for him (and what stranger came to that city who did not?) the natural answer was, " Go into such a quarter, and where you see a crowd of poor people you will find him." It might be imagined that such lavish bounty was sufficient to exhaust even all the means which could be obtained from an extensive business and from royal munificence ;

---

[5] " Fabricabat in usum Regis utensilia quamplurima ex auro et gemmis : sedebat fabricans indefesso, et contra eum * * * * vernaculus ejus . . . . qui magistri sequens vestigia, et ipse postmodum venerabilem vitam duxit. Sedens ergo * * * * ad opus prædictum, codicem sibimet præ oculis præparabat apertum, ut quoquo genere laborans divinum perciperet mandatum." His biographer farther says, " Habebat itaque in cubiculo suo multa sanctorum dependentia pignora, necnon et sacros libros in gyro per axem plurimos, quos post psalmodiam et orationem revolvens, et quasi apis prudentissima diversos ex diversis flores legens, in alvearium sui pectoris optima quæque recondebat." I cannot help supposing that this revolving was more than what is usually meant by turning over the leaves of a book, and refers to some contrivance by which he could bring a variety of books within his reach ; though it does not appear to have been so understood by any moderns whose notice of him I have seen. Perhaps I may have some readers to whom it is right to state that, in writers of the middle age, such an expression as " sacros libros," even if it had been " scripturam sacram," would not necessarily imply the Bible. I do not doubt that what we properly call Holy Scripture was meant to be included in this case, and elsewhere in this history ; but without being aware that such phrases were used to designate " religious books " in general, the student of church history would be liable to fall into error.

though the king seldom refused him any request, not so much, I am afraid, from any real zeal for religion as from an hereditary attachment to the goldsmith, and because he knew that in giving him anything he was conferring a benefit, not on one, but on many. But, in fact, the goldsmith had other and, I suppose, much greater expenses. One of these arose from what his time and circumstances rendered a very obvious Christian duty. His mode of performing it might now be considered singular and unwise ; and perhaps, as it was not adopted by some of those who have, in modern times, felt most strongly (or, at least, talked and written most fiercely) about the abolition of slavery, it may be liable to serious objections, which I do not perceive. To me, a very poor judge in such matters, and perhaps somewhat prejudiced, it seems that his plan, whatever faults it might have, was the most simple, certain, and expeditious—he put his hand in his pocket, and paid the price of redemption. It was not the grandest way of doing the thing; but he lived in a dark age, when, even if the thing itself could have been successfully carried on, the collateral benefits of philanthropy and political agitation were little understood. Right or wrong, however, his biographer tells us that when he heard of a sale of slaves, he set off immediately, and bought as many as twenty or thirty, or even fifty or an hundred at a time. When he had got them, the next business was to carry them before the king, and set them at full liberty with all the forms of law. When they had thus become their own masters, he suggested to them three courses, and helped them to take which they pleased, if they chose to take either. In the first place, if they chose to return home, he was ready to give them all the assistance in his power,—secondly, any who wished to remain with him, he willingly allowed to do so ; and it was rather on the footing of brethren than of servants,—thirdly, if he could persuade them to become monks, he

treated them with great respect, honoured them as
a class superior to that to which he belonged, supplied them with clothes, and all other necessaries,
sent them to different monasteries, and took a great
deal of care of them.

All this was, no doubt, very expensive; but it
was not all. He asked the king to give him a certain town that he might there build a ladder by
which they might both get to heaven. His majesty
granted it at once; and he built a monastery
capable of receiving a hundred and fifty monks. He
spent upon it "all that he had, all that he could get
from the king, all that he could honestly come by in
any way, and all that the great were willing to
give." His biographer says, " You might see wag-
gons heavily laden with vessels of brass and wood
for all purposes, bedding, table linen, a great
number of religious books, and, indeed, everything
necessary for the monastery; in so much that some
evil-minded persons were moved to envy;"[6] and,
having himself inspected the place, he speaks in
high terms of the order and discipline maintained
in it. He adds, " There is now a great company
there, adorned with all the flowers of various graces.
There are also many artificers skilled in divers arts,
who, being perfected in the fear of Christ, are
always prepared to yield ready obedience. No man
there claims anything as his own; but (as we read
in the Acts of the Apostles) all things are, in all
respects, common. And the place is so fertile and
so beautiful that anybody going there, amidst its

---

[6] Ipse vero tanta se devotione, tantoque amore eodem loco
diffudit, ut quidquid, habere potuisset, ut quidquid Regi auferre,
quidquid digne comparare, quidquid etiam gratuito ei a potentibus
largitum esset, cuncta prædicto loco destinaret. Videres plaustra
vehere onera copiosa vascula utique usibus necessaria, ærea simul
et lignea : vestimenta etiam lectuaria ac linteamina mensalia,
necnon et *volumina sacrarum scripturarum quamplurima*, sed et
omnia quæ erant Monasterii usibus necessaria, in tantum ut pravi
quique ingenti ex hoc succenderentur invidia.

wide orchards and pleasant gardens, might well exclaim, ' How goodly are thy tents, O Jacob, and thy tabernacles, O Israel! like shady woods, as cedar trees beside the waters, as gardens by the river side.' It is of such that Solomon has said, ' The habitations of the righteous shall be blessed;'"[7] and he goes on to describe how it was surrounded by an enclosure (not, indeed, a stone wall, but a bank, with hedge and ditch—sphærico muro, non quidem lapideo; sed fossatum sepe munitum), about a mile and a quarter in circumference; and how the excellent river on which it was situated, with all the beauties of wood, water, and precipice, combined (perhaps one should say contrasted) with the enclosure of the monastery, entirely filled with fruit-bearing trees, might almost make the spectator fancy that he saw paradise before him.

" Yes, the monks took care to make themselves comfortable." No doubt they did; and I dare say, if the truth were known, the reader does the same; and I believe that, if he observes the course of things, he will find that no man can rationally seek his own comfort without promoting the comfort of others. At any rate, I restrain myself with difficulty from expressing a very familiar train of thought, now excited by this peep at the enclosed monastery. Very often it has been awakened; and I know of nothing in the history of the dark ages more admirable and adorable than the visible Providence of God over-ruling not only the better sense and feelings, but even the weakness and whims, the folly, the fanaticism, the sin, of the monks, and actually making their infirmities and vices the means of spreading not only religion, but civilization; and setting forth in a dark and desolate age, in lands ravaged by fire and sword, among men wild and turbulent and cruel—setting forth, in characters of peace and sunshine, the great truth that godliness

---

[7] Prov. iii. 33.

hath the promise of this life as well as of that to come. I hope, some time or other, to show this, with no other difficulty than what arises from selecting out of the abundant materials which are furnished by monastic history.

To return, therefore, to the goldsmith; and it will be a very natural mode of transition if I say a few words of his foreman—at least I suppose him to have held that rank from his being placed first in the list of the goldsmith's workmen, which his biographer gives, and the statement that he used to sit opposite his master at work, as may be seen in a foregoing note. He was a foreigner of good family, who had been brought away from his own country in his childhood, and sold as a slave. Happily for him, he was purchased by the goldsmith, who sent him to this new monastery which he had founded, to be educated, and then took him back, and they worked and read together.[8] So matters went on, until the goldsmith gave up business; and then what could the foreman do but go back to the scene of his youth, and turn monk? At least he did so; and, by direction of his old master, he became a priest also. Whether it was out of respect to their founder, or whether the same qualities which had endeared him to his master won the affection and respect of the abbot and monks, or whether it was commanded by the mild virtues and rigid austerities which had become habitual to him, I cannot tell; but, in fact, he received so much attention and

---

[8] " Quem vir sanctus "—that is, the abbot (says the biographer of the foreman) " sicut in mandatis acceperat, cum omni diligentia sub pietatis studio enutrivit, sacris literis erudivit, evangelicis atque apostolicis documentis roboravit; " and then sent him back to his master, to work at his business. He kept him constantly about his person; and the young captive " alter Elisæus, Eliæ felix virtutum ejus heres et successor, Deo donante futurus famulabatur obsequiis. Fabricabant ambo simul indefesse apertos præ ocellis semper codices habentes, geminum inde fructum capientes, ut videlicet manus usibus hominum, mentes vero usibus manciparentur divinis."

honour that he did not know what to do with himself in the monastery,[9] and seems to have remained there only out of respect for his benefactor; for, as soon as ever he heard of his death, he fairly ran away. Two texts of Scripture seem to have harassed his mind, and made him fear lest in his popularity with men he should lose the favour of God[1]— "They that please men; they are ashamed because God hath despised them" (Ps. liii. 5); and the words of the Apostle—"If I yet pleased men, I should not be the servant of Christ." (Gal. i. 10.) He wandered alone through desert places until he found a remote, and almost inaccessible, spot among the rocks, which he could only approach on his hands and knees, but which offered the necessary supply of wild fruits and water. "There he lived," says his biographer, "always singing in his heart that of David—'Oh that I had wings like a dove; for then would I fly away, and be at rest. Lo! then would I wander afar off, and remain in the wilderness'[2]— 'As the hart panteth after the water brooks, so panteth my soul after thee, O God. My soul thirsteth for God, for the living God: when shall I come and appear before God?' For he was such a man as Jeremiah describes when he says, 'It is good for a man that he bear the yoke in his youth. He sitteth alone and keepeth silence, because he hath borne it upon him;'[3] and elsewhere, 'I sat alone because of thy hand, for thou hast filled me with indignation.'"[4] Knowing, however, the dangers of idleness, and the apostolic injunction, that he who would not work should not eat, he employed himself in cultivating the earth; and soon found farther occupation in

---

[9] Whether they made him abbot I do not know. Who is to decide when Mabillon and the Bollandists disagree?

[1] "Qui hominibus placent confusi sunt quoniam Deus sprevit eos."—*Vulg.*

[2] Ps. lv. 6.

[3] Lam. iii. 27, 28.

[4] Jer. xv. 17.

preaching to the multitudes who came to visit him, and to seek his prayers and instruction. I believe that only one of his sermons is in print. That it is quite original I do not vouch; neither will I take upon me to say that it contains all and omits nothing that it should contain, for that is more than I can say of any sermon that I ever saw or heard; but I am not writing controversially, and merely wish, on this occasion, to tell the reader, as a matter of fact, what he did say; and according to the specimen given by his biographer, it was as follows:—" Brethren, hear what I say with attention; and sedulously meditate on it in your hearts. God the Father, and his Son our Lord Jesus Christ, who gave his precious blood for us, you must love with all your soul, and with all your mind. Keep your hearts clean from wicked and impure thoughts; maintain brotherly love among yourselves, and love not the things that are in the world. Do not think about what you *have*, but what you *are*. Do you desire to hear what you are? The prophet tells you, saying—' All flesh is grass; all the goodliness thereof as the flower of the field.'[5] Consider how short the present life is; always fearing, have the day of judgment before your eyes. While there is opportunity, redeem your sins by alms and good works." Such, says his biographer, were his discourses; and if the reader cannot agree with him in adding, " sermo ejus mellifluus sufficienti sale erat conditus," he may yet join me in hoping that he spoke truly in saying, that " no corrupt or idle discourse at any time proceeded out of his mouth; never was anything on his lips but Christ, and peace, and mercy."

As he grew old, his thoughts turned again to the monastery which he had twice left, and he besought the abbot to build a little cell near it in honour of its founder, and to let him live there. The abbot

---

[5] Is. xl. 6.

accordingly built one, rather more than half a mile
from the monastery; and there the old man lived,
constantly employed in reading or praying, or some
work of Christian duty or benevolence, or some
handicraft, until he was ninety-four years old.   I do
not know that he ever pretended to work miracles.
One of his biographers gives them to him by whole-
sale; but another account is not only very sparing
on that point, but relates an anecdote which has
quite an opposite aspect.   When a certain woman,
who was grievously wounded, went to the gate of
the monastery, asking to see him, " he would by no
means see her, but sent her back this message :—
' Woman, why do you ask my help?   I am a mortal,
and your associate in infirmity ; but, if you believe
in Christ, whom I serve, go away and pray to God
according to your faith, and you will be healed.'
Immediately she went away believing; and having
without delay called on Jesus, returned home
healed."

To proceed, however, with our story.   Up to the
point at which we digressed from the goldsmith's
affairs, one history might have served for master
and man ; but then a great difference began.   When
the servant became a monk, the master became a
bishop.   But I ought to have mentioned several
things before this, only I write under a constant
dread of being tedious.   One hears so much of
" wading through "—not thick folios and cubical
quartos—but even magazine articles on subjects
more popular than mine, that I am always tempted
to omit those details which in my own opinion give
interest to history, and enable one to understand,
and remember, and use it.   But for this I should
have told of the opposition which the goldsmith
and his noble convert and biographer, though both
laymen, made to the simony which was too prevalent
in their part of the world—how they also opposed
heresy, and drove it out of the kingdom without
personal injury to the heretics—and how the gold-

smith converted a mansion in the capital, which his royal master had given him, into a convent for three hundred nuns, who lived there under the superintendence of an abbess, who was appropriately (but, as far as I see, accidentally) named *Aurea.* She was not, I believe, the daughter of the goldsmith, nor do I find or suppose that he had any children; but he is said to have had a god-daughter; and were it not for the reasons just mentioned, I should run into a story about her. As it is, even, I cannot help briefly mentioning one or two particulars of her history; for the truth of which, however, as to matter of fact, I by no means vouch. I quote it for the illustration of our subject; should it be a contemporary and literally true story, it is worth our attention—or indeed whether it is truth or fiction; and if it belongs to a later period (of which, I suppose, there can be no doubt), it is still more deserving of notice. It is, I mean, more to our purpose to read the romance, if it be one, of a writer of any period within the limits to which the production in question must belong than to learn the real adventures of a young woman.

I pass over the account of her noble birth, and her betrothal in her infancy to one of equal rank, and how at a marriageable age she persuaded him to accompany her to Rome; and how, while he was rambling about to see the rarities of the city, she took the opportunity of throwing herself at the pope's feet, and declaring her determination to become a nun—it is sufficient to say that she did so, and that after returning thanks to God, his holiness addressed her :—"'Of what nation art thou, and from what country dost thou come, maiden? And say also, what is thy name, and the creed of thy people; for I suppose thee to have been born of noble race, and instructed in sacred learning from thine infancy.' Whereupon she, with most serene mind and countenance, and with downcast look, began :—' If you inquire, O father and lord, con-

cerning my nation, I am a * * * * my name is
* * * * I was born in the district of * * * *,
whence I came hither. I was educated by Christian
parents; and, contrary to my own will (and I
believe to the will of God), I was betrothed to a
young man, whom I give up, and turn from, being
bound by the love of Christ, through whose
guidance and favour I remain free from all pollu-
tion in body and mind. I devote myself to Him
who created all things; and that faith of which you
inquire, I keep unbroken to Him—which faith, if
you really wish to hear it, most excellent father, I
will rehearse; for though I am a barbarian by
nation, we, notwithstanding, profess that true and
holy faith which was brought to us in the end of
time from this holy apostolical see and catholic
mother church. For truly, when your holiness
inquires after our creed, it seems like Christ's
asking water from the Samaritan woman, in that
while He vouchsafed to honour her with such a
discourse, He covertly insinuated that no nation
could exclude anyone from the faith. As, therefore, we blush not for our creed, so we are not
confounded by reason of our nation; for David
commands that all peoples should clap their hands,
and rejoice before God with the voice of praise, &c.
But since we are admonished by the apostolical injunction to give a reason concerning the hope and
charity that is in us to all who ask us, I will no
longer delay to set forth before your holiness, in few
words, the glory of our faith. We believe, then,
and confess a chief and unlimited (summum et in-
circumscriptum) Spirit, without beginning of time
or ending, to be the one omnipotent God; as Moses
has said, 'Hear, O Israel, the Lord thy God is one.'
There is, I say, one Father, unbegotten; one Son,
his only begotten; one Holy Spirit, proceeding from
both, co-eternal with the Father and the Son; but
that always the Father is God; the Son, God; and
the Holy Ghost, God; by whom, through whom,

and in whom, are all things, and without whom
nothing was made. This tripartite conjunction,
and conjunct division, both excludes unity in the
persons, and produces unity notwithstanding the
distinction of persons. But while we believe in
three persons, we do not believe in three Gods; but
we confess one Godhead in three persons. We believe in a Holy Trinity of subsistent persons; but
in an unity as to the nature, majesty, and substance
of God. We, therefore, divide all that exists into
two parts; and, except only the Trinity, all that
has power, action, or motion in heaven, earth, or
sea, we believe and confess to be a creature, and
God the only Creator. Moreover, we believe that the
Son of God was, in the last times, conceived of the
Holy Ghost, and born of the Virgin Mary, and took
upon him the flesh and soul of human nature. In
which flesh we believe and confess that he was
crucified and buried, and arose from the dead; and
that in that same flesh, though of another glory,
after his resurrection, he ascended into heaven, from
whence we expect him to come as the Judge of the
quick and the dead. We also confess an entire and
perfect resurrection of our flesh in which we now
live and move in this present life; and that in it we
shall either receive the reward of good things for
good actions, or sustain punishment for evil actions.
Repentance of sins we confess with the fullest faith,
and receive as a second grace, according to what the
apostle says to the Corinthians—'I was minded to
come unto you before, that ye might have a second
benefit'⁶ (*secundam gratiam*). This is the treasure
of our faith, which we keep sealed with the seal of
the creed of the church which we received in baptism. Thus before God we believe with our hearts;
thus before all men we confess with our mouths;
that the knowledge of it may give faith to men, and
that his image may bear testimony to God."

---

⁶ 2 Cor. i. 15.

Such, we are told, was this virgin's confession ;
and I have endeavoured to translate it as literally as
possible, without addition or diminution. Should
any reader observe that she did not say (or, if he
pleases, that the more modern, lying, forging,
legend-maker, does not make her say) anything
about transubstantiation, or purgatory, or prayers
for the dead, or worshipping the Virgin Mary, or
the saints, or relics, or indeed any of the subjects
with which it might have been supposed that a
candidate for the veil would have entertained the
pope in a "barbarous age" like hers, when "religion
lay expiring under a motley and enormous heap of
superstitious inventions," I cannot help it. Neither
am I concerned to explain to system-makers how it
was that the great western Antichrist, instead of
opening his "mouth, speaking great things" to
blaspheme God and his saints, should have given
utterance to the prayer which followed her confession—or, rather, the benediction of her veil, and
the other habits which she was to assume :—" ' Look
down, O Lord, on this thine handmaid, that the purpose of holy virginity which, by thy inspiration, she
hath formed, she may, under thy governance, keep.
May there be in her, O Lord, by the gift of thy
Spirit, a prudent modesty, a serious gentleness, a
chaste freedom. May she be fervent in charity, and
love nothing beside Thee (*extra te*). May she study
so to live as that she may deserve praise without
being ambitious of it. In thy fear may she love
Thee above all things, and in love may she fear
Thee in all things. Be thou, O Lord, her rejoicing ;
thou her comfort in sorrow ; thou her counsel in
doubt. Be thou her defence against injury ; in
poverty, abundance ; in fasting, food ; in sickness,
medicine. What she has professed, may she keep ;
so that she may overcome the old enemy, and purify
herself from the defilement of sin ; that she may be
adorned with fruit an hundredfold, with virgin
beauty, and the lamps of virtues, and may be

counted worthy to join the company of the elect virgins.' And when they had all answered ' Amen,' the holy pontiff, kissing the forehead of the holy virgin * * * *, dismissed her in peace."

As to all these collateral matters, however, I content myself, for the present, with noticing them more briefly than I could wish. This paper is already longer than I expected it to have been, and than it ought to be, considering that it is written in what I hope the reader considers the worst possible style—without any name of person or place, or any date, or a single reference to any authority whatever. If he has fairly got thus far, there is perhaps little use —I wish there may be any courtesy—in telling him that he might have skipped it; that it is entirely parenthetical, and intended only as an introduction to another paper, in which I hope to explain why I have written it, and to excuse myself for writing it in such a manner.

No. VII.

THE goldsmith,[1] as I have already said, became a bishop. It is not very surprising, and some perhaps will say, "Yes, that was, of course, what he was aiming at." For my own part I should very much doubt it; at least, if he desired a bishopric, I do not see any reason to suppose that he did so from sordid or unworthy motives. The lowest calculation (for the point is disputed) makes him more than fifty years of age when he was consecrated—of money he seems to have possessed unlimited command—the love of power, if he had it (though I really know of nothing to show that he had), might have been better gratified at court than in his diocese, which can scarcely be supposed to have contained such luxuries as the times afforded, and as he might have enjoyed where he was. There is, moreover, another circumstance to which I cannot help

---

[1] Here again I trust that I shall be pardoned if I retain the note which Mr Rose appended to this paper, at its first publication. "It may be doubted whether anything will induce many persons in *this* age to read for themselves. If anything could, surely the simple statement in this paper ought to have that effect. Here we find not only an individual *traduced*, but, through him, the religious character of a whole age *misrepresented*, and this misrepresentation now *generally believed*. We find men leaving out what a writer says, and then reproaching him and his age *for not saying it*. We find Mosheim, Maclaine, Robertson, Jortin, White, *mangling*, misusing, and (some of them) traducing a writer whose works not one of them, except Mosheim (if even he), *had ever seen*. These things are very serious. We may just as well, or better, not read at all, if we read only second-hand writers, or do not take care that those whom we do trust read for themselves, and report honestly. We, in short, trust a painter who paints that *black* which is *white*, and then think we have a clear idea of the object.—Ed."

attaching considerable importance, both as it regards this point, and as a mark of his character in general. On the proposal being made, and whatever reluctance he might feel being overcome, he insisted on a delay of two years, and during that period he exercised the office of an ordinary priest. From a consideration of all these circumstances, I am not inclined to believe that he had any flagrant desire to become a bishop, or was influenced by any sordid or ambitious motive.

But, after all, how much there is in a name. No doubt it is correct to say that he became a bishop; but the real idea would be much better conveyed by saying that he turned missionary; and, forsaking all that the world had to offer, went to preach the gospel among pagan barbarians. In fact, having received episcopal consecration at the same time as his noble young convert, he set off for his diocese, and began to visit it diligently. At first, we are told, the people, sunk in idolatry, received him with hostility; but, being gradually softened by his preaching, a great part of them renounced idolatry, and embraced Christianity.

But from this point what need is there to pursue the details of his history? The rest is known, perhaps, at the antipodes; at least, from the Ohio to the Ganges, every reader of popular books has been told *how* he preached. It is really curious to observe by what apparently trifling incidents people become notorious. Comparatively few persons take the trouble to read about Clotaire and Dagobert, and their goldsmith, and his noble convert Dado (or St. Owen), and his foreman Tillo or St. Theau the Saxon, and his god-daughter St. Hunegundis, and the Abbess St. Aurea. But what reader of Robertson's Charles the Fifth, or Mosheim's History, or Jortin's Remarks, or White's Bampton Lectures, or other popular books (to say nothing of living writers), has not heard of St. Eligius or Eloy, Bishop of Noyon? And all because Mosheim—the

only one of the writers mentioned who can be suspected of knowing anything about him—was pleased
to record that he had preached a bad sermon, and
to give a specimen of it. This scrap, as Dr. Lingard
has truly said, " holds a distinguished place in every
invective which has been published against the
clergy of former ages ; and the definition of a good
Christian has been echoed a thousand times by the
credulity of writers and their readers."[2] Indeed,
the story has been so widely circulated, and, I
apprehend, so influential, that on coming to Robertson's statement in the note next to that on which I
have been hitherto commenting, I cannot help
wishing and endeavouring to put the matter in a
truer light. Though, strictly speaking, it does not
immediately relate to that period of which I professedly write, yet this " hack story " should be
exposed, because many persons have read it
without knowing or attending to its date, and also

---

[2] I copy these words from a note signed " Editor," and printed
on a cancel in the edition of Mosheim, Lond. 1826, vol. ii. p. 159.
When the leaf was changed I do not know, as it is only lately that
I met with the copy in which I saw it. I wish I could give the
space which the whole note would require; but the following
certificate in favour of Dr. Lingard I cannot persuade myself to
omit, not for his sake, but for the reader's :—" We are bound to
state, because we have ascertained the point, that he [Dr.
Lingard] has quoted the original *fairly* and *correctly*, according
to the best edition of the Spicilegium.—(Paris, 1723, 3 vols.
folio.)   We are induced to mention this circumstance because
some protestant divines have been so eager to exculpate Dr.
Mosheim, that they have accused Dr. Lingard of following a
spurious edition, in which various interpolations *might have been*
made by the Romanists to support the credit of the early church.
We are aware that papists *seem* to have a fellow-feeling with their
religious ancestors [something, I suppose, connected with what
an old document calls " the communion of saints "], and are
frequently hurried by their zeal into misrepresentation, sometimes
into gross deviations from truth ; but it is certainly illiberal to
suspect them without cause [which he says there is], or to condemn
them without inquiry."

because many—perhaps most—of those who do
know its date, have a general idea that matters, far
from improving, grew worse and worse for some
centuries. It seemed, however, desirable first to give
some account of this most unfortunate bishop, and
accordingly I did so in the preceding number, in
which I ventured to give his story anonymously,
because I was afraid that in some, at least, I should
excite unconquerable prejudice, if I mentioned a
name which has acquired such evil notoriety.[3]

But let us now inquire about his preaching.
Robertson had said in his text :—

" Even the *Christian religion,* though its precepts are delivered,
and its institutions are fixed in Scripture with a precision which
should have exempted them from being misinterpreted or corrupted,
degenerated during those ages of darkness into an *illiberal superstition.* The barbarous nations when converted to Christianity
changed the object, not the spirit of their religious worship. They
endeavoured to conciliate the favour of the true God by means not
unlike to those which they had employed in order to appease their
false deities. Instead of aspiring to sanctity and virtue, which
alone can render men acceptable to the great author of order and
of excellence, they imagined that they satisfied *every obligation* of
duty by a scrupulous observance of external ceremonies. Religion,
according to their conception of it, comprehended *nothing else ;*
and the rites, by which they persuaded themselves that they could
gain the favour of Heaven, were of such a nature as might have
been expected from the rude ideas of the ages which devised and
introduced them. They were either so unmeaning as to be altogether unworthy of the Being to whose honour they were consecrated, or so absurd as to be a disgrace to reason and humanity."
—(p. 19.)

A sad picture of religion truly, when it comprehended *nothing else* beside what was either *un-*

---

[3] The facts which I have stated respecting St. Eloy are to be
found in his Life, written by St. Owen, Archbishop of Rouen, in
D'Achery's Spicilegium, tom. ii. p. 76. Those which relate to St.
Tillo, or Theau, the foreman, and St. Hunegundis, the god-
daughter, are in the second volume of Mabillon's A. S., 954, 977

meaning, or so *absurd* as to disgrace reason and
humanity ; but it is a note on the word " ceremonies," in the foregoing passage, with which we
are at present concerned ; he begins it by saying —

" *All* the religious *maxims* and *practices* of the dark ages are a
proof of this. I shall produce one remarkable testimony in confirmation of it, from an author canonized by the church of Rome,
S. Eloy or Egidius,[4] Bishop of Noyon, in the seventh century."—
(p. 236.)

But as he, and everybody else I believe, was
indebted to Mosheim, it may be as well at once to

---

[4] So it stands in the original edition ; whether it has been
corrected in those which have followed I do not know ; nor can I
tell whether Robertson (who was not, I imagine, very familiar
with either St. Eloy or St. Giles) thought that he was correcting
a mistake by turning *Eligius* into *Egidius ;* but I cannot help
suspecting Maclaine of some such conceit when he turned the *S.
Piato* of Mosheim into *St. Plato,* as it stands in all editions which
I know, Cent. VII. part ii. c. 3, in a note which by itself might
settle the character of the " learned and judicious translator," as
Robertson calls him. It affords matter highly illustrative not
only of his learning and judgment, but of his taste. [The note
referred to is retained in the new edition of Dr. Murdock, edited
by Mr. Soames, since these papers were published, but with some
diminution of its low and filthy blackguardism ; but even as it now
stands, is such a phrase as " carcass-hunter of saints " proper ?
Surely the most bitter puritanism might be satisfied to direct its
wrath against those who give undue, or give any, reverence to the
relics of God's saints ; but is it right to speak thus of the bodies
in which the Apostles of Christ shall be raised ? But how
singular it is that those who write in this way generally stamp
their performances with some plain mark of ignorance. None of
the parties to the translation seem to have heard of Father
D'Achery. Maclaine takes it as it stands in Mosheim, and speaks
of " Dacherius' Spicilegium." Dr. Murdock, I suppose, translated
at a venture ; but reinforced himself a little from the original,
where he found LVCAE DACHERII, which (without assigning a full
equivalent to the Christian name) he put down as " Lu. Dachier."
Of course there is no credit in knowing Father D'Achery's works,
and no discredit in not knowing them ; but can those who really
do not know his name, have qualified themselves (whatever their
erudition of other kinds may be) with *such* knowledge as is needed
to write, to translate, or even to edit the Church History of the
middle ages ?]

give the original as it stands in his work, placing beside it the passage as it stands in Robertson's work :—

Mosheim.	*Robertson.*
" Bonus Christianus est, qui ad ecclesiam frequentius venit, et oblationem, quæ in altari Deo offeratur, exhibet, qui de fructibus suis non gustat, nisi prius Deo aliquid offerat, qui quoties sanctæ solemnitates adveniunt, ante dies plures castitatem etiam cum propria uxore custodit, ut secura conscientia ad Domini altare accedere possit, qui postremo symbolum vel orationem Dominicam memoriter tenet. - - - Redimite animas vestras de pœna dum habetis in potestate remedia - - oblationes et decimas ecclesiis offerte, luminaria sanctis locis juxta quod habetis exhibete - ad ecclesiam quoque frequentius convenite, sanctorum patrocinia humiliter expetite - - - Quod si observaveritis, securi in die judicii ante tribunal æterni judicis venientes dicetis : Da, Domine, quia dedimus."—p. 269.	" He is a good Christian who comes frequently to church ; who presents the oblation which is offered to God upon the altar ; who doth not taste of the fruits of his own industry until he has consecrated a part of them to God ; who, when the holy festivals shall approach, lives chastely even with his own wife during several days, that with a safe conscience he may draw near to the altar of God ; and who, in the last place, can repeat the creed and the Lord's prayer. Redeem, then, your souls from destruction while you have the means in your power ; offer *presents* and tythes to *churchmen ;* come more frequently to church ; humbly implore the patronage of the saints ; for if you observe these things, you may come with security in the day to the tribunal of the eternal Judge, and say, ' Give to us, O Lord, for we have given *unto Thee.*' "—Vol. i. p. 236.

This, then, according to Robertson, is a " remarkable testimony in confirmation " of his assertion that " *all* the maxims and practices of the dark ages " are a proof that men " instead of aspiring to sanctity and virtue, ... imagined that they had satisfied *every obligation* of duty by a scrupulous observance of external ceremonies." Let us, then, look at it as it stands. Some of it appears to me quite unobjectionable, and indeed, as far as I can judge, there are only, or (to say the least) chiefly, three points at which protestants would take offence.

1. "Redeem, then, your souls from destruction while the means are in your power; offer presents and tithes to churchmen." Pretty advice, truly— it shows the cloven foot at once; and the sordid, grasping churchman stands out as plain as Robertson, or Jortin, or any modern radical, could wish. I say nothing, however, of Robertson's translating "oblationes et decimas ecclesiis offerte," by "offer *presents* and tithes to *churchmen*," for that (however indicative of the *animus*) is quite unimportant compared with his connecting the two things in such a way as if Eligius had made the gift of presents and tithes to churchmen the means of redeeming men's souls. Mosheim acts more fairly, for he places two hyphens after the word "remedia," from which his copyists should have learned that something was omitted. In fact, the sentence stands, "Redimite animas vestras de pœna dum habetis in potestate remedia; eleemosynam juxta vires facite," &c., and the reference is evidently to Dan. iv. 24 (our version 27), "peccata tua eleemosynis redime."

2. "Humbly implore the patronage of the saints," is certainly an injunction which may properly offend protestants; but I need not, I presume, say that it is not peculiar to St. Eligius or the dark ages—that the error which it countenances had assumed foul shapes of sin centuries before he was born, and still flourishes in these enlightened days. I am not undertaking to defend all that Eligius said, but only to show the absurdity of bringing it forward as peculiarly characteristic of *his* preaching, or of *his* age. That it was not so, will as clearly appear from the next point.

3. "Give to us, O Lord, for we have given unto Thee." The words "unto Thee," are neither expressed nor implied in the original, but inserted by Robertson without any warrant whatever. The idea, however, and even the mode of expressing it,

was not characteristic of the age of St. Eligius. Strange as it may seem in these days of high education and profuse literature, it cannot be denied that during the dark ages preachers did sometimes make bold to borrow a homily, or part of one, from their predecessors ; and, in fact, this sermon of St. Eligius (or part of it, including that with which we are at present concerned) had belonged to Cæsarius, Bishop of Arles, who died about a hundred years before Eligius became a bishop.[5] He begins a Homily on Almsgiving by saying that a gracious and merciful God has provided a variety of ways by which men may be enabled to procure the pardon of their sins—" quibus possumus sine grandi labore ac difficultate peccata nostra redimere," and he afterwards says, " Let him to whom God has given more than necessaries hasten to redeem his sins with his superfluity ; and let him who has it not in his power to redeem captives, or to feed or clothe the poor, harbour no hatred in his heart against any man; but let him love, and never cease to pray for them ; certain of the promise, or the mercy of his Lord, with a free conscience he will be able to say, ' Give, Lord, for I have given ; forgive, for I have forgiven.' "[6]

This was the language of Cæsarius ; and I adduce it merely to show the absurdity of bringing forward the words as characteristic of St. Eloy and his age, and in this view it may be worth while to add that

---

[5] Cæsarius was born in A.D. 469, and became Bishop of Arles in A.D. 502, and died A.D. 542. Eligius became Bishop of Noyon, according to the earliest date which I have seen assigned, in A.D. 635 (*Chron. Elnon. ap. III. Mart.* 1392) ; or, according to the latest, which Cave states to be the most common, in the year 646. He thinks, however, that Le Cointe has proved that the right date is 640 ; and adds, that according to the same authority, Eloy lived until A.D. 659 ; according to the most commonly received opinion till 665 ; and according to others till 663.

[6] Bib. Pat. ii. 285.

the language of some earlier, and more respected, fathers did not, as far as I can see, very materially differ from it.

The charge, however, against Eligius is not only, and perhaps not principally, that his doctrine is popishly heretical, but that it is grossly defective; he is much to blame, we are told, for what he says, but much more to blame for what he does not say. Robertson tells us, " The *learned* and *judicious* translator of Dr Mosheim's Ecclesiastical History, from one of whose additional notes I have borrowed this passage, subjoins a *very proper* reflection—' We see here a *large and ample* description of a good Christian, in which there is not the least mention of the love of God, resignation to his will, obedience to his laws, or of justice, benevolence, and charity towards men.' " Jortin says, " As to true religion, here is the *sum and substance* of it as it is drawn up for us by Eligius, one of the principal saints of that age ; " and, in his table of contents, this scrap is referred to as " Eligius's *system of religion.*" White, in the notes to his Bampton Lectures (if they should be called his), tells us that, " no representation can convey stronger ideas of the melancholy state of religion in the seventh century than the description of the character of a good Christian by St. Eligius, or Eloi, Bishop of Noyon."[7]

As to defectiveness, then, let it be observed in the first place, that this scrap is but a very small part— as nearly as I can calculate not a hundredth part —of a very long sermon ; or rather, as one might suppose, from its prolixity and tautology, even if the language of St. Eloy's biographer did not suggest it, of several sermons mixed up into one great homily. If it were printed like Bishop Horsley's Sermons, it would, I believe occupy just about the fifty-six octavo pages which contain the first three of them. Candour would suggest a possi-

---

[7] Bampton Lectures, notes, p. 5.

bility that the other ninety-nine parts might contain
something that would go towards supplying the
deficiencies of the scrap.

But this is not all; or even what is most important. Mosheim printed the passage in such a way
as to show that there were *some* omissions, though
he did not indicate *all*. In Jortin's *translation* only
one mark of omission is retained; and that is, between the words " prayer " and " Redeem." In the
version given by Robertson, *all* such indications are
removed, and the scrap stands as one continuous
passage. White goes a step farther, and prints
the *Latin text* without any break or hint of omission.
Let us, therefore, see what is omitted in the part
which is professedly quoted; and as that part is not
far advanced in the sermon, it will be best to begin
at the beginning. The part actually extracted by
Mosheim I mark by *italics* :—

" I beseech you, most dear brethren, and admonish you with
great humility, that you would listen attentively to those things
which I desire to suggest to you for your salvation. For Almighty
God knows that I offer them with fervent love towards you, and
were I to do otherwise I should undoubtedly be held to have failed
in my duty. Receive, then, what I say, not for my sake, who am
of little account, but for your own salvation, willingly; at least,
in such a way that what you receive by the ear you may fulfil in
practice, so that I may be counted worthy to rejoice with you in
the kingdom of heaven, not only by my obedience, but through
your profiting by it. If there is any one of you who is displeased
that I persist in preaching to you so frequently, I beg him not to
be offended with me, but rather to consider the danger to which I
am exposed, and to listen to the fearful threatening which the
Lord has addressed to priests by his prophet,—' If thou dost
not speak to warn the wicked from his way, that wicked man shall
die in his iniquity ; but his blood will I require at thine hand.
Nevertheless, if thou warn the wicked of his way to turn from it;
if he do not turn from his way, he shall die in his iniquity ; but
thou hast delivered thy soul.'—Ezek. xxxiii. 8. And that,
' Cry aloud, spare not, and show my people their sins.'—Is.
lviii. 1.

" Consider therefore, brethren, that it is my duty incessantly to
stir up your minds to fear the judgment of God, and to desire the
heavenly reward, that, together with you, I may be counted worthy

to enjoy perpetual peace in the company of angels. I ask you, therefore, always to hold in dread the day of judgment; and every day to keep before your eyes the day of your death.

" Consider how far you would be fit to be presented before angels, or what you would receive in return for your deserts, and whether you will be able in that day to show that the promise of your baptism has been kept unbroken. Remember that you then made a covenant with God, and that you promised in the very sacrament of baptism to renounce the Devil and all his works. Whosoever was able then made this promise in his own person and for himself. If any was unable, his sponsor, that is, he who received him at his baptism, made these promises to God for him, and in his name.

" Consider, therefore, what a covenant you have made with God, and examine yourselves whether after that promise you have been following that wicked Devil whom you renounced. For you did renounce the Devil, and all his pomps, and his works ; that is, idols, divinations, auguries, thefts, frauds, fornications, drunkenness, and lies, for these are his works and pomps. On the contrary, you promised to believe in God the Father Almighty, and in Jesus Christ, his only Son, our Lord, conceived of the Holy Ghost, born of the Virgin Mary; that he suffered under Pontius Pilate, rose from the dead on the third day, and ascended into heaven ; and then you promised that you would believe also in the Holy Ghost, the holy catholic church, the remission of sins, the resurrection of the body, and the life everlasting. Without all doubt this your covenant and confession which you then made will never be lost sight of by God ; and, therefore, most dearly beloved, I warn you that this your confession or promise should always be kept in your own memory, that so your bearing the Christian name, instead of rising in judgment against you, may be for your salvation. For you are made Christians to this end, that you may always do the works of Christ ; that is, that you may love chastity, avoid lewdness and drunkenness, maintain humility, and detest pride, because our Lord Christ both showed humility by example and taught it by words, saying —' Learn of me, for I am meek and lowly in heart ; and ye shall find rest to your souls.' (Matt. xi. 30.) You must also renounce envy, have charity among yourselves, and always think of the future world, and of eternal blessedness, and labour rather for the soul than for the body. For the flesh will be only a short time in this world ; whereas the soul, if it does well, will reign for ever in heaven ; but, if it does wickedly, it will burn without mercy in hell. He, indeed, who thinks only of this life is like the beasts and brute animals.

" It is not enough, most dearly beloved, for you to have received the name of Christians, if you do not do Christian works. To be called a Christian profits him who always retains in his mind, and fulfils in his actions, the commands of Christ ; that is, who does not commit theft, does not bear false witness, who neither tells lies nor swears falsely, who does not commit adultery, who does not hate anybody, but loves all men as himself, who does not render evil to his enemies, but rather prays for them, who does not stir up strife, but restores peace between those who are at variance. For these precepts Christ himself has deigned to give by his own mouth, in the gospel, saying—' Thou shalt do no murder, Thou shalt not commit adultery, Thou shalt not steal, Thou shalt not bear false witness, Thou shalt not swear falsely nor commit fraud, Honour thy father and thy mother : and, Thou shalt love thy neighbour as thyself.' (Matt. xix. 18, 19.) And also, ' All things whatsoever ye would that men should do to you; do ye even so to them : for this is the law and the prophets.' (Matt. vii. 12.)

"And he has given yet greater, but very strong and fruitful (valde fortia atque fructifera) commands, saying—' Love your enemies, do good to them that hate you,' and ' pray for them which despitefully use you and persecute you.' (Matt. v. 44.) Behold, this is a strong commandment, and to men it seems a hard one ; but it has a great reward ; hear what it is—' That ye may be,' he saith, ' the children of your Father which is in heaven.' Oh, how great grace ! Of ourselves we are not even worthy servants ; and by loving our enemies we become sons of God. Therefore, my brethren, both love your friends in God, and your enemies for God; for ' he that loveth his neighbour,' as saith the apostle, ' hath fulfilled the law.' (Rom. xiii. 8.) For he who will be a true Christian must needs keep these commandments ; because, if he does not keep them, he deceives himself. He, therefore, is a good Christian who puts faith in no charms or diabolical inventions, but places all his hope in Christ alone ; who receives strangers with joy, even as if it were Christ himself, because he will say—' I was a stranger, and ye took me in,' and, ' inasmuch as ye have done it unto one of the least of these my brethren, ye have done it unto me.' *He*, I say, *is a good Christian* who washes the feet of strangers, and loves them as most dear relations ; who, according to his means, gives alms to the poor ; *who comes frequently to church : who presents the oblation which is offered to God upon the altar ; who doth not taste of his fruits before he hath offered somewhat to God ;* who has not a false balance or deceitful measures ; who hath not given his money to usury ; who both lives chastely himself, and teaches his sons and his neighbours to live chastely and in the fear of God ; *and, as often as the holy festivals occur, lives continently even with his own wife for some days previously, that he may, with safe conscience, draw near to the altar of God ; finally, who can repeat the Creed or the Lord's Prayer*, and teaches the same to his sons and servants. He who is such an one, is, without doubt, a true Christian, and Christ also dwelleth in him, who hath said, ' I and the Father will come and make our abode with him.' (John xiv. 23.) And, in like manner, he saith, by the prophet, ' I will dwell in them, and walk in them,

132   ST. ELIGIUS   [NO. VII.

and I will be their God, and they shall be my people.' (2 Cor. vi.
16.)

" Behold, brethren, ye have heard what sort of persons are good
Christians ; and therefore labour as much as you can, with God's
assistance, that the Christian name may not be falsely applied to
you ; but, in order that you may be true Christians, always meditate
in your hearts on the commands of Christ, and fulfil them in your
practice ; *redeem your souls from punishment while you have the
means in your power ;* give alms according to your means, maintain peace and charity, restore harmony among those who are at
strife, avoid lying, abhor perjury, bear no false witness, commit no
theft, *offer oblations and gifts to churches, provide lights for sacred
places according to your means*, retain in your memory the Creed
and the Lord's Prayer, and teach them to your sons. Moreover,
teach and chastise those children for whom you are sponsors, that
they may always live with the fear of God. Know that you are
sponsors for them with God. *Come frequently also to church ;
humbly seek the patronage of the saints ;* keep the Lord's day in
reverence of the resurrection of Christ, without any servile work ;
celebrate the festivals of the saints with devout feeling ; love
your neighbours as yourselves ; what you would desire to be done
to you by others, that do to others ; what you would not have done
to you, do to no one; before all things have charity, for charity
covereth a multitude of sins ; be hospitable, humble, casting all
your care upon God, for he careth for you ; visit the sick. seek out
the captives, receive strangers, feed the hungry, clothe the naked ;
set at nought soothsayers and magicians, let your weights and
measures be fair, your balance just, your bushel and your pint fair ;
nor must you claim back more than you gave, nor exact from any
one usury for money lent. *Which, if you observe, coming with
security before the tribunal of the eternal Judge, in the day of Judgment, you may say ' Give, Lord, for we have given ;* show mercy,
for we have shown mercy ; we have fulfilled what thou hast commanded, do thou give what thou hast promised.'"

I feel that by this extract I do very imperfect
justice to the sermon of St. Eloy ; of which, indeed,
I might say that it seems to have been written as if
he had anticipated all and each of Mosheim's and
Maclaine's charges, and intended to furnish a
pointed answer to almost every one. I feel it to
be most important to our forming a right view of
the dark ages, that such false statements respecting
the means of instruction and of grace should be
exposed ; but with so wide a field before us, I am

unwilling, at present, to give more space than this
to one case, especially as I am anxious to get beyond
that part of the subject which consists in merely
contradicting misstatement ; but I cannot do so
until I have offered some remarks on the work
of a popular historian whom I have not as yet
noticed.

(*Addition to the Second Edition.*)

The passage in Mosheim which gave rise to this
paper is still retained without qualification or explanation in the "New and literal translation from the
original Latin, with copious additional notes,
original and selected, by James Murdock, D.D.,
edited, with additions, by Henry Soames, M.A.,
rector of Stapleford Tawney, with Thoydon Mount,
Essex," and published by Messrs. Longman and
others in the year 1841. I am tempted, therefore,
to give some further extracts which I made when
the paper was written, but which would have occupied too much room in the magazine. But for
this I should then have produced proofs and illustrations of my statement, that the sermon seemed as
if it had been written to anticipate and refute the
charges of Mosheim.

In this new translation the passage to which the
note on St. Eligius is appended, stands as follows :—

"During this century, true religion lay buried
under a senseless mass of superstitions; and was
unable to raise her head. The earlier Christians
had worshipped only God, and his Son ; but those
called Christians in this age, worshipped the wood
of a cross, the images of holy men, and bones of
dubious origin. The early Christians placed heaven
and hell before the view of men ; these latter
depicted a certain fire prepared to burn off

the imperfections of the soul. The former
taught, that Christ had made expiation for the sins
of men, by his death and his blood; the latter
seemed to inculcate, that the gates of heaven would
be closed against none who should enrich the clergy
or the church with their, donations."—Vol. ii.
p. 93.

Now at this distance of time I do not pretend to
speak positively respecting the contents of this long
rambling discourse, which it is not worth while to
search over again minutely, in order to say whether
it contains one word about the wood of the cross, or
the images of the saints, or the dubious bones. I
really believe there is nothing of the kind; but the
extracts which I have by me were, I think, made to
meet the statement that instead of having heaven
and hell set before them, the people were told about
a certain fire that was "to burn off the imperfections of the soul." The reader will therefore
understand that I give them as illustrative of the
preacher's doctrine (if he can be said to have had
any) of purgatory; though at the same time they
may show us what he taught on some other subjects;
and lead the reader very reasonably to disbelieve the
other charges made against him, all of which could
hardly be answered without extracting the greater
part of the Homily.

"Those whom you see to be good, do you imitate; those whom
you see to be bad, chasten and rebuke; that you may have a
double reward. And let him who has hitherto lived free from the
aforesaid evils rejoice, and give God thanks, and take care for the
future, and persevere with alacrity in good works; but let him who
has hitherto lived in sin, quickly correct himself, and repent with
his whole heart before he departs this life; for if he dies without
repentance he will not enter into rest, but will be cast into hell fire
(in gehennam ignis), whence he will never get out through all
eternity" (unde nunquam exiet in sæcula sæculorum).—p. 98 a.

After addressing magistrates, he says—"Considering these
things, brethren, both you who govern and you who are subject,
ground yourselves in the fear of God. Retain what has been said,

do what is commanded, have Christ always in your mind, and his mark on your forehead. Know that you have many adversaries who are eager to impede your course ; therefore in all places and at all times arm yourselves with the sign of the cross, fortify yourselves with the standard of the cross ; for this alone they fear, this alone they dread, and this is given you as a shield whereby you may quench all the fiery darts of the wicked one. For the mark of Christ is a great thing and the cross of Christ, but it profits those only who keep the precepts of Christ. That it may profit you, therefore, strive to fulfil his precepts with all your might ; and whether you sit or walk, or eat, or go to bed, or get up, always let the mark of Christ guard your forehead, that by the recollection of God it may both protect you while waking and keep you while asleep ; and as often as you wake in the night and sleep flies from your eyes, immediately let the sign of the cross occur to your lips and let your minds be occupied in prayers, and revolve the commandments of God in your hearts, lest the enemy should suddenly creep into your stupid breasts, or the eager adversary twist himself into your soul through your foolish carelessness. And when he suggests to your sense any evil thought, set before yourself the future judgment of God, the punishment of hell, the pains of Gehenna, the darkness of Tartarus, which the wicked endure. If you do this, the evil thought will immediately vanish, and the power of Christ will not desert you ; for that which the prophet has said is true, ' He that trusteth in the Lord, mercy shall compass him about.' " (Ps. xxxii. 10).—p. 98 b.

" Redeem yourselves while you live, for after death no one can redeem you " (quia post mortem nemo vos redimere potest).—p. 99 b.

" In all these works of goodness which the Lord has commanded you to perform, he seeks nothing from you but the salvation of your souls, and that you may fear him always and keep his commandments [then after referring to and in great measure repeating the blessing and the curse given by Moses, he proceeds :] These things, therefore, brethren, always keep in mind, these words repeat to your sons and your neighbours, remember them when you sit in your houses, and when your walk, neither forget them in your prosperity, but always fear God, and serve him alone, lest his fury be kindled against you. Know that he keepeth covenant and mercy towards those who love him and keep his commandments, and heals all their sicknesses. Consider that, as the apostle John forewarns, 'it is the last hour,' and therefore do not now love the world, for it soon passeth away, and all the lust thereof with it. But, do you do the will of God, that you may remain for ever, and may have confidence when he shall appear, and not be confounded at his coming. Let no man deceive you. He that doeth righteousness is righteous, and he that committeth sin is of the devil ; and certainly every sin, whether theft, or adultery, or lying, is not committed without diabolical agency. Consider, I beseech you, what a destructive thing it is to do the works of the devil, and to become partaker with him, not in rest, but in the punishment of gehenna. Therefore, whenever you sin, do not wait in mortiferous security until your wounds putrefy, nor add others to them, but immediately by the confession of repentance hasten to obtain a remedy."—p. 100 *a*.

" Now, according to his unspeakable mercy, the Lord not only admonishes, but entreats that we would be converted to him. Let us therefore listen to him when he asks, lest if we do not, he should not listen to us when he judges. Let us listen also to the Scripture, which crieth out, ' My son, have pity on thine own soul, pleasing God.'[8] What wilt thou answer to this, O human frailty? God entreats thee to pity thyself, and thou wilt not ; how shall he hear thee supplicating in the day of necessity, when thou wilt not hear him entreating for thyself? If you now neglect these things, brethren, what will you do in the day of judgment, or to what refuge will you fly? If, I say, you now neglect such exhortations of God, you will not then escape the torments of hell, nor can gold or silver deliver you, nor those riches which you now secrete in corners, and through the pride of which you become negligent of your salvation. For hence, God saith by the prophet, ' I will visit you with evil, and I will cause the arrogancy of the wicked to cease, and will lay low the haughtiness of the terrible.' (Is. xiii. 11.) And again he admonishes, saying, ' Bring it again to mind, O ye transgressors ; cease to do evil, learn to do well ; relieve the oppressed, defend the poor, and the widow, and the orphan ; deal not by oppression with the stranger.'[9] These things, therefore, brethren, keep in mind. Hasten to observe them with all your might. Fight as those who are separated from the devil. Be joined to God, who has redeemed you. Let the Gentiles be astonished at your conversation, and if they slander you, and even if they mock you for performing the duties of Christianity, let not that trouble you, for they shall give an account to God. Place, therefore, all your hope in the mercy of Christ, and not only abstain from every impure act, but also guard your minds from evil thoughts ; for the Lord God is a righteous judge, and judgeth of evil thoughts."—p. 101 *b*.

---

[8] " Miserere animæ tuæ placens Deo." Ecclus. xxx. 23. Our English version is, " Love thine own soul, and comfort thy heart ; remove sorrow far from thee." v. 23. I give the Douay in the text.

[9] The passage stands, " Redite prævaricatores ad cor ; quiescite agere perverse, discite benefacere ; succurrite oppresso, defendite pauperem et viduam, et pupillum ; et advenam nolite calumniari." It will be seen that it is made up from Is. xlvi. 8, and i. 16, 17, and Ezek. xxii. 7.

" Moreover, that which is threatened by the voice of truth in the gospel : ' they,' it saith, ' that do iniquity shall be cast into a furnace of fire, where there shall be weeping and gnashing of teeth.' Consider, then, how fierce, how much to be dreaded that fire is; and let him who could not now bear to put even one of his fingers in the fire, fear to be tormented there with his whole body for ever " (in sæcula).—p. 102 *b*.

" But know that the soul when it is separated from the body, is either immediately placed in paradise for its good deserts, or certainly precipitated directly into hell for its sins."—p. 103 *b*.

Love therefore with all your hearts that eternal life which through all ages you shall never bring to an end. Hasten thither, where you shall ever live, and never fear death. For if you love this wretched, fleeting life which you maintain with such labour—in which by running about and bustling, by the sweat of your brow, and working yourselves out of breath, you can scarcely provide the necessaries of life—how much more should you love eternal life in which you shall have no labour at all, where there is always the highest security, secure happiness, happy freedom, free blessedness ; where shall be fulfilled that which our Lord saith in the gospel, ' Men shall be like unto the angels ;' like, indeed, not in substance, but in blessedness ? And that, ' then shall the just shine forth as the sun in the kingdom of their Father.' What, think you, will then be the splendour of souls, when the light of bodies shall have the brightness of the sun ? There shall then be no sorrow, no labour, no grief, no death ; but perpetual health shall endure. There no evil shall arise, no misery of the flesh, no sickness, no need of any kind ; there shall be no hunger, no thirst, no cold, no heat, no faintness of fasting, nor any temptation of the enemy ; nor then any will to sin, any possibility of defection ; but there shall be fulness of joy, and exultation in all things ; and men, associated with angels, shall be ever young in freedom from all fleshly infirmity. There, therefore, shall be solid joy, there secure rest, there pleasure infinite ; where if it be once attained, there shall be no chance of losing it throughout eternity, in that blessedness in which what is once gained shall be kept for ever. Nothing is there more magnificent than that place, nothing more glorious, nothing more bright, more beautiful, more true, more noble, nothing more pure in excellence, nothing more abundant in fulness. There always peace and the highest rejoicing. There is true and certain happiness. There shall no longer be feared that most fierce enemy who continually desires to destroy souls, nor shall the fiery darts of the devil, or any temptations of the adversary, be any longer dreaded. The cruelty of barbarians shall no more strike terror, nor shall any adversity be thenceforth apprehended. There shall be no fear of the sword, of fire, or the savage countenance of the tormentor. No one in that glorious place shall want clothing ; for there is there no cold nor heat, nor any change of climate. No one there hungers, none is sad, none is a stranger ; but all who

shall be counted worthy to attain to that place shall live secure as
in their own country. The flesh shall no longer war against the
spirit, nor shall any danger be feared, but unspeakable rewards
with the angels shall be given by Christ; and 'what the eye hath
not seen,' saith the apostle, 'nor the ear heard, neither hath it
entered into the heart of man to conceive, what God hath prepared
for those who love him.' Behold what blessedness he will lose
who refuses now while he hath opportunity to amend himself. Let
us therefore, brethren, for whom so great blessedness is prepared
in heaven, disdain (the Lord being our helper) to be any longer
the servants of sin. While, then, there is time, let us hasten to
obtain the favour of God, let us despise earthly things, that we
may gain those which are heavenly ; let us think of ourselves as
pilgrims in this world, that we may the more cheerfully hasten
towards heaven ; for all the things which are here seen quickly
pass away, and will be gone like a shadow."—p. 103 *b*.

After quoting Matt. xxv. of our Lord's advent,
he proceeds :—

" Then when all are looking, he will show the wounds and the
holes of the nails in that body undoubtedly the same in which he
was wounded for our transgressions ; and addressing the sinners
he will then say—' I formed thee, O man, with my hands from the
dust of the earth, and placed thee amidst the delights of a paradise, which thou didst not deserve ; but thou, despising me and
my commands, didst prefer to follow a deceiver ; wherefore, being
condemned to just punishment, thou wast appointed to the torments of hell. Afterwards, pitying thee, I became incarnate, I
dwelt on earth among sinners, I bare scorn and stripes for thee.
That I might save thee, I underwent blows and spitting. That I
might gain for thee the sweets of paradise, I drank vinegar and
gall. For thee I was crowned with thorns, fastened to the cross,
wounded with the spear. For thee I died, was laid in the grave,
and descended into hell. That I might bring thee back to paradise, I went to the gates of hell ; that thou mightest reign in
heaven, I penetrated the infernal deep. Acknowledge, then, oh
human impiety, how much I have suffered for thee. Behold the
wounds which I received for thee, behold the holes of those nails
fastened by which I hanged on the cross. I bare thy griefs, that I
might heal thee ; I underwent punishment, that I might give thee
glory ; I submitted to death, that thou mightest live for ever; I
lay in the sepulchre, that thou mightest reign in heaven. All
these things I bare for you ; what more than these things should
I have done for you that I have not done ? Tell me now, or show
me, what you have suffered for me, or what good you have done for
yourselves. I when I was invisible did, of my own will, become

incarnate on your account; though I was impassible, for you I condescended to suffer; when I was rich, for your sakes I became poor. But you, always despising both my humility and my commandments, have followed the seducer rather than me; and now behold my justice cannot adjudge to you anything else than what your works deserve to receive. Take, then, what you have chosen; you have despised light, possess darkness; you have loved death, go into perdition; you have followed the devil, go with him into eternal fire.' What, think you, will then be the grief, what the lamentation, what the sadness, what the distress, when this sentence shall be given against the wicked? For then shall be to the wicked a grievous separation from the sweet company of the saints; and, being delivered over to the power of demons, they will go in their own bodies with the devil into eternal punishment, and will remain for ever in lamentation and groaning. For being far exiled from the blessed country of Paradise, they will be tormented in hell, never again to see light, never to obtain a time of refreshing, never to end their punishment, never to arrive at rest; but through thousands of thousands of years to be tormented in hell, nor ever, through all eternity, to be delivered. Where he that torments is never tired, and he that is tormented never dies. For there the fire so consumes that it still reserves; torments are so inflicted as that they may be for ever renewed. According to the quality of his crimes, however, each one will there suffer the punishments of hell; and those who are guilty of the like sins will be associated together in punishment. Nothing will be heard there but weeping, and wailing, and gnashing of teeth. There will be no consolation, nothing but flames and the terrors of punishments, and the wretched ones will burn without end in eternal fire through all ages. But the just shall go into life eternal, and without doubt in that very same flesh which they here had, and shall be associated with holy angels in the kingdom of God, appointed to perpetual joys, never again to die, no more to see corruption, but always filled with the joy and sweetness of Christ, they shall shine as the sun in the brightness and glory which God has prepared for those who love him. And the more obedient to God any one hath been in this life, so much the larger reward shall he receive; and the more he hath loved God here, the more nearly shall he then see him.

" Behold, most dearly beloved, I have foretold you plainly, so that you may understand what things shall happen to every one. No one can now plead ignorance, for life and death are set before you; the punishments of the wicked and the glory of the just are told you,—now it remains for your choice to take which you please; for each will surely then possess that which he hath desired and endeavoured after here."—p. 104 b.

These are not all the passages which might be

quoted to the same effect; but surely they are more than enough, and such in quality as to warrant my saying that they seem as if they had been written purposely to anticipate, and refute, the charge that the preachers, of whom St. Eloy is given as a specimen, instead of placing " heaven and hell before the view of men," only " depicted a certain fire prepared to burn off the imperfections of the soul."

No. VIII.

" A modern author, who writes the history of ancient times, can have no personal knowledge of the events of which he writes ; and consequently he can have no title to the credit and confidence of the public, merely on his own authority. If he does not write romance instead of history, he must have received his information from tradition—from authentic monuments, original records, or the memoirs of more ancient writers—and therefore it is but just to acquaint his readers from whence he *actually* received it. "— HENRY.

IN the preceding paper, I expressed my design to go on from Robertson to another popular writer ; and I now beg to call the reader's attention to the historian from whom I have borrowed my motto.   In that part of his History of England which treats of the tenth century, Henry compassionately says :—

" That we may not entertain too contemptible an opinion of our forefathers, who flourished in the benighted ages which we are now examining, it is necessary to pay due attention to their unhappy circumstances.   To say nothing of that contempt for letters which they derived from their ancestors, and of the almost incessant wars in which they were engaged, it was difficult, or rather impossible, for any but the clergy, and a very few of the most wealthy among the laity, to obtain the least smattering of learning ; because all the means of acquiring it were far beyond their reach.   It is impossible to learn to read and write even our own native tongue, which is now hardly esteemed a part of learning, without books, masters, and materials for writing ; but in those ages, all these were so extremely scarce and dear, that none but great princes and wealthy prelates could procure them.   We have already heard of a large estate given by a king of Northumberland for a single volume ; and the history of the middle ages abounds with examples of that kind.   How, then, was it possible for persons of a moderate fortune to procure so much as one book, much less such a number of books as to make their learning to read an accomplishment that would reward their trouble ? It was then as difficult to borrow books as to buy them. It is a sufficient proof of this that the king of France was obliged to deposit a considerable quantity of plate, and to get one of his nobility to join with him in a bond, under a high penalty, to return it, before he could procure the loan of one volume, which may now be purchased for a few shillings. Materials for writing were also very scarce and dear, which made few persons think of learning that art. This was one reason of the scarcity of books ; and that great estates were often transferred from one owner to another by a mere verbal agreement, and the delivery of earth and stone, before witnesses, without any written deed. Parchment, in particular, on which all their books were written, was so difficult to be procured, that many of the MSS. of the middle ages, which are still preserved, appear to have been written on parchment from which some former writing had been erased."— Book ii. ch. iv. vol. iv. p. 80.

After what I have said in former papers, it is, I trust, quite unnecessary to make a single remark on all this ; which I transcribe and set before the reader, instead of asking him, as I should otherwise have done, to turn back to the statements of Robertson, which I have from time to time quoted, and to see how far, when read off without any explanation, they are calculated to give a true view of things. Henry has, however, one "hack story," of which I must take particular notice ; for, notwithstanding the false impression conveyed by such absurd matter as that which I have just quoted, there is really more mischief done by the little pointed anecdotes with which some popular writers pretend to prove or to illustrate their sweeping statements. These stories are remembered by their readers, and the semblance of particular and detailed truth in one instance, gives sanction and weight to a whole string of false and foolish assertions about the general state of things. Perhaps it might be enough to refer the reader back to the instance of the Abbot Bonus ;[1] but instead of that we will have an entirely new story, from Henry.

[1] See No. IV. p. 63.

Having told us that—

" All the nations of Europe were involved in such profound darkness during the whole course of the tenth century, that the writers of literary history are at a loss for words to paint the ignorance, stupidity, and barbarism of that age"—(Book ii. c. 4. vol. iv. p. 67).

and having, in proof of this, referred to " Cave Histor. Literar. p. 571, Brucker Hist. Philosoph. t. 3. p. 632," he adds on the next page—

" The clergy in this age were almost as illiterate as the laity. Some who filled the highest stations in the church could not so much as read ; while others, who pretended to be better scholars, and attempted to perform the public offices, committed the most egregious blunders ; of which the reader will find one example, *out of many*, quoted below."

At the foot of the page, we find the following note :—

" Meinwerc, Bishop of Paderborn, in this century, in reading the public prayers, used to say,—' Benedic Domine regibus et reginis mulis et mulabis [*sic*] tuis :—' instead of ' famulis et famulabis ; [*sic*]' which made it a very ludicrous petition.— *Leibniz Coll. Script. Brunswic.*, t. i. p. 555."

Very ludicrous indeed — What an odd person Bishop Meinwerc must have been, and what a very strange habit to fall into—but, without attempting to account for it, farther than by saying, " it was his way," may we not draw three inferences from it —first, that if Meinwerc habitually made this blunder, he made a thousand others like it ; secondly, that what *he* did, all the other bishops did ; thirdly, that if the bishops were so ignorant, the priests and deacons, to say nothing of the laity, were infinitely worse ? Are not these fair deductions ? And yet, to say the truth, when I consider that my inquiry is not whether there were any ignorant, stupid, incompetent persons in the dark ages ; but whether there were not some of a different character, I feel inclined to claim, or at least to cross-examine, this witness. I cannot but think that the story, even as it stands, may be fairly made to say something in my favour. If the bishop did make this blunder, it seems that he had, at least, one hearer who knew that it was a blunder, and who thought it worth while to note it down as such ; which, moreover, that hearer would hardly have done if conscious that he was the only person capable of seeing its absurdity. Besides, if this is only " one example out of many," there must have been persons in various places equally competent to detect such errors ; and who, like the critic of Paderborn, thought them worth recording. So that, in proportion as the recorded blunders of this kind are numerous, we may be led to suspect a thicker and more extensive sprinkle of better-instructed persons. I know not how else to account for the fact that such things were seen and recorded as errors ; unless, indeed, we assume the existence of some one individual " George Seacoal," whose reading and writing in this dark age came " by nature ;" and suppose him to have circuited about with " the lanthorn " which he had in charge, in order to " comprehend all vagrom men " who broke the bounds of grammar, and who has certainly acted up to the very letter of his instructions, by letting his reading and writing " appear where there is no need of such vanity ;" for what in the world did it matter to Bishop Meinwerc's flock whether he said *mulis* or *famulis*, if neither he nor they knew the difference ?

We cannot, however, well understand this story without paying some attention to the circumstances of the bishop ; and it is quite within the limits— indeed in the very heart—of our subject, to inquire into the proceedings of any prelate who was born in the tenth century, though not (as Henry makes him) a bishop until the eleventh. I might fairly inflict on the reader a long pedigree, and trace up the Bishop of Paderborn to the great Duke Witikind ; but it may suffice for our present purpose to say, that he was born in the reign of the Emperor Otho II., and was his second cousin once removed ; Theoderic, the father of the Empress Matilda, the wife of Henry the Fowler, being their common ancestor. His father, Imed, intending that Thiederic, the elder of his two sons, should succeed him in his honours and possessions, devoted Meinwerc, at an early age, to the clerical function, and offered him, in his childhood, in the Church of St. Stephen, at Halberstadt. There he received the first rudiments of his education ; but was afterwards removed to Hildesheim, where, among many other schoolfellows, who afterwards took a leading part in the world, he had his third cousin, Henry, Duke of Bavaria, afterwards Emperor, better known under the title of St. Henry.[2]

---

[2] I should have thought that there was such a difference between the ages of Meinwerc and the emperor, as could not have allowed of their being school-fellows. But the author of the life to which Henry refers, so distinctly states not only that it was so, but that it was in the time of Otho the *Second*, that I do not know how to dispute it, though I cannot reconcile it even with the dates which he gives himself in various parts of his work. He says that Meinwerc went to Hildesheim, " ubi Heinricus filius Ducis Bajoariæ Henrici, cum aliis plurimis honori et decori ecclesiæ Christi suo tempore profuturis, secum theoriæ studiis continuam operam dedit. . . . Acceptus autem de scholis, vixit in prædicta Halverstadensi Ecclesia sub Præposito canonicæ legis, omnibus carus et amabilis, aspectu et colloquio affabilis, actu et eloquio irreprehensibilis. Eo tempore monarchiam Romani Imperii Otto ejusdem nominis *secundus* strenue gubernabat."—p. 519. It is not worth while to discuss the chronology of the matter. If it be a mistake to suppose that the emperor and the bishop were school-fellows, it is beyond all doubt that they were cousins and play-fellows.

Otho II. died in A.D. 983, and was succeeded by
his son, Otho III.; who called his kinsman, Meinwerc, to court, and made him his chaplain. In this
situation he is said to have been esteemed and
respected by all, and particularly beloved by his
royal master and cousin, who enriched him with
most liberal presents, in proof of his affection—
" quod videlicet suam vitam diligeret ut propriam."
On the death of that Emperor, in A.D. 1002, among
many candidates for the empire, the successful one
was Henry of Bavaria, who was related to Meinwerc
in precisely the same degree as his predecessor in
the empire had been, and who was perhaps bound
to him by what is often the closer and stronger tie
of school-fellowship. The chaplain became the inseparable companion of his royal master—" de Karo
fit Karissimus ; factusque est ei in negotiis publicis
et privatis comes irremotissimus."

After some time—that is to say, in the year 1009
—the see of Paderborn became vacant by the death
of Rhetarius, who had been bishop for twenty years.
Messengers from the church announced the fact to
the emperor, who was then at Goslar, and prayed
him to appoint a successor. This, however, was
not so easy a matter; for, about nine years before,
the city of Paderborn had been burned; and the
noble monastery, containing the cathedral, had been
all but entirely destroyed. Rhetarius had, indeed,
done what he could with the pope, and the Emperor
Otho III.; and had obtained from them (what was,
no doubt, very important as far as it went) a full
confirmation to the church of all the rights and
property which it had possessed before the conflagration; but it does not appear that he got anything from them towards repairing losses. When,
however, Henry, his successor, came to the throne
of the empire, he made it his study and his business
to advance the interests of the church; and when
Rhetarius applied to him, he gave him a forest.

When he came at another time to beg for his
church, the emperor not having (as the historian
says with great simplicity) at the moment anything
which he could conveniently give him (rege autem
in promptu quod daret non habente), his chaplain,
Meinwerc, gave his royal master a farm, which
belonged to himself, which the emperor immediately
transferred to the bishop.

Still, notwithstanding the exertions of Rhetarius,
the see remained in a state of wretched poverty as
long as he lived; and it was difficult to know how
to fill up the vacancy occasioned by his death. The
emperor having, however, convened such bishops
and princes as attended him at Goslar, consulted
with them as to the appointment of a bishop who
should be most suited to the circumstances of time
and place. After long deliberation, and canvassing
the merits of a good many persons, all agreed that
Meinwerc was the fittest man. In coming to this
decision, they were avowedly influenced by his rank
and wealth; but it is only justice to him to say,
that I find nothing against his moral character, nor
even anything which should authorize me to say
that he had not a true zeal for God, though it might
not be, in all respects, according to knowledge.
The council, however, were unanimous; and the
emperor (faventibus et congratulantibus omnibus)
sent for the chaplain; and, when he came, smiling
with his usual kindness, he held out a glove, and
said—" Take this." Meinwerc, who can hardly be
supposed to have been quite ignorant of what was
going on, and who understood the nature of the
symbol, inquired what he was to take. " The see
of Paderborn," replied the emperor. The chaplain,
with all the freedom of a kinsman and old schoolfellow, asked his royal master how he could suppose
that he wished for such a bishopric, when he had
property enough of his own to endow a better.
The emperor, with equal frankness, replied that

that was just the very thing that he was thinking of
—that his reason for selecting him was that he
might take pity on that desolate church, and help it
in its need. "Well, then," said Meinwerc, heartily,
"I will take it on those terms;" and then and there
—namely, at Goslar, on the next Sunday, being the
second Sunday in Lent, and the thirteenth of March,
1009—he was consecrated Bishop of Paderborn, by
Willigisus, Archbishop of Mentz, and the other
bishops who were there.

"Being therefore," says his biographer, "raised to
the episcopal office, he constantly watched over the
flock committed to him; and, fearing lest he should
incur the reproach of the slothful servant, who hid
his lord's money in a napkin, he did nothing
remissly. As to external duties, in the general
government of the clergy and people, he laboured
diligently with heart and body in his episcopal
superintendence; and, as to internal labours, he
without ceasing made intercession to God for them
all, by watchings, fastings, and the sacrifice of
prayers." He immediately made over his hereditary property to the see; and on the third day
after his arrival he pulled down the mean beginnings
of a cathedral, which his predecessor had built up,
and erected one at great expense, and with singular
magnificence — sumptu ingenti et magnificentia
singulari. His personal attention to the work, and
his kindness to the workmen, made the building go
on rapidly; and he did not fail to call upon the
emperor, who frequently came to Paderborn, and
took great interest in its proceedings, for his
full share of the expense; and Henry and his
empress, Chunigunda, contributed largely and
willingly.

A circumstance which occurred during one of
the emperor's visits tends so much to illustrate the
character of the bishop, and of the times, that I am
induced to transcribe it. It quite belongs to our

subject ; and, indeed, to our immediate purpose, so far as it shows that Meinwerc was rather a severe disciplinarian, and that if he performed the services of the church disreputably himself, he did not allow others to do it, or even to run the risque of it, with impunity. There was in those days an eccentric saint—or the church of Rome has made him one since—named Heimrad. He was a native of Swabia, and, as far as I know, a good sort of fanatic. After wandering about, and doing a great many strange things, he settled down in a little cell, or hut, at Hasungen. Previously to this, however, in the course of his rambles, he came to Paderborn, and suddenly made his appearance before the bishop ; who, being startled at the sight of his sickly countenance and his long figure, rendered ghastly and unsightly by fasting and rags, inquired whence "that devil" had risen. Heimrad having meekly replied that he was not a devil, the bishop inquired if he was a priest; and learning that he had that day celebrated mass, he immediately ordered that the books which he had used should be produced. Finding that they were written in a slovenly manner, and were of no value (incomptos et neglectos et nullius ponderis aut pretii), he caused them to be immediately put in the fire ; and, by command of the Empress, who sympathized with the "just zeal" of the bishop, he farther ordered that the unlucky priest should be flogged.

After this, Count Dodico, of Warburg (a person of some consequence in the early history of the see of Paderborn), invited the bishop to keep the feast of St. Andrew, at his castle ; and on the very eve of the festival, whom should the bishop see seated opposite to him, at supper, but this identical Heimrad. He was not a little moved, and inquired what could induce a man of his host's respectability to keep such company ; and then, breaking out into severe abuse of the poor solitary, he called him a crazy apostate. Heimrad took it all very quietly, and said not a word ; but Count Dodico began to apologize to the bishop, for whom he had a sincere respect, and endeavoured to soothe him by assurances that he had no idea that the recluse was in any way offensive to him. All his endeavours were, however, in vain, and the bishop was not to be appeased. On the contrary, he declared that as people chose to consider Heimrad as a saint, he would put him to the test ; and, in the presence of all the company, he ordered that he should sing the *Hallelujah* at mass the next day, on pain of being flogged. The Count at first attempted to beg him off ; but finding that he only added fuel to the flame, he took the recluse apart, as soon as lauds were over, and endeavoured to console him. He besought him to bear this trial as one of those which are appointed for the purification of the saints—to make the attempt, beginning in the name of the Trinity, and trusting in God for the event. Heimrad did not at all like the prospect, and earnestly requested leave to creep away quietly to his cell at Hasungen ; but at length, overcome by the Count's entreaties, he acquiesced. When the time came, another attempt was made to beg him off ; but the bishop continuing inexorable, he began, and in fact chanted the whole with such propriety, and in so agreeable a manner, that the company were astonished, and declared that they had never heard sweeter modulation from any man. The bishop, as soon as mass was over, taking Heimrad aside, fell at his feet, and having humbly asked, and quickly obtained, pardon for his conduct towards him, became, from that time forth, his constant and faithful friend.

But, though I give these anecdotes as characteristic of the bishop and the times, and therefore illustrative of our subject, it will be more immediately to our present purpose to give one or two which show

the terms on which the bishop stood with the
emperor, and some passages which occurred between
them. Those terms cannot, perhaps, be more
briefly or more clearly explained, than by saying
that these two schoolfellows still behaved to each
other rather more in the manner of schoolboys than
was quite becoming in a bishop and an emperor, as
will appear ; but first, let me premise that from the
time when he became Bishop of Paderborn, Meinwerc seems to have devoted himself—that is, his
property, his time, his thoughts, words, and deeds,—
to the aggrandizement of his see. He was, his
biographer tells us, skilful in getting all that was to
be had, as well as faithful in taking care of what he
had got—" in acquirendis utilis, in conservandis
fidelis."[3]

As to the latter point, many stories are recorded
which show that he laboured most energetically in
conducting the affairs of his diocese, which he seems
to have governed with an extraordinary degree both
of severity and kindness, so as to have been, in a
peculiar degree, a terror to evil-doers, and a praise
to those who did well. He superintended, in person,
the buildings which the circumstances already
mentioned required, until he had got them so far
advanced that he could be spared to look after the
country estates of the diocese ; and then perpetually
visiting them, from time to time, he took care that
all things were managed decently and in order, and

---

[3] It might perhaps be said of him, as it was of an abbot of much
the same period—" cum esset vir strenuus, et suam rempublicam
semper augmentare toto anhelaret desiderio."—*Mab.* A. S. *tom.* vi.
p. 405. Such hints as these contain a good deal, and are a key to
a good deal more, and must be borne in mind when we read such
notes as I have adverted to in the note, p. 124, about carcass-hunt-
ing bishops who wanted " to amass riches."   What did they want
the riches for ?

raised the serfs to a degree of comfort which they had not before enjoyed. Once, riding through one of the farms belonging to the bishopric, he told some of his companions to ride their own, or to turn some loose, horses into some corn, which was being thrashed under cover; saying, that if the serfs were faithful, they would resist them, but if they were unfaithful to the steward, they would rejoice in a mischief which would bring loss upon him. The serfs, however, under pretence of paying their obeisance to the bishop, all ran away; and the horses began to devour and trample on the corn. The bishop immediately taxed the labourers with their want of faith, had them severely flogged, and then gave them an uncommonly good dinner (ciborum copiis abundantissime reficiens), and a paternal admonition on fidelity to their master; all which together had so excellent an effect, that when he next visited the place he found himself shut out by their faithful vigilance, and was obliged to make his way into the premises by stealth. Having done so, he heard the woman of the house complaining that the labourers on that farm had nothing but a very spare allowance of meal; whereupon he ordered that two of the gammons of bacon which the steward was bound to furnish every year should be detained for them.

I should like to gossip on with an account of his visits to other farms, and to tell how he once got into the kitchen of his monastery by himself, and investigated the contents of the pots which were boiling at the fire, in order to see that his monks had proper food; and how, at another time, he went there in a lay habit, to have a little chat on the same subject with the cook, who, in reply to his inquiries, informed him that the living there was very good as concerning the soul, but very poor in respect of the body; and how—for he seems always to have been

on the alert—he went through his diocese in the dis-
guise of a pedlar, in order that he might see for
himself how things were going on.   I should like, I
say, to transcribe some of these anecdotes, for they
are really—not like some which we find produced
as such—characteristic of the times; but I am
afraid of being tedious; and whatever might be his
care in preserving, it is more to our purpose to show
that he was diligent in acquiring. In that matter, he
did not spare his imperial schoolfellow.   Indeed,
there seems to have been an understanding—or,
in the language of the schools, they seem to have
" made it fair "—between them, that the bishop
should get all he could by force or fraud, and that
in return the emperor should love him heartily,
growl at him occasionally, and now and then make
a fool of him.   As to the latter point, however, the
emperor seems generally to have had the worst of it
in the long run, as will appear from one or two
instances.

Once, when Henry was going to hear mass at the
cathedral, he ordered the altar to be decked with the
costly apparatus of royalty, and bade his people keep
a sharp look-out, lest the bishop should get hold of
anything, as he was very apt to do.   Meinwerc said
mass himself, and after the *Agnus Dei*, he entered
the pulpit, and began to discuss the difference
between the imperial and sacerdotal dignity, and
the superiority of the latter, affirming that matters
of divine right were above human authority, and
showing by the canons that whatsoever was consecrated to the uses of divine service was under the
sacerdotal jurisdiction.   He therefore put under a
bann all the ecclesiastical ornaments and priestly
vestments which had just been used, and threatened
with excommunication any person who should remove
them.

On another occasion, the emperor sent him, after
vespers, his own golden cup, of exquisite workman-

ship, full of drink,[4] charging the messenger not to
see his face again without the cup. The bishop
received the present with many thanks, and got the
messenger into a long chat, during which he seems
to have forgotten the business which brought him
there, and the emperor's charge—at least, somehow
or other, he went away without the cup—and the
bishop, taking care to have the doors fastened after
him, sent immediately for his goldsmiths, Brunhard,
and his son, Erpho, and in the course of the night,
which immediately preceded Christmas-day, the cup
was converted into a chalice. One of the emperor's
chaplains, who officiated as sub-deacon at mass the
next day, recognized the cup, and took it to the
emperor, who charged the bishop with theft, and told
him that God abhorred robbery for burnt-offering.
Meinwerc replied that he had only robbed the vanity
and avarice of Henry, by consecrating their subject
to the service of God; and dared him to take it
away. " I will not," said the emperor, " take away
that which has been devoted to the service of God;
but I will myself humbly offer to him that which is
my own property; and do you honour the Lord,
who vouchsafed as on this night to be born for the
salvation of all men, by the performance of your own
duties."

At another time, the emperor had a mantle of
marvellous beauty, and exquisite workmanship.
Meinwerc had often begged it for his church in
vain; and therefore, on one occasion, when the
emperor was intent on some particular business, he
fairly snatched it from his person, and made off with
it. The emperor charged him with robbery, and

---

[4] The laxity with which writers of this age use the word
" sicera " sanctions the ambiguous expression which I use. If
not very elegant, it is better than talking of beer between such
parties.

threatened to pay him off for it some time or other.
Meinwerc replied that it was much more proper that
such a mantle should hang in the temple of God,
than on his mortal body, and that he did not care
for his threats.   They were, however, carried into
execution in the following manner :—" The emperor
knowing that the bishop, being occupied in a great
variety of secular business, was now and then guilty
of a barbarism, both in speaking and in reading
Latin, with the help of his chaplain effaced the
syllable *fa* from the words *famulis* and *famulabus*,
which form part of a collect in the service for the
defunct, in the missal ; and then called on the bishop
to say a mass for the souls of his father and mother.
Meinwerc, therefore, being unexpectedly called on to
perform the service, and hastening to do it, read on
as he found written, *mulis* and *mulabus*, but, perceiving the mistake, he repeated the words correctly.
After mass, the emperor said, in a sarcastic manner,
to the bishop, ' I asked you to say mass for my
father and mother, not for my male and female
mules.'   But he replied, ' By the mother of our
Lord, you have been at your old tricks, and have
made a fool of me again ; and now, in no common
way, but in the service of our God.   This he who is
my Judge has declared that he will avenge ; for that
which is done to him he will not pass by unpunished.'
Thereupon, he immediately convened the canons in
the chapter-house of the cathedral, ordered the
emperor's chaplain, who had been a party to the
trick, to be most severely flogged ; and then, having
dressed him in new clothes, sent him back to the
emperor to tell him what had happened."[5]

---

[5] " Sciens autem Imperator, episcopum sæcularibus negotiis
multipliciter occupatum, tam latinitatis locutione quam in lectione
barbarismi vitia non semel incurrere, de missali in quadam collecta
pro defunctis *fa* de *famulis*, et *famulabus*, cum capellano suo delevit,
et episcopum pro requie animarum patris sui et matris missam

And here, good reader, you have, I believe, the
whole and sole foundation for the notable story of
Bishop Meinwerc and his mules. If you have been
at church as often as you should have been in these
five years past, perhaps you have heard King George
prayed for by men who were neither stupid nor
careless ; but who were officiating from a book which
had not been corrected. I am sure I have heard it
within these six months ;—but there is no need to
apologize for the bishop.

"Oh! but he '*used* to say' this." Well, that is
one of those things which, as they admit of only one
reply, very commonly receive none at all from civil
people. "But it is only 'one example out of *many*.'"
Perhaps so ; but I really do not recollect any story
like it, except the notorious *mumpsimus,* and one
which looks almost like another version of what we
have just had, and which I know only from its being
quoted by Lomeier,[6] in connection with another

---

celebrare rogavit. Episcopus igitur ex improviso missam celebrare
accelerans, ut scriptum reperit *mulis* et *mulabus* dixit; sed errorem
recognoscens, repetitis verbis, quod male dixerat, correxit. Post
missam insultans Imperator Pontifici, ' Ego,' inquit, ' patri meo et
matri, non mulis et mulabus meis, missam celebrari rogavi.' At
ille, ' Per matrem,' ait, ' Domini, tu more solito iterum illusisti
mihi, et non quoquo modo, verum in Dei nostri servitio. Cujus ero
vindex, en promittit meus judex. Namque sibi factum non
pertransibit inultum.' Illico canonicis in capitolium principalis
ecclesiæ convocatis, capellanum Imperatoris, hujus rei conscium,
durissime verberibus castigari jussit, castigatumque novis vestibus
indutum ad Imperatorem, nuntiaturum quæ facta fuerant, remisit."
I suspect that the reply of Meinwerc, from the word " Cujus," &c.,
is a quotation from some hymn ; though it is printed like prose,
and certainly can hardly be called verse.

[6] De Bibliothecis, cap. viii., de Bibliothecis sub ipsa barbarie, p.
147. [It is a pity not to have as many such good stories as we
can, and therefore I add one which I have met with since I wrote
the foregoing paragraph. Bruno, in his account of the Emperor
Henry IV., who reigned from A.D. 1056 to A.D. 1106, tells us, that

dark-age anecdote which is too good to be passed
by, and which shows, in dismal colours, the horrible
ignorance of the clergy. " A certain bishop, named
Otto, is said to have recommended a clerk to
another bishop for an ecclesiastical office in these
terms—' *Otto Dei gratia, rogat vestram clementiam,
ut velitis istum clericum conducere ad vestrum
diaconum.*' The words being abbreviated, the
clerk, who was directed to read it to the bishop,
read thus :—' *Otto Dei gram rogat vestram clam ut
velit istum clincum clancum convertere in vivum diabo-
lum.*' " The other story is of a clerk, who turned
Sueno, king of Norway, into a mule by the same
mistake as Meinwerc's. As to the truth or falsehood
of these statements, I have never inquired ; and I
have not, at present, the means of consulting the
author to whom Lomeier refers.

But is it not lamentable that learned men should
credit and circulate such stories ? I do not mean
Henry ;[7] for, notwithstanding what he says, and
what I have quoted at the head of this paper, I do
not believe that he really took the story from the
book to which he refers. I think I know where he

---

among his other wicked deeds, he appointed to the see of Bamberg
(tam rebus exterius divitem, quam sapientibus personis intus
venerabilem) an ignoramus, who read out in divine service (coram
sapientibus clericis) that the earth, instead of being void, *vacua*,
was a cow, *vacca.* " Ipse," adds the indignant historian, " nimirum,
licet bipes, *vacca* bruta et omni probitate *vacua.*"—(*Saxon.
Belli Hist. ap. Freh. Ger. Rer. Scr.* Tom. I. p. 179 ; old Ed.
p. 105.) Surely there must have been *some* critical ears in those
days.]

[7] And still less Mr. Andrews, already introduced to the reader as
a retailer of such things. He prefaces this perverted story by
saying, "The prelates set examples of the most gross want of
common literature. Mein-*hard*, Bishop of Paderborn, used to
read," &c. Yet he gives no reference but to the original. Does
anybody believe that he had seen it ?

picked it up ; and I believe it is more charitable—
at least it is imputing what is, of the two, least
disgraceful—to suppose that he took the story
(notwithstanding his profession quoted as the motto
to this paper) from a respectable writer, than to
suppose that he made up the falsehood himself from
such an original as he refers to, and I have just
transcribed.   He had (as I have stated near the beginning of this paper, p. 143) almost immediately
before quoted Brucker's History of Philosophy, Vol.
III. p. 632, and on the 634th page of that same
volume, and in the section entitled " Facies literarum
et philosophiæ sæculo X.," stands this very story
of Meinwerc in these terms—" Meinwercum episcopum Paderbornensem ne recte legere quidem potuisse, et in psalterio legisse : *Benedic Domine regi-*
bus et reginis mulis et mulabus tuis, pro famulis et
famulabus tuis."   Brucker's reference is, " In eius
vita in LEIBNIZ. Coll. Script. Brunsuic. T. I. p. 555."
And, really, if it were in any way possible, I should
believe that Brucker had had some other edition, or
some other authority, for the story. He tells us that
it was in the *psalter*, and affects to give us the
words.   Henry seems to have been sensible of the
absurdity of this ; and, not knowing what particular
part to substitute, he says, it was " in the public
prayers."   I speak thus, because I cannot doubt
that he took it from Brucker, though not perhaps
immediately ; and my belief is strengthened by a
trifling circumstance, which is perhaps worth
mentioning, because it is desirable to trace error
when we can.   Who has not heard of Leibnitz ?
Thousands have known the philosopher by name or
character, who never took the trouble to learn that
he was librarian of the Royal and Electoral Library
of Brunswick-Luneburg, and who never had the
pleasure of reading his three folios containing the
" Scriptores Rerum Brunsvicensium illustrationi in-
servientes ; "—his name is familiar ; but how often

have they seen it spelt (by any writer of English,
to say the least) without a *t*? He calls himself, on
the title-page of this work, " Leibnitius; " and I do
not remember ever to have seen his name without
the *t*, except in this very volume of Brucker, and in
Henry's reference.

I must, however, notice that Brucker adds to his
account of the matter, " unde vix credi potest quod
idem vitæ Meinwerci scriptor refert, ' *studiorum
multiplicia sub eo floruisse exercitia, et bonæ indolis
juvenes et pueros strenue fuisse institutos.* ' " Incredible as this might appear to Brucker, it is
certainly true that the same authority which tells
us that Meinwerc was guilty of occasional bar-
barisms in speaking and reading Latin (which implies that he was not unfrequently called on to do
both), also assures us that he was a promoter of
education. Indeed, the foolish trick which has
given rise to all this discussion, was not such as to
have been worth playing, or as was likely to have
been even thought of, among perfectly illiterate
barbarians. What wit or fun could there be in
leading a man into a blunder, which nobody could
know to be a blunder? The same authority tells
us, that the schools of Paderborn, then founded,
became more famous in the time of Imadus, who
was the nephew and successor of Meinwerc, and
brought up by him; " sub quo in Patherbornensi
ecclesia publica floruerunt studia : quando ibi *musici*
fuerunt et *dialectici*, enituerunt *rhetorici*, clarique
grammatici; quando magistri artium exercebant
trivium, quibus omne studium erat circa *quadrivium;*
ubi *mathematici* claruerunt et *astronomici*, habebantur
physici, et *geometrici:* viguit *Horatius*, magnus et
Virgilius, *Crispus* ac *Salustius* et *Urbanus Statius:*
Ludusque fuit omnibus insudare versibus, et dicta-
minibus jocundisque cantibus. Quorum in *scriptura*
et *pictura* jugis instantia claret multipliciter hodierna
experientia dum studium nobilium clericorum usu

perpenditur utilium librorum." Make what allowance you like for exaggeration, but let the words
have *some* meaning ; and if you do this you
will never be able to make them square with the
letter, still less with the spirit, of these absurd
stories.

No. IX.

" *LI*. Attate ! modo hercle in mentem venit.
Nimis vellem habere perticam. *LE*. Quoi rei ? *LI*. Quî ver-
berarem Asinos."—PLAUTUS.

THERE is one of Robertson's proofs and illustrations,
which I intended to notice, but I really forgot it
when I passed on to Henry's history of England—a
blunder the more stupid, because it is another note
immediately following the note respecting St. Eloy ;
and I actually quoted the text to which it belongs,
and in which Robertson tells us, that " the external
ceremonies, which then formed the whole of religion,
were either so unmeaning as to be altogether unworthy of the Being to whose honour they were
consecrated, or so absurd as to be a disgrace to
reason and humanity." The note is as follows :—

" It is no inconsiderable misfortune to the church of Rome,
whose doctrine of infallibility renders all such institutions and
ceremonies as have been once universally received immutable and
everlasting, that she must continue to observe in enlightened times
those rites which were introduced during the ages of darkness and
credulity. What delighted and edified the latter, must disgust
and shock the former. Many of these rites appear manifestly to
have been introduced by a superstition of the lowest and most
illiberal species. Many of them were borrowed, with little variation, from the religious ceremonies established among the ancient
heathens. Some were so ridiculous, that, if every age did not
furnish instances of the fascinating influence of superstition, as
well as of the whimsical forms which it assumes, it must appear
incredible that they should ever be received or tolerated. In
several churches of France, they celebrated a festival in commemoration of the Virgin Mary's flight into Egypt. It was called
the feast of the Ass. A young girl richly dressed, with a child

in her arms, was set upon an ass superbly caparisoned. The ass
was led to the altar in solemn procession. High mass was said
with great pomp. The ass was taught to kneel at proper places ;
a hymn no less childish than impious was sung in his praise : And,
when the ceremony was ended, the priest, instead of the usual
words with which he dismissed the people, brayed three times like
an ass ; and the people, instead of their usual response, We bless
the Lord, brayed three times in the same manner. Du Cange,
voc. Festum v. iii. p. 424. This ridiculous ceremony was not, like
the festival of fools, and some other pageants of those ages, a
mere farcical entertainment exhibited in a church, and mingled, as
was then the custom, with an imitation of some religious
rites ; it was an act of devotion, performed by the ministers
of religion, and by the authority of the church. However,
as this practice did not prevail universally in the Catholic Church,
its absurdity contributed at last to abolish it."—p. 237.

I copy this note, not so much as a specimen of
broad, barefaced falsehood, or gross mistake, such
as I have before presented to the reader's notice,—
though, as it regards the misrepresentation of facts,
it is worth looking at,—as for some other reasons,
which will, I hope, appear satisfactory.

First, however, as to the fact,—which it is always
well to examine in such cases,—that is, in all
" wonderful-if-true " stories, told by persons of
whose knowledge or veracity we have any doubt.
The reader is welcome to put this rule in practice
with regard to myself, and my communication, for
he may naturally be somewhat incredulous when I
tell him that the Feast of the Ass was not " a
festival in commemoration of the Virgin Mary's
flight into Egypt,"—that the Virgin Mary had
nothing to do with the matter, and, so far as
appears, was not even mentioned in it,—and that
the Ass from whom the festival derived its name
was not that on which she fled into Egypt (if,
indeed, any such ass ever existed), but the ass of
Balaam. Of this whoever pleases may satisfy
himself by turning to Du Cange, as cited by
Robertson.

Secondly, as to the fact.—Though Robertson

cites Du Cange, it is not for the Feast of the Ass, but for the story about the "young girl richly dressed," &c. ; which (though Robertson has confounded the two things) had nothing whatever to do with the Feast of the Ass, and is not mentioned, or even alluded to, by Du Cange. I do not mean to be hypercritical, or quibbling.   There is an account of this folly at the volume and page of the book which we may familiarly call "Du Cange,"— that is, the Benedictine edition of Du Cange's Glossary, which expanded his three folios into ten, —but it is important to observe, that the account of this custom formed no part of the original work ; and that, therefore, the custom itself may be presumed to have been unknown to Du Cange ; and how far anything of that kind, which was at all general, or of long standing, was likely to have escaped him, those who are even slightly acquainted with his Glossary will be able to judge.

Thirdly, as to the fact.—Du Cange does give, from the Ordinal of the Cathedral of Rouen, the office (or more properly, the rubric—or, more properly still, the stage-directions of the office) appointed for the Feast of Asses ; which was a sort of interlude performed in some churches at Christmas. I do not know whether it would be possible now to learn what was said or sung by the various characters, as the account of Du Cange contains only the rubric, and the initiatory words of each part ; but the dramatis personæ appear to have been numerous and miscellaneous ; and I can only account for the total absence of the Virgin Mary by supposing that it arose from superior respect.   There were Jews and Gentiles as the representatives of their several bodies, Moses and Aaron, and the Prophets, Virgilius Maro, Nebuchadnezzar, the Sibyll, &c.   Among them, however, was Balaam on his ass ; and this (not, one would think, the most important or striking part of the show)

seems to have suited the popular taste, and given
the name to the whole performance and festival.
I should have supposed, that Nebuchadnezzar's
delivering over the three children to his armed men,
and their burning them in a furnace made on
purpose in the middle of the church, would have
been a more imposing part of the spectacle; but I
pretend not to decide in matters of taste, and
certainly Balaam's ass appears to have been the
favourite.[1] The plan of the piece seems to have
been, that each of the persons was called out in his
turn to sing or say something suitable to his
character ; and among others, " *Balaam ornatus
sedens super asinam* (hinc festo nomen) *habens
calcaria, retineat lora, et calcaribus percutiat asinam,
et quidam juvenis, tenens gladium, obstet asinæ.
Quidam sub asina dicat,* Cur me calcaribus miseram
sic læditis ? *Hoc dicto Angelus ei dicat,* Desine
Regis Balac præceptum perficere. *Vocatores Balaun,*
Balaun, esto vaticinans. *Tunc Balaun respondeat,*
Exibit ex Jacob rutilans," &c.

I am afraid that some persons give me credit for
defending a good deal of nonsense ; and, therefore,
let me say at once, that I am not going to defend
this. I acknowledge that it was nonsense—nonsense
that came very near, if not to actual, profaneness,
at least to something like the desecration of holy
things. The age, I admit, was dark; the performers
were probably ignorant; in short, the reader may

---

[1] Indeed, he seems to be always a favourite with the public, and
to give the tone and the title wherever he appears. The ass is
the only link which unites these two stories, and in each he seems
to be put forth as the principal character. So it was, when, in the
twelfth century, an order of monks was formed, whose humility (or
at least their Rule) did not permit them to ride on horseback.
The public (I hope to the satisfaction of the humble men) entirely
overlooked them, eclipsed as they were by the animals on which
they rode, and called it *Ordo Asinorum.*

say what he pleases of the Feast of Asses, and of all the animals, biped or other, concerned in it, if he will only bear in mind one other fact,—a fact almost incredible, perhaps, to those who do not know how Robertson muddled the chronology of his proofs and illustrations, yet very true,—namely, that, notwithstanding all he had said about the period from the *seventh* to the *eleventh* century, and the immediate connexion about heathen converts retaining their barbarous rites—notwithstanding all this, the Ordinal of Rouen, which is Du Cange's sole authority on the subject, is a MS. of the *fifteenth* century. How long the Feast of Asses had been celebrated at that time I really do not know ; and I shall be obliged to anybody who will tell me [2]—nor do I know how long it was suffered to continue— but that it flourished when this MS. was written seems clear ; and to bring it forward as a special and characteristic sin of the dark ages, is too bad.

Fourthly, as to the fact.—Though the Feast of Asses had nothing to do with the flight of the Virgin, yet that latter event was celebrated, it appears, in some churches in the diocese of Beauvais,

---

[2] The following passage from Warton's History of Poetry has been cited against me :—" Grosthead, bishop of Lincoln in the eleventh century, orders his dean and chapter to abolish the FESTUM ASINORUM, *cum sit vanitate plenum, et voluptatibus spurcum*, which used to be annually celebrated in Lincoln Cathedral, on the Feast of the Circumcision.   Grossetesti Epistol. xxxii. apud Browne's Fascicul. p. 331. edit. Lond. 1690. tom. ii. Append. And p. 412." *Vol. II. p.* 367.   Beside the general issue that Warton's authority in such matters is not worth a rush, it may be pleaded in this particular case, first, that Bishop Grosteste's letter does not belong to the *eleventh*, but the *thirteenth* century ; and, secondly, that it says not a word of the Feast of Asses, but only of the Feast of Fools, which was a totally different matter.   I believe that this blunder is corrected in the octavo edition of Warton's History, published in 1840.

on the 14th of January, with some of the absurdities
mentioned by Robertson. This, at least, is stated
by the editors of Du Cange; who give no account
of their authority, or any idea of its date, except
that for the "hymn no less childish than impious"
which they quote, they say that they have the
authority of a MS. five hundred years old; which
of course throws the matter back into the *thirteenth*
century.[3] They add, that the same silly ceremony
was performed in the diocese of Autun; but for
this they give no authority at all. Such appears to
have been the extent of the custom; as to its
duration I am unable to judge. It may have
existed through all the dark ages, but I do not
remember to have met with any trace of either
custom; and the fact, that neither Du Cange nor
his editors appear to have known of their earlier
existence, is ground for a presumption that they did
not, in fact, exist before the times which have been
mentioned.

One more observation as to the fact—"The ass
was taught to kneel at proper places." I must say
I doubt it. It may not be impossible, but I suspect
it is very difficult, to make that class of animals do
such a thing. Indeed, I think the reader who turns
to Robertson's authority will agree with me in
supposing, that he was led to make this statement
merely by his misunderstanding the marginal direction annexed to one verse of the hymn, "*hic
genuflectebatur.*"

But having thus observed on the *facts*, let us now
notice the *animus* and the *modus* ;—the *facts* are, as
we have seen, absurdly misstated; but what are we

---

[3] Should this meet the eye of any gentleman whose reading in
early French has enabled him to judge, from the *language*, as to
the date of the song in question, I should feel much obliged by his
referring to it, and communicating his opinion.

to say of the design, and the manner, of introducing
those facts ? It is really necessary to say very
little on this point, though it is principally for this
that the matter is worth noticing at all. Who can
help seeing the absurdity of introducing this asinine
business by a sober reflection on the practical evils
of assuming infallibility, with its attributes of per-
petuity and immutability ; and then telling us, that
what is apparently given as an example (for why,
else, is it given at all ?) never was general, and was,
after a while, abandoned. But what is the obvious
animus ?   Why did not Robertson, instead of
throwing the whole odium of this nonsense on the
church, tell his readers that this ass was patronized
by the people—that he was the pet of the laity—
and that, with natural and characteristic obstinacy,
and, cheered by the love and sympathy of his lay
friends, he kept his ground against the ecclesiastical
powers which would have turned him out of the
church ?   Why did he not add the statement of
those from whom he borrowed the story—" Hæc
abolere censuris ecclesiasticis non semel tentarunt
episcopi, sed frustra, altissimis quippe defixa
erat radicibus donec supremi Senatus accessit
auctoritas, qua tandem hoc festum suppressum
est ? "
    Having said thus much of Asses, let us proceed
to speak of Fools. Robertson says, just in the way
of passing allusion, that the Feast of Asses " was
not, like *the Festival of Fools,* and some other
pageants *of those ages,* a mere farcical entertainment,
exhibited in a church, and mingled, *as was then the
custom,* with an imitation of some religious rites."
In saying that these festivals differed, Robertson is
right. The Feast of the Ass, and the more ridiculous custom of the girl at Beauvais, which he
describes, were, I believe, instituted by Christians
in a comparatively late age of the church. From
what has been said, at least, it appears that the

Feast of Asses flourished in the fifteenth, and the other follies in the thirteenth century, in some part of France. But the Feast of Fools was a more ancient and more widely celebrated festival; which may, perhaps, be more or less traced in all ages of the church, and in all parts of Christendom. Even now, I suppose, there is hardly a parish church in our protestant country which does not annually exhibit some trace or relic of it. Notwithstanding the decrees of Councils, and the homilies of Fathers, the Christmas evergreen,—the *viriditas arborum*,— which they denounced, still keeps its ground.

The Feast of Fools (the *Festum Fatuorum*, or *Stultorum*) was, in fact, the old heathen festival of the January Calends. Some ingenious persons have employed themselves in showing that every ceremony and observance of the Romish church (that is, every ceremony and observance which they do not see in their own day, and their own parish church or meeting) is a genuine pagan rite, adopted from the heathen. Others, with as much facility and truth, prove that every particular is Jewish. I have neither the taste nor the learning required for such an undertaking, and if I had it would be sadly out of place here. The same persons would, I hope, be consistent enough to admit that the people of the dark ages, whatever ceremonies or observances they might introduce, did not borrow either from pagans or Jews—for who knew the classics—who read the bible—in *those* days? So it, evidently, is not my present business; but I wish that someone would give us a true and full account of the insinuation, modification, or extirpation, of gentilisms in the Christian church, at the same time tracing their causes, history, and effects. As to our present business, however, I will pass over all the earlier councils and fathers;[4] but as I should wish to give

[4] The reader who wishes to follow out this subject will find abundant indication of sources by referring to Du Cange in v.

a specimen of the resistance made by the church to this pagan folly, I am glad to be able to give at the same time a farther extract (it happens to be the immediate continuation of what I gave at p. 132) from the well-known, or at least much talked-of, sermon of St. Eloy. I have already stated that, about the year 640, he became the bishop of a people, many of whom were newly and scarcely converted from heathenism. If I carry on the quotation a few lines farther than the matter for which it is especially quoted, and the immediate subject of this paper may seem to require, those who have read Nos. VI. and VII., and who at all understand my motive, and the drift of these papers, will perceive my reason for doing so.

" Before all things, however, I declare and testify unto you, that you should observe none of the impious customs of the pagans ; neither sorcerers,[5] nor diviners, nor soothsayers, nor enchanters ;

Kalendæ ; or by looking at Bingham's Antiquities, b. xvi. ch. iv. sect. 17, and b. xx. ch. i. sect. 4. In less than two hours, however, he may become pretty well acquainted with this part of the subject by reading the Homily of Asterius, which is, of all that I know, the thing best worth reading, and which he may find in the Bibliotheca Patrum, tom. xiii. p. 590, of the Paris ed. of 1633, or a Latin translation of it in Raynaud's edition of Leo Magnus. Next to this in value (and it may be found in the same edition of Leo, and, I believe, in the largest Bib. Pat., but I am sorry to say I have not the means of ascertaining), is the Homily on the Circumcision, by Maximus Taurinensis, at p. 198 of his Homilies ; and if the reader has Mabillon's Museum Italicum, let him look at tom. i. par. ii. p. 17. The same edition of Leo also contains the sermons of Petrus Chrysologus, the 155th of which is worth reading. These, with the 62nd canon of the council in Trullo (Lab. Conc. vi. 1169), will, I think, put the reader in possession of most that is known on the subject. It may seem a good allowance for two hours ; but, in fact, I might have said one, for all the things referred to are very short.

[5] The following note was appended by Mr. Rose to this passage : —" If anyone will take the trouble to refer to the writers of the eleventh century, especially Peter of Blois, he will find a constant

nor must you presume for any cause, or any sickness, to consult or
inquire of them ; for he who commits this sin immediately loses
the sacrament of baptism. In like manner, pay no attention to
auguries and sneezings ; and, when you are on a journey, do not
mind the singing of certain little birds. But, whether you are
setting out on a journey, or beginning any other work, cross yourself in the name of Christ, and say the Creed and the Lord's
Prayer with faith and devotion, and then the enemy can do you no
harm. Let no Christian observe the day on which he leaves, or
returns, home; for God made all the days. Let none regulate the
beginning of any piece of work by the day, or by the moon. Let
none on the Calends of January join in the wicked and ridiculous
things, the dressing like old women, or like stags,[6] or other
fooleries, nor make feasts lasting all night, nor keep up the custom
of gifts [7] and intemperate drinking. Let no Christian believe in

---

condemnation of superstitious usages and customs ; and if he will
go back much farther, to Theodore's *Pœnitentiale*, in the seventh
century, he will find the same doctrine.—Ed."

[6] *Vetulas aut cervolos.*—The council of Auxerre (an. 378) had
decreed—" Non licet Kalendis Januarii vetula aut cervolo facere."
Lab. Con. v. 917. Some would read this as *vitulas*, and suppose
it to mean assuming the appearance, or sacrificing, a calf. But
certainly the wearing of female attire by men was one great feature
of the festival. Isidore (about the end of the sixth century) says
—" Tunc enim miseri homines, et, quod pejus est, etiam fideles,
sumentes species monstruosas, in ferarum habitu transformantur ;
alii fœmineo gestu demutati virilem vultum effœminant." *De
Eccl. Offic. lib. ii. c.* 40. (*Bib. Pat.* x. 200.) Alcuin, nearly two
centuries after, has almost the same words; but it is worth while
to remark that he changes *transformantur* and *effœminant*, into
transformabant and *effœminabant*; in fact, he says,—" Domino
largiente, hæc a fidelibus pro nihilo habentur, licet quantulæcunque
similitudines, quod absit, adhuc lateant in feris hominibus." *De
Div. Off.* (*Ibid.* p. 229.) The reader will observe that I put some
words of the extract in the text in italics without any note, by
which I wish to express that I do not know what they mean. This
is not the place to discuss the conjectures of others, or to offer my
own.

[7] *Strenas.*—What Asterius says on this point is worth reading.
When he says that children were taught to love money by being
permitted to go round from house to house collecting it, in return
for nominal presents, one is led to think of *Christmas-boxes ;*
which, indeed, as well as new year's gifts, seem to be genuine
remains of the custom.

puras, nor set amidst their singing, for these are the works of the Devil. Let no one on the festival of St. John, or on any of the festivals of the saints, join in *solstitia*, or dances, or leaping, or *caraulas*,[8] or diabolical songs. Let none trust in, or presume to invoke, the names of dæmons; neither Neptune, nor Orcus, nor Diana, nor Minerva, nor Geniscus, nor any other such follies. Let no one keep Thursday as a holy-day, either in May, or at any other time (unless it be some saint's day), or the day of moths and mice, or any day of any kind, but the Lord's Day. Let no Christian place lights at the temples, or the stones, or at fountains, or at trees, or *ad cellos*, or at places where three ways meet, or presume to make vows. Let none presume to hang amulets on the neck of man or beast ; even though they be made by the clergy, and called holy things, and contain the words of Scripture ; for they are fraught, not with the remedy of Christ, but with the poison of the Devil. Let no one presume to make lustrations, nor to enchant herbs, nor to make flocks pass through a hollow tree, or an aperture in the earth ; for by so doing he seems to consecrate them to the Devil. Let no woman presume to hang amber beads on her neck ; or in her weaving, or dyeing, or any other kind of work, to invoke Minerva, or the other ill-omened persons ; but let her desire the grace of Christ to be present in every work, and confide with her whole heart in the power of His name. If at any time the moon is darkened, let no one presume to make a clamour; for, at certain times, it is darkened by the command of God. Neither let anyone fear to set about any work at the new moon ; for God has made the moon on purpose to mark the times, and to temper the darkness of the nights, not to hinder anybody's work, nor that it should make any man mad, as foolish persons think, who suppose that those who are possessed by devils suffer from the moon. Let none call the sun or moon 'Lord;' nor swear by them, for they are creatures of God ; and, by the command of God, they are subservient to the necessities of men. Let no man have his fate or his fortune told, or his nativity, or what is commonly called his horoscope, so as to say that he shall be such as his horoscope shall indicate ; for God will have all men to be saved, and come to the knowledge of the truth, and wisely dispenses all things even as He hath appointed before the foundation of the world. Moreover, as often as any sickness occurs, do not seek enchanters, nor diviners, nor sorcerers, nor soothsayers, or make devilish amulets at fountains, or trees, or cross-roads; but let him who is sick trust only ín the mercy of God, and receive the sacrament of the body and blood of Christ with faith and devotion ; and faithfully seek

---

[8] I will not here repeat the arguments of those who make this word mean *charms* or *dances*, but I cannot help thinking of and mentioning Christmas *carols*.

consecrated oil from the church, wherewith he may anoint his body
in the name of Christ, and, according to the apostle, ' the prayer
of faith shall save the sick, and the Lord shall raise him up ; ' and
he shall receive health not only of body but of mind, and there
shall be fulfilled in him that which our Lord promised in the
gospel, saying, ' for all things whatsoever ye shall ask in prayer,
believing, ye shall receive.'

  " Before all things, wherever you may be, whether in the house,
or on a journey, or at a feast, let no filthy or lewd discourse proceed out of your mouths ; for, as our Lord declares in the gospel,
for every idle word which men shall speak on earth, they shall give
account in the day of judgment. Forbid also the performance of
all diabolical games, and dances, and songs of the heathen. Let
no Christian perform them, because by them he becomes a heathen ;
for indeed it is not right that from a Christian mouth, which
receives the sacraments of Christ, and which ought always to
praise God, diabolical songs should proceed. And therefore,
brethren, eschew with your whole heart all inventions of the Devil,
and fly from all the impieties which I have mentioned, with horror.
You must show reverence (venerationem exhibeatis) to no creature
beside God and His saints. Destroy the fountains which they call
sacred ; forbid them to make the images of feet which they place
at the parting of roads, and if you find them, burn them with fire.
Believe that you cannot be saved by any other means than by calling on Christ, and by His cross. For what a thing it is that if
those trees, where these miserable men pay their vows, fall down,
they will not use them to make their fires. And see how great the
folly of the men is, if they pay honour to an insensible and dead
tree, and despise the commands of Almighty God. Let not any
man, then, believe that the heaven, or the stars, or the earth, or,
in short, any creature whatsoever, is to be adored (adorandam)
except God ; because He, by Himself alone, created and arranged
them. The heaven, indeed, is high, the earth great, the sea
immense, the stars are beautiful ; but He who made all these things
must needs be greater and more beautiful. For if these things
which are seen are so incomprehensible—that is, the various
produce of the earth, the beauty of the flowers, the diversity of
fruits, the different kinds of animals—some on the earth, some in
the waters, some in the air—the skill of the bees, the blowing of
the winds, the showers of the clouds, the noise of thunder, the
change of seasons, and the alternation of day and night—all which
things the human mind hath never yet been able by any means to
comprehend. If therefore these things, which we see, without
being able to comprehend them, are such, how ought we to
estimate those heavenly things which we have not yet seen ? And
what is the Creator of them all, at whose nod all were created, and
by whose will all are governed ? Him then, brethren, above all
things, fear ; Him in all things adore ; Him beyond all things

love ; cling to His mercy, and never lose your confidence in His loving kindness."

Notwithstanding the statement of Alcuin, which was, I dare say, true, as far as his knowledge went —and his means of knowledge render his authority respectable—we are not to suppose that this heathenism was entirely rooted out. If it was so modified as to be lost sight of, and to have become comparatively harmless, in old Christian societies, the accession of barbarous nations, or heathenish communities, from time to time, rendered it necessary to watch against, and denounce it. Whether on this account, or merely to make his Capitulare more complete, Atto (Bishop of Vercelli, as late as A.D. 960) inserted a prohibition against the heathenish celebration of the Calends;[9] though it is not improbable that this superstition might maintain its ground, in its more barefaced form, up to a later period in Italy than elsewhere. It is curious to observe that Boniface, the apostle of Germany, not long before the time when Alcuin wrote, found his new converts much scandalized by reports which travellers brought from Rome, of what went on in the pope's own city, and " hard by the church of St. Peter." In his letter of congratulation to Pope Zachary, he told his Holiness (or rather, " his Paternity "—it is the pope who calls Boniface " your Holiness ") that when the laity and secular persons among the Germans, Bavarians, and Franks, saw these things performed at Rome, it was vain to denounce them as sins, or to attempt to persuade people that they had not ecclesiastical sanction. The pope replied that he considered it an abomination, and had (like his

---

[9] Can. 79, ap. Dach. Spicil. i. 410.

predecessor, Gregory) done all that he could to put a stop to it.[1]

But I am not writing the history of this folly. The question forces itself upon one—What had *this* heathen foolery to do with the church, more than any other invention of the world, the flesh, or the devil? It was " juxta ecclesiam sancti Petri "— " hard by " St. Peter's ; but did it get in? Council after council attests that all regular ecclesiastical authority perpetually opposed it ; and, though I know less than I could wish about the particulars, and the time of its intrusion into sacred places, and its admixture with sacred things, yet I believe that it did not become " a farcical entertainment, exhibited in a church," during the period with which we are concerned. The only account which I have met with of any participation by the church in this " libertas Decembrica," as it was also called, is that which is given by a writer, who is said to have belonged to the church of Amiens, and to have been

---

[1] The pope's reply is dated 1st of April, 743 ; but I do not know that the precise date of Boniface's letter can be fixed. Having inquired respecting dispensations, respecting marriage, which some maintained to have been granted by the pope, he adds —" quia carnales homines idiotæ, Alamanni, vel Bajuarii, vel Franci, si juxta Romanam urbem aliquid fieri viderint ex his peccatis quæ nos prohibemus, licitum et concessum a sacerdotibus esse putant ; et dum nobis improperium deputant, sibi scandalum vitæ accipiunt. Sicut affirmant se vidisse annis singulis, in Romana urbe, et juxta ecclesiam Sancti Petri, in die vel nocte quando Kalendæ Januarii intrant, paganorum consuetudine choros ducere per plateas," &c. The pope, after expressing his abomination of such proceedings, says—" quia per instigationem diaboli iterum pullulabant, a die qua nos jussit divina clementia (quanquam immeriti existamus) apostoli vicem gerere, illico omnia hæc amputavimus. Pari etenim modo volumus tuam sanctitatem populis sibi subditis prædicare atque ad viam æternæ perducere vitæ."— *Lab. Conc.* vi. 1497—1500.

living in A.D. 1182.[2]   He tells us that there were
some churches in which it was customary for the
bishops and archbishops to join in the Christmas
games which went on in the monasteries in their
dioceses, and even so far to relax as to play at ball.
If I grant that this was "desipere," may I not
plead that it was "in loco," and that it was not
quite so bad as what went on at Rouen and Beauvais
in more enlightened times?

For when did this festival become the regular
Feast of Fools, with the Bishop of Fools, and the
Abbot of Fools, and foolery sacred and profane in
perfection?   Let us hear Du Cange, to whom
Robertson remits us—"Licet, inquam, ab ecclesia
non semel proscriptæ fuerint, indictis ad hanc diem
jejuniis et litaniis de quibus suo loco, quibus eæ
quodammodo expiarentur, et ut ludicræ et impiæ
festivitatis loco vera ac solida succederet; non
potuere tamen tam alte radicatæ prorsus evelli,
*adeo ut extremis etiam temporibus plus solito vires
acceperint*, et non a secularibus dumtaxat; sed et ab
ipsis episcopis et sacerdotibus legantur usurpatæ:

---

[2] His words are—"Sunt nonnullæ ecclesiæ, in quibus usitatum
est, ut vel etiam Episcopi et Archiepiscopi in cœnobiis cum suis
ludant subditis, ita ut etiam sese ad lusum pilæ demittant;" and
he afterwards says—"quanquam vero magnæ ecclesiæ ut est
Remensis, hanc ludendi consuetudinem observent, videtur tamen
laudabilius esse, non ludere."—*Ap. Du Cange in v. Kalendæ.* The
only writer before the year 1200, mentioned in the continuation of
the article by the editors, is Petrus Capuanus, who wrote in A.D.
1198.   He is the earliest writer, as far as I have seen, who speaks
of this, or any festival, under the title of the Festum Fatuorum.
He is here said to have testified its existence in the church of
Paris, and elsewhere; but with what rites it was celebrated does
not appear. He wrote, as cardinal-legate, to Odo, Bishop of Paris,
and to some of the canons, requiring them to put down the
custom; and it appears that they issued an ordinance for that
purpose.

[imo, cum ab iis omnino abstinuissent laici, eas obstinate retinuisse clericos, atque ab iis solis usurpatas fuisse, testantur theologi Parisienses in Epist. encyclica ann. 1444. 'Quid quæso fecissent' (Episcopi) 'si solum clerum sicut hodie his observantiis vacantem vidissent?']" The part between brackets is so printed by the editors, to show that is their own addition to the statement of Du Cange, who proceeds to say that, in modern times, beside its old title, it came to be called the Feast of Subdeacons; not because that order of the clergy alone took part in it, but from the ambiguity of the word "*Soudiacres* id est ad literam *Saturi Diaconi*, quasi *Diacres Saouls*." He also refers to the fourth council of Constantinople, to show that something like the mock consecration of the Bishop of Fools was performed in the east, in the ninth century, by some of the laity in derision of the clergy; and that it was forbidden by the church. This council declares it to be a thing before unheard of; and whether it was thence imported into the west, and, if so, at what time, it might be curious to inquire; but the editors of Du Cange skip at once from the ninth to the fourteenth century. What they quote from the Ceremonial of Viviers, written in A.D. 1365, from the council of Rouen, in A.D. 1445, or the Inventory of York, in A.D. 1350; or even the more scanty references to the council of Paris, in A.D. 1212, or that of Cognac, in A.D. 1260, and the Constitutions of our Archbishop Peckham in A.D. 1279, it is not to our present purpose to notice; but I wish that some of those gentlemen who understand all about the march of intellect would explain, how it happened that these profane follies began—if not to exist, at least to flourish and abound—at, and after, and along with, the revival of letters. If not, I may, perhaps, attempt something of the kind; but, in the meantime, I hope (having, perhaps, said enough about popular misrepresentations for the present) to go on to some of the points which I proposed to investigate with reference to the earlier—for really, after such a discussion, I do not like to call them the darker—ages of the church.

No. X.

" Habet unumquodque propositum principes suos. Romani
duces imitentur Camillos, Fabritios, Regulos, Scipiones. Philosophi
proponant sibi Pythagoram, Socratem, Platonem, Aristotelem.
Poetæ, Homerum, Virgilium, Menandrum, Terentium. Historici,
Thucydidem, Sallustium, Herodotum, Livium. Oratores, Lysiam,
Gracchos, Demosthenem, et ut ad nostra veniamus, episcopi et
presbyteri habeant in exemplum Apostolos et Apostolicos viros :
quorum honorem possidentes, habere nitantur et meritum. Nos
autem habeamus propositi nostri principes, Paulos, et Antonios,
Julianos, Hilarionem, Macarios."—Hieronymus.

" The monks were abominably illiterate "—Well,
good friend, and if you are not so yourself, be
thankful in proportion as you are sure that you
are the better for your learning. But suppose it
were otherwise—suppose *you* were " abominably
illiterate "—would you like me and all other writers
in great books and small, in magazines and newspapers, to rail at you and run you down, as a creature
not fit to live ? If you were too modest to speak in
your own behalf, it is likely that some of your
friends might suggest such redeeming qualities as
would show that you were not only tolerable, but
useful, in the world. " Very true, very true," says
the march-of-intellect man, " I dare say he may be
a very good Christian, a good subject, a good hus-
band or father or landlord, a person of great integrity
and benevolence, and all very well in his way, but
he is abominably illiterate, and I will throw it in his
teeth whenever I come within a mile of him." Now
surely the compassion of a mere by-stander would
lead him to say, " Well, suppose he is abominably
illiterate, do let him alone ; he makes no pretence to
learning."

But did not the monks pretend to it ? Certainly
not. " C'est une illusion de certaine gens, qui ont
écrit dans le siècle précédent que les monastères
n'avoient esté d'abord établis que pour servir d'écoles
et d'academies publiques, où l'on faisoit profession
d'enseigner les sciences humaines." Very true, Dom
Mabillon, and it is very right that you should contradict in plain terms a vulgar error, which, for want
of proper discrimination on the part of the public,
has been confirmed rather than corrected, by the
labours of yourself and Montfaucon, and other of
your brethren in the Benedictine Order. The
" Editio Benedictina et Optima," which figures in
every bookseller's catalogue, has a tendency to mis-
lead even those who do not take the trouble to inquire
who the Benedictines of St. Maur were, or why
their editions of books cost three times as much as
others. This by the way, however; for it is here
only necessary to say, that the abuse heaped on
monks for being unlearned is altogether unjust and
absurd.

The monastic life, whatever it might have of good
or bad, was, I apprehend, that point of rest in which
the minds of men settled after they had been driven,
partly by fierce persecution, and partly by the
natural tendency of man towards extremes, into a
mode of life purely solitary. At that stage of the
world, man might have known from experience, as
well as from the Word of God, without making a
fresh trial, that it was not good for him to be alone;
and that it was as truly, if not as great, a sin to live
without man, as without God, in the world—that is,
to renounce the second great commandment, under
pretence of keeping the first. The eremitical life
was contrary to nature, reason, and religion, and
seems only to have been permitted in order to the
introduction of a system which was, to say the least,
more rational—namely, that of societies, not individuals, forsaking the world, and living in seclusion.

The solitary ascetic, by his self-constructed, self-imposed, rule (self in all things, self the boundary of his horizon), was required to renounce the duties, the charities, the sympathies, of life, and to cut himself off from all the means of grace which God has given to man in his fellows ; but, in the monastery, the idea was to carry out into some remote place of safety one mind dispersed and diversified in various bodies, guiding many hands and uniting many hearts, and directing, sanctifying, and governing the various gifts of the many members of one body, whose head was Christ. Such was the idea ; and when once suggested it spread rapidly. Small companies nestled down in solitude—to study the classics ?—to stimulate the march of intellect ? No such thing—" tota rusticitas, et extra psalmos silentium est. Quocunque te verteris, arator stivam tenens, alleluia decantat. Sudans messor psalmis se avocat, et curva attondens vitem falce vinitor, aliquid Davidicum canit. Hæc sunt in hac provincia carmina ; hæ, ut vulgo dicitur, amatoriæ cantiones. Hic pastorum sibilus : hæc arma culturæ." Solitude, labour, silence, and prayer—these were the elements of monastic life ; and the question was not how the monk might most effectively gather and diffuse learning, but—when, indeed, any question came to be raised—whether he might lawfully cultivate learning at all.

"Tout le monde sait"—says Dom Vincent Thuillier ; but it is certainly quite a mistake of his,—or if it was true when he wrote it, it has long since ceased to be so,—for there are plenty of people, who are very far from being abominably illiterate, who nevertheless know nothing about the " Contestation sur les Etudes Monastiques," of which he undertook to be the historian. If he had said that most people have heard of De Rancé, of his noble birth, his profligate life, his sudden and mysterious conversion, his persevering austerities—of the solitary and silent horrors of La Trappe, and of a great deal of picturesque truth so like romance that one can hardly imagine the hero sitting at a wooden table, with a real pen and ink, writing a book—if Father Thuillier had said this, we might have assented; but to tell us outright that everybody knows that De Rancé's "Traité de la Sainteté et des Devoirs de la Vie Monastique" began the fray between him and Dom Mabillon, is too much, seeing that there are, as I have said, a great many very well-informed persons, who do not know that these two famous men ever had any controversy about monastic studies, or even, perhaps, that there were any such studies to dispute about.

The work of De Rancé, I am told (for I have never seen it), was professedly written for his own monks, and represented to them that the pursuit of literature was inconsistent with their profession, and that their reading ought to be confined to the Scriptures and a few books of devotion. This seemed like—some thought it was meant to be—an attack on the Benedictine monks of St. Maur—for that they were learned everybody knew—and they were urged to reply. They, however, remained very quiet; and it was long before they could be persuaded to take the field. The Benedictine historian whom I have mentioned, and to whom I am indebted, suggests as a reason for this, that the Benedictines really were (and everybody knew they were) following the footsteps of their learned predecessors in the cultivation of letters, and that they thought it quite sufficient to tell those who talked to them on the subject, that the abbot of La Trappe had his own reasons for what he did[1]—that he had

---

1 " Et pour toute réponse à ceux qui les excitoient à se défendre, ils alleguérent que le Pere Abbé *avoit ses vûes particuliéres*, qu'il n'avoit droit de décision que sur sa Maison, qu'il y étoit le maître,

no authority except in his own convent—that
there he really was master—and no one had a
right to blame him if, in order to conduct his
own flock to heaven, he prescribed paths somewhat
singular under the conviction that they were the
safest.

Father Thuillier is not, perhaps, quite an un-
prejudiced historian ; and I hope I am not unchari-
table in thinking that he might have added, that
although these good fathers of St. Maur were in fact
following the steps of their predecessors in the order
of St. Benedict, yet, considering that they had had
predecessors in that order for nearly twelve hundred
years, and that during the lapse of that period many
things had altered both in and out of the cloister,
they felt it rather awkward to be sharply recalled to
the naked letter of their Rule. They were in no
haste to meet an opponent of great influence from
family, connexion, character, and the singular
circumstances of his life—a man, acute, eloquent,
fervid, and fully persuaded that he was maintaining
the cause of pure and primitive and spiritual religion,
against the incursions of vain, worldly, and mischievous pursuits. One might forgive them if they
were not eager to fight such a battle, with such an
adversary, before an enlightened public, who, which-
ever side might gain the victory, would be sure to
make themselves merry with the battle of the
monks.

Be this as it may, however, a considerable time

---

et qu'on ne pouvoit trouver à redire, que pour conduire son
troupeau au Ciel, il se fît des routes singuliéres, puisqu'il les
croioit les plus sures." Mabill. Op. Post. Tom. I. p. 366. The
words which I have marked by *italics* seem capable of an invidious
construction ; but the notorious circumstances of the case were
such that it can hardly have been intended.

elapsed—I do not know in what year De Rancé published his book, and therefore cannot tell whether it was with a view to be specific, or to show his own classical reading, that Father Thuillier tells us that more than nine years had passed before the Benedictine reply came out; but in fact Dom Mabillon's "Traité des Etudes Monastiques" was published in the year 1691. It was, of course, learned, wise, and modest. It proved that there had been a succession of learned monks from almost the very beginning of monasticism, that they had learned and taught as much as they could, and that, on the general principles of religion, reason, and common sense, they were quite right in so doing; but, as to the RULE, he did not get on quite so well; because it must be obvious to everyone who inquires, that none of the monastic legislators ever contemplated the formation of academies of learning and science. This Mabillon of course knew, and I doubt whether he could have carried on his argument (for I do not believe that he would have done what he considered dishonest), had it not been for a full persuasion of his mind which, though it may not bear to be stated as an argument, peeps out occasionally in a very amusing manner, and gives a colour to the whole line of defence.—" Not study? why, how could they help it?"—or, thrown into a more logical form, " You acknowledge that the monks lived in their monasteries; but it is impossible for people to live without study; therefore the monks studied." Some caviller might say that the Rule did not tell them to study; and the good father would perhaps have smiled and answered that it did not tell them to breathe.

The work was, however, popular; for who would not wish to be ranged with the admirers and advocates of learning and science? and a second edition was printed the next year after the first. It was quickly translated into Italian by Father Ceppi,

an Augustinian monk[2], but was very near being
prohibited, not on account of anything connected
with the dispute, but for some things which
appeared too liberal ; among others, a commendation of Archbishop Ussher's Annals. Father Ceppi,
however, managed to soften the Master of the
Sacred Palace, and so got a conditional *imprimatur*
in 1701. A German translation of it was published
by Father Udalric Staudigl in 1702 ; and a Latin
one by Father Joseph Porta in 1704.

It is not, however, my present business to trace
this controversy through the reply of De Rancé,
and the rejoinder of Mabillon. I mention it here to
show that, even so recently as little more than a
century ago, it was a question sharply contested
between men of the highest monastic eminence,
whether a monk might lawfully be a learned man.
I do this with a view to remove what I believe to be
a very common misapprehension as to the origin and
nature of monastic institutions. I know, as well as
Mabillon did—that is, as to full conviction that it
was so, not as to the facts which his almost

---

[2] I learn from Father Ossinger's Bibliotheca Augustiniana, that
this Father Ceppi was, " singularis venerator nostri S. Nicolai de
Tolentino," and that " ad promovendam devotionem erga hunc
universæ Ecclesiæ Patronum in lingua Italica typis mandavit,
' Maraviglie trecenta ed una operate da Dio per li meriti del Santo
Protettore di Santa Chiesa Nicolo di Tolentino. In Roma,
1710.' " And also another work, with the same design, " Il
sangue miracoloso del Santo Protettore di Santa Chiesa Nicolo di
Tolentino, dedicata all' Eminentissimo, e Reverendissimo Prencipe
il Signor Cardinale Nicolo Coscia. Romæ, 1725, in 8." I
acknowledge that this has nothing to do with the period under
our consideration ; for Ceppi wrote in the *eighteenth*, and this St.
Nicholas (his patron, or patronized) lived in the *fourteenth*,
century ; but may I not be pardoned if, having to say so much of
the dull, legendary, and lying works of the Dark Ages, I enliven
the subject by an occasional reference to the wiser literature of
more enlightened times ? *See Note* A.

unbounded learning might have furnished in proof
or illustration—that the monks were the most
learned men; and that it pleased God to make
monastic institutions the means of preserving
learning in the world, and I hope to show this; but
before I do so, I wish to come to a clear understanding with those who, instead of thanking the
monks for what they did, find sufficient employment
in abusing them for not doing what they never
undertook to do, and were, in fact, no more bound
to do than other people. With this view I am also
desirous to say something of the Rule of St. Benedict.
" I would not have answered him," said De Rancé
to Father Lamy, when the Duchess of Guise, who
took a vast interest in the matter, had gone to La
Trappe, and got these two fathers face to face, to
fight the matter out before her [3]—" I would not
have answered him, if he had not carried the matter
up to the time of Pachomius." It *was* too bad;
and I am not going to imitate it by speaking here
of any earlier Rule than St. Benedict's. To be
sure, even that was born before the dark ages, and
has survived them; but its almost universal adoption
in the west, and its incalculable influence, as being
the Rule by which almost all the monasteries of
Europe were governed, and by which therefore
every individual monk in them had solemnly bound
himself, render it a matter of much interest and

---

[3] Father Lamy went, because Mabillon could not be persuaded
to go; " Il se rendit donc à la Trappe auprès de son A. R. Elle
avoit sans doute prévenu sur son chapitre le P. Abbé, car on ne
peut pas plus d'egards, plus d'honnêtez, plus de soins et d'assiduitez
qu'il reçut et de deux de ses Religieux. Après les premiers com-
plimens son A. R. les fit asseoir dans une ruelle, l'un, dit-elle
agréablement, a titre de goute sciatique, et l'autre a titre de pierre,
et puis Elle les obligea d'entrer en matiere sur le grand différent
des Etudes."—p. 376.

importance to those who would understand the
spirit of monastic institutions, and their real circumstances during the Dark Ages. For our present
purpose, it may be sufficient to extract the prologue,
and the fourth chapter; the former of which is as
follows :—

"Hear, O my son, the precepts of a master; and incline the
ear of thine heart; and cheerfully receive, and effectually fulfil,
the admonition of an affectionate father; that, by the labour of
obedience, thou mayest return to him, from whom thou hast
departed by the sloth of disobedience. To thee therefore my discourse is now directed—whosoever, renouncing the desires of self,
and about to serve as a soldier of the Lord Christ, the true
King, dost assume the most powerful and noble arms of obedience.

"In the first place, you must, with most urgent prayer, entreat
that whatsoever good thing you take in hand, may through Him
be brought to completion; that He who hath condescended now to
reckon us in the number of his sons, may not be obliged to grieve
over our ill conduct. For He is ever to be served by us, with
those good things which are his own; so served by us as that not
only He may not, as an angry father, disinherit his sons,—but
that He may not, as a Master who is to be feared, be so in-
censed by our sins, as to deliver over to eternal punishment,
as most wicked servants, those who would not follow Him to
glory.

"Let us, however, at length arise; for the Scripture arouses
us, saying, 'That now it is high time to awake out of sleep;' and,
our eyes being opened to the divine light, let us hear with
astonished ears the voice which every day admonishes us, 'To-day,
if ye will hear his voice, harden not your hearts;' and again, 'He
that hath ears to hear, let him hear what the Spirit saith to the
churches;' and what saith He? 'Come, ye children, hearken
unto me: I will teach you the fear of the Lord'—'Run while
ye have the light of life, lest the darkness of death overtake
you.'

"And the Lord, seeking for his workman among the multitude
of the people, whom He thus addresses, saith again, 'What man
is he that desireth life, and will see good days?' And if when
you hear this you answer 'I,' God saith unto you, 'If thou wilt
have life, keep thy tongue from evil, and thy lips that they speak
no guile. Depart from evil, and do good; seek peace and pursue
it.' And when you shall have done this, 'my eyes are upon you,
and my ears are towards your prayers; and before ye call upon
me I will say unto you "Here am I."' Most dear brethren,

what is sweeter than this voice of the Lord inviting us? Behold, in his mercy, the Lord points out to us the way of life.

" Our loins therefore being girded, and our feet shod with faith and the observance of good works, let us, under the guidance of the gospel, go forth on his ways, that we may be counted worthy to see Him who hath called us, in his kingdom. In the tabernacle of whose kingdom, if we desire to dwell, we can by no means attain our desire, except by running in the way of good works. But let us inquire of the Lord with the Prophet, and say unto Him, ' Lord, who shall dwell in thy tabernacle, and who shall rest in thy holy mountain?' After this inquiry, Brethren, let us hear the Lord replying, and showing us the way of his tabernacle, and saying, ' He that walketh uprightly, and worketh righteousness, and speaketh the truth in his heart ; he that backbiteth not with his tongue, nor doeth evil to his neighbour, nor taketh up a reproach against his neighbour.' Who turning away the eyes of his heart from the wicked Devil who tempts him, and from his temptation, hath brought him to nought, and hath taken the young thoughts which he hath bred and dashed them to pieces on Christ.[4] Who, fearing the Lord, are not puffed up by their good works ; but who, considering that those good things which are in them could not be wrought by themselves, but by the Lord, magnify the Lord who worketh in them, saying with the Prophet, ' Not unto us, O Lord, not unto us, but unto thy name give glory.' Like as the Apostle Paul reckoned nothing of his preaching, saying, ' By the grace of God I am what I am ;' and again he says, ' He that glorieth let him glory in the Lord.'

" Hence also it is, that our Lord saith in the gospel, ' Whosoever heareth these sayings of mine, and doeth them, I will liken him unto a wise man, which built his house upon a rock : and the floods came, and the winds blew, and beat upon that house ; and it fell not : for it was founded upon a rock.' While the Lord does all this, He expects every day that we should respond to his holy admonitions, by our actions. Therefore it is, that the days of this life are extended as a respite for the emendation of what is evil ; as the Apostle says, ' Knowest thou not that the long suffering of God leadeth thee to repentance?' For the merciful God hath said, ' I desire not the death of a sinner, but that he should be converted and live.'

" When therefore, my brethren, we inquire of the Lord, ' who shall abide in thy tabernacle?' we thus hear the rule of habitation ; and if we fulfil the duty of an inhabitant, we shall be heirs of the

---

[4] The allusion is to Psalm cxxxvii. 9. " Filia Babylonis . . . beatus qui tenebit et allidet parvulos tuos ad petram."

kingdom of heaven. Therefore our hearts and bodies are to be
prepared to go forth to the warfare of holy obedience to the commandments ; and, because it is impossible to our nature, let us ask
the Lord of his grace that He would assist us with his help. And
if, flying from the pains of hell, we desire to obtain eternal life,
while yet there is opportunity and we are in this body, and
space is afforded to fulfil all these things by this life of light,
we must now run and labour for that which shall profit us for
ever.

  "We must, therefore, institute a school of service to the Lord ;
in which institution we trust that we shall appoint nothing harsh
or burdensome. If, however, anything a little severe should, on
reasonable grounds of equity, be enjoined for the correction of
vices, and the preservation of charity, do not in sudden alarm fly
from the way of safety, which can only be begun by a narrow
entrance. In the progress, however, of our conversation and faith,
the heart being enlarged with the ineffable sweetness of love, we
run the way of God's commandments, so that never departing from
his governance, remaining under his teaching in the monastery
until death, we through patience are partakers of Christ's suffer-
ings, that we may be counted worthy to be partakers of his
kingdom."

The first chapter of the Rule is on the various
kinds of monks—the second, on the qualifications
and duties of an abbot—the third, on the duty of
the abbot to take counsel with the brethren—and
the fourth is headed, "Quæ sint instrumenta
bonorum operum." This title has given some
trouble to commentators; and the reader may
translate it as he pleases. It is not my business to
criticize it, especially as the chapter itself is intelligible enough. It contains seventy-two brief injunctions, from whence we may form some general
opinion as to what those who bound themselves by
this Rule did, and did not, undertake. Most of the
other seventy-two chapters of the Rule consist
of regulations respecting the organization and
management of their society, which would, of
course, occupy the most room ; but it seems
to me that this single fourth chapter should
at least qualify the statements of those who pro-

fess to have found nothing but a body of heartless
forms.[5]

" 1. In the first place, to love the Lord God with the whole
heart, whole soul, whole strength.   2. Then his neighbour as himself.   3. Then not to kill.   4. Then not to commit adultery.
5. Not to steal.   6. Not to covet.   7. Not to bear false witness.
8. To honour all men.   9. And what anyone would not have done
to him, let him not do to another.   10. To deny himself, that he
may follow Christ.   11. To chasten the body.   12. To renounce
luxuries.   13. To love fasting.   14. To relieve the poor.   15. To
clothe the naked.   16. To visit the sick.   17. To bury the dead.
18. To help in tribulation.   19. To console the afflicted.   20. To
disengage himself from worldly affairs.   21. To set the love of
Christ before all other things.   22. Not to give way to anger.
23. Not to bear any grudge.   24. Not to harbour deceit in the
heart.   25. Not to make false peace.   26. Not to forsake charity.
27. Not to swear, lest haply he perjure himself.   28. To utter
truth from his heart and his mouth.   29. Not to return evil for
evil.   30. Not to do injuries ; and to bear them patiently.   31. To
love his enemies.   32. Not to curse again those who curse him ;
but rather to bless them.   33. To endure persecutions for
righteousness sake.   34. Not to be proud.   35. Not given to wine.
36. Not gluttonous.   37. Not addicted to sleep.   38. Not sluggish.
39. Not given to murmur.   40. Not a slanderer.   41. To commit
his hope to God.   42. When he sees anything good in himself, to
attribute it to God, and not to himself.   43. But let him always
know, that which is evil in his own doing, and impute it to himself.   44. To fear the day of judgment.   45. To dread Hell.
46. To desire eternal life, with all spiritual longing.   47. To have
the expectation of death every day before his eyes.   48. To watch
over his actions at all times.   49. To know certainly that, in all
places, the eye of God is upon him.   50. Those evil thoughts
which come into his heart immediately to dash to pieces on Christ.
51. And to make them known to his spiritual senior.   52. To keep
his lips from evil and wicked discourse.   53. Not to be fond of
much talking.   54. Not to speak vain words, or such as provoke
laughter.   55. Not to love much or violent laughter.   56. To give
willing attention to the sacred readings.   57. To pray frequently.
58. Every day to confess his past sins to God, in prayer, with

---

[5] About this time the monastic rules of Benedict were established, which afterwards were received through the western
churches.   They are full of forms, and breathe little of the spirit
of godliness.   The very best thing that I can find recorded of the
superstitious founder, is the zeal with which he opposed idolatry.
—*Milner's History of the Church of Christ*, Cent. VI., ch. iv.

tears and groaning ; from thenceforward to reform as to those sins.
59. Not to fulfil the desires of the flesh ; to hate self-will. 60. In
all things to obey the commands of the abbot, even though he himself (which God forbid) should do otherwise; remembering our
Lord's command, ' What they say, do ; but what they do, do ye
not.' 61. Not to desire to be called a saint before he is one, but
first to be one that he may be truly called one. 62. Every day to
fulfil the commands of God in action. 63. To love chastity.
64. To hate nobody. 65. To have no jealousy ; to indulge no
envy. 66. Not to love contention. 67. To avoid self-conceit.
68. To reverence seniors. 69. To love juniors. 70. To pray for
enemies, in the love of Christ. 71. After a disagreement, to be
reconciled before the going down of the sun. 72. And never to
despair of the mercy of God."

I apprehend that these injunctions are better than
some readers would have expected to find; and
should it appear that, on the whole, they are defective either as to doctrine, or instruction, let it be
remembered that St. Benedict did not intend that
his Rule should supersede the Holy Scriptures.
He did not mean to give his disciples the traditions
of men *instead* of the word of God. He told them
plainly that the most perfect Rule of life was contained in the Old and New Testament;[6] and that he
expected them to be assiduous in reading the Scriptures, and the works of some of the Fathers, is clear.
This species of study, and this only, he enjoined
upon them ; and as to their practice in this respect
I hope to speak hereafter. In the meantime, I just
observe that thus to read (or to be read to, if he
could not read) was all that was required of a
monk.

It may, however, be said, that supposing the
monks to have kept to their original state, and to
have lived in all things according to their Rules,
they might not, perhaps, have been so much to

---

[6] " Quæ enim pagina, aut quis sermo divinæ auctoritatis veteris
ac novi Testamenti, non est rectissima norma vitæ humanæ," &c.
Cap. lxxiii; which is entitled " De eo quod non omnis observatio
justitiæ in hac sit Regula constituta."

blame for the want of learning, but that, by the times with which we are concerned, most of them were priests, and that the clergy—well, I fully admit that as clergy they were bound to be more learned than other men ; but at present, as Jerome says, " quod loquor, non de episcopis, non de presbyteris, non de clericis loquor; sed de monacho."[7] I desire, first, to place the question on its right footing, and trust that I shall not be found reluctant to acknowledge that the clergy ought to be the most learned class in the community. In fact, they always were so, and this I hope to show.

[7] Ad Paulin.

No. XI.

" Alia, ut ante perstrinxi, monachorum est causa : alia clericorum.
Clerici pascunt oves; ego pascor."—HIERONYMUS.

IT will be readily admitted that those who profess
to teach others should be more learned than the
rest of the community. This was, however, the
very point of difference between the monks and the
clergy—" monachus non docentis, sed plangentis
habet officium," said Jerome, and a monk, as such,
had no business, and did not, in fact, pretend, to
teach anything or anybody. This, though strictly
applicable only to the original state of things, may
be, in some degree, applied to the subsequent condition of monastic institutions, when most of the
monks were priests ; because the real and practical
difference is between those who live in the world
with, and for the sake of, the cure of souls, and
those who, either for devotion or for any other
reason, live out of the world—in the cell or the
cloister.[1]

[1] That which St. Jerome so pithily expressed, is more diffusely
stated by St. Ambrose—" Namque hæc duo in adtentiore chris-
tianorum devotione præstantiora esse quis ambigat, clericorum
officia, et monachorum instituta? Ista ad commoditatem et
moralitatem disciplina, illa ad abstinentiam adsuefacta atque
patientiam : hæc velut in quodam theatro, illa in secreto : spectatur
ista, illa absconditur . . . . Hæc ergo vita in stadio, illa in
spelunca ; hæc adversus confusionem sæculi, illa adversus carnis
appetentiam : hæc subjiciens, illa refugiens corporis voluptates :
hæc gratior, illa tutior : hæc seipsam regens, illa semet ipsam
coercens : utraque tamen se abnegans, ut fiat Christi ; quia per-
fectis dictum est : ' Qui vult post me venire, abneget seipsum sibi,
et tollat crucem suam, et sequatur me.' . . . Hæc ergo dimicat,
illa se removet : hæc illecebras vincit, illa refugit : huic mundus
triumphatur, illi exsulat : huic mundus crucifigitur, vel ipsa mundo,
illi ignoratur : huic plura tentamenta, et ideo major victoria ; illi
infrequentior lapsus, facilior custodia."—Ep. lxiii. tom. ii. p.
1039.

Notwithstanding—or, perhaps, I ought rather to say, by reason of—this, the monks took the lead in learning. It is not worth while here to enter into all the reasons of this, while there is one that is so obvious—namely, that they led quiet, retired, and regular lives; and that if they could not be originally, or at all times, said to have more leisure than the secular clergy, their employments and habits were of a nature less unfriendly to study. Instead, therefore, of now entering into this matter, let us come at once to a question which must be met if we are to understand each other or the subject,—for I cannot help fearing that, while speaking of the dark ages, I and some, at least, of my readers may be thinking of very different things, under the same name—What is learning? or, to put the question in a more limited and less troublesome form—What did the people of the dark ages think on this subject? It might, I think, be shown that there were a good many persons in those ages not so destitute of all that is now called learning as some have asserted, and many, without much inquiry, believe. I might ask, how does it happen that the classics, and the older works on art or science, have been preserved in existence? and I might, with still greater force (but obviously with intolerable prolixity), appeal to the works of writers of those ages to show that they knew the meaning of that which, no one can deny, they preserved and multiplied. But this is not to our present purpose; and the proper answer is, that people in those days were brought up with views respecting profane learning which it is necessary for us to understand before we form our judgment of the men ; and, as I have never seen these views clearly stated, I will take leave to say a few words about them.

"Quid ergo Athenis et Hierosolymis? quid Academiæ et Ecclesiæ? quid hæreticis et Christianis? Nostra institutio de porticu Salomonis est: qui et ipse tradiderat, Dominum in simplicitate cordis esse

quærendum. Viderint qui Stoicum, et Platonicum,
et Dialecticum Christianismum protulerunt. Nobis
curiositate opus non est post Christum Jesum, nec
inquisitione post evangelium. Cum credimus, nihil
desideramus ultra credere. Hoc enim prius credimus, non esse, quod ultra credere debemus." These
are not the words of a monk of the tenth century,
if not of a priest of the second. How far it might
have been better or worse if the Christian church
had maintained, and acted on, the feeling which
Tertullian expresses, this is not the place to discuss.
In point of fact, the rigour of the law here laid
down was soon softened,—or perhaps I should say
that an excuse was soon provided for those who
were enamoured of profane learning. They were
not to go down to Egypt for help. Undoubtedly,
that was quite clear ; but it was equally clear that
they might spoil the Egyptians, and bring that
silver and gold which, wherever they may be found,
are the Lord's, into the camp of His people. They
were not to contract alliances with the heathen.
Certainly not ; but if, in the course of war, they
should see among the spoil a beautiful captive, it
was lawful to bring her home ; and, when her head
had been shaved, and her nails pared, to take her to
wife. These fancies were, as far as I know, excogi-
tated by Origen,—the man, perhaps, of all others
most bound, and best able, to devise some excuse
for a practice which the severe and exclusive
purity of primitive Christianity had condemned.[2]

---

[2] In his letter to Gregory (tom. i. p. 30), he suggests that this
might be really intended by the command given to the Israelites
to borrow from the Egyptians. As to the captive, after quoting
the law (Deut. xxi. 10), he says—" And to say the truth, I also
have frequently gone out to battle against my enemies, and there
I have seen, among the spoil, a woman beautiful to behold. For
whatever we find that is well and rationally said in the works of
our enemies, if we read anything that is said wisely and according
to knowledge, we ought to cleanse it, and from that knowledge
which they possess to remove and cut off all that is dead and use-

Whether it was entirely valid or not, however, this was, for more than a thousand years, the standing excuse for those who were conscious (not to say vain) of their heathenish acquirements. Take, for instance—and as a specimen of the feeling at a

---

less,—for such are all the hair of the head, and the nails of the woman taken out of the spoils of the enemy,—and then at length to make her our wife, when she no longer has any of those things which for their infidelity are called dead. Nothing dead on her head or in her hands : so that neither in senses, nor in action, she should have anything that is unclean or dead about her." *In Levit. Hom.* VII. tom. ii. p. 227. If Origen's plaything were not the Word of God, one might often be amused with his childish fooleries ; but when we consider what mischief has been done to truth by the way of allegorizing (or, as it is now called, spiritualizing) the Bible, it cannot be looked on without disgust. Of course, the next step is to despise and get rid of the letter of Scripture, as Jerome does most unceremoniously (not to say blasphemously) in this very case. After telling us that the husks, in the parable of the prodigal son, may mean poetry, rhetoric, and the wisdom of this world, he adds—" Hujus sapientiæ typus et in Deuteronomio sub mulieris captivæ figura describitur : de qua divina vox præcipit : ut si Israelites eam habere voluerit uxorem, calvitium ei faciat, ungues præsecet, et pilos auferat : et cum munda fuerit effecta tunc transeat in victoris amplexus. Hæc si secundum literam intelligimus nonne *ridicula* sunt ? Itaque et nos hoc facere solemus quando philosophos legimus," &c.—*Ad Damas.* tom. iii. p. 44, M. My object here, however, is only to show whence certain opinions and feelings of the dark ages were derived. The reader who thinks what I have said insufficient may see the account which Jerome gives, in his Epistle to Eustochium, of his being brought before the judgment-seat, and punished as a Ciceronian. The story is too long to be extracted here, and too well known, perhaps, to require it. At all events, it was well known in the dark ages. He introduces it by saying—" Quæ enim communicatio luci ad tenebras ? qui consensus Christo cum Balial ? Quid facit cum Psalterio Horatius ? cum Evangeliis, Maro ? Cum Apostolis, Cicero ?" &c.—tom. i. p. 51, C. To this we may add, the first book of Augustine's Confessions, c. 12, and thenceforth. Stronger things than these fathers wrote are not, I believe, to be found in the writings of the dark ages. Some of what Jerome says it would hardly do to produce in the present day—for instance, " At nunc etiam sacerdotes Dei, omissis evangeliis et prophetis, videmus comœdias legere, amatoria Bucolicorum versuum verba canere, tenere Virgilium : et id quod in pueris necessitatis est, crimen in se facere voluptatis," &c.

period with which we are at present more concerned
than with that of Tertullian or Origen—a letter and
answer which passed between a prior and an abbot
in the year 1150 :—

"To his Lord, the Venerable Abbot of ——, R. wishes health
and happiness. Although you desire to have the books of Tully,
I know that you are a Christian and not a Ciceronian. But you
go over to the camp of the enemy, not as a deserter, but as a spy.
I should, therefore, have sent you the books of Tully which we
have De Re Agraria, Philippics and Epistles, but that it is not
our custom that any books should be lent to any person without
good pledges. Send us, therefore, the Noctes Atticæ of Aulus
Gellius, and Origen on the Canticles. The books which we have
just brought from France, if you wish for any of them, I will send
you."

The Abbot replied—

" Brother ——, by the grace of God what he is in the Catholic
Church, to his friend R., the venerable Prior of H ——, blessing
and life eternal. You have rightly reminded me, brother, that
though I may have the books of Cicero, yet I should remember
that I am a Christian ; and as you have written (and as your
Seneca says of himself) I go over sometimes to the enemy's camp,
not as a deserter or traitor, but as a spy, and one who is desirous
of spoil, if haply I may take prisoner some Midianitish woman,
whom, after her head has been shaved, and her nails have been
pared, I may lawfully take to wife. And though I deserve only to
be a stranger—or, indeed, an exile—in a far country, nevertheless
I desire rather to be filled with that bread which came down from
heaven, than to fill my belly with the husks which the swine do
eat. The dishes prepared by Cicero do not form the principal, or
the first, course at my table ; but if, at any time, when filled with
better food, anything of his pleases me, I take it as one does the
trifles which are set on the table after dinner. For it is even a
kind of pleasure to me not to be idle. Nor, indeed (to say nothing
of any other reasons), can I bear that that noble genius, those
splendid imaginations, such great beauties both of thought and
language, should be lost in oblivion and neglect; but I want to
make into one volume all his works which can be found; for I have
no sympathy with those who, neglecting all liberal studies, are
careful only for transitory things ; and who collect that they may
disperse, and disperse that they may collect. They are like men
playing at ball—they catch eagerly, and throw away quickly ; so
that they have no moderation either in catching or in throwing
away. Although their doctrine is praised by secular persons of
bad character, yet if you love me, you will avoid it as poison, and
the death of the soul. I have sent you as pledges for your books,

Origen on the Canticles, and instead of Aulus Gellius (which I could not have at this time) a book which is called, in Greek, Strategematon, which is military."

It must be observed, however, that this excuse would scarcely serve—indeed, strictly speaking, it could not be admitted at all—for reading heathen works of fiction. The Midianitish captive might have beauty, and might be loved, if she assumed the form of philosophy or history, art or science. Truth, wherever found, is truth and beauty; but when the captive appeared in the meretricious form of poetry, and that, too, poetry about false gods— or, more plainly, nonsense about nonentities—or even coarsely, as they would have expressed it, lies about devils—when this was the case they thought that the less Christians had to do with it the better. Beside this, they thought that Virgil and Horace (to say nothing of some others) spoke of things whereof it is a shame to speak—things which children should not be taught, and which it were better that Christian men should not know. This was their feeling and conviction; and on this they acted. It was not, as modern conceit loves to talk, that they were ignorant that such books existed, or that they were men so destitute of brains and passions as not to admire the language in which the heathen poets described, and the images in which they personified, ambition, rage, lust, intemperance, and a variety of other things which were quite contrary to the Rules of St. Benedict and St. Chrodegang.

I grant that they had not that extravagant and factitious admiration for the poets of antiquity which they probably would have had if they had been brought up to read them before they could understand them, and to admire them as a necessary matter of taste before they could form any intellectual or moral estimate of them. They thought, too, that there were worse things in the world than false quantities, and preferred running the risque of

them to some other risques which they apprehended;[3]
but yet there are instances enough of the classics
(even the poets) being taught in schools, and read
by individuals ; and it cannot be doubted that they
might have been, and would have been, read by
more but for the prevalence of that feeling which I
have described, and which, notwithstanding these
exceptions, was very general. Modern, and, as it
is supposed, more enlightened, views of education
have decided that this was all wrong ; but let us not
set down what was at most an error of judgment
as mere stupidity and a proof of total barbarism.
If the modern ecclesiastic should ever meet with a
crop-eared monk of the tenth century, he may, if he
pleases, laugh at him for not having read Virgil ;
but if he should himself be led to confess that,
though a priest of Christ's catholic church, and
nourished in the languages of Greece and Rome till
they were almost as familiar to him as his own, he

---

[3] When our Archbishop Lanfranc was a monk at Bec, but at a
time when the most renowned teachers of Latin were coming to
him for instruction—clerici accurrunt, Ducum filii, nominatissimi
scholarum latinitatis magistri—he was one day officiating as reader
at table, when the prior corrected, or thought that he corrected,
him for a false quantity. " It was," says his biographer, " as if he
had said docēre with the middle syllable long, as it is ; and he [the
prior] would have corrected it by shortening the middle syllable to
docĕre, which it is not, for that prior was not learned.   But the
wise man, knowing that obedience was due to Christ rather than to
Donatus, gave up the right pronunciation, and said as he was
improperly told to say.   For he knew that a false quantity was not
a capital crime, but that to disobey one who commanded him in
God's stead (jubenti ex parte Dei) was no trifling sin."—*Mab. A. S.*
IX. 635.   By way of a set-off to some things which I have quoted,
and a specimen of the exceptions of which I speak, I may add
what the biographer of Herluin (who was abbot of Bec at this
time) says of this confluence of learned men.   He tells us that the
monastery increased in a variety of ways, as to fame, revenue, &c.
—" Viris litteratis undecumque confluentibus cum ornamentis et
spoliis quibus spoliaverant Ægyptum, que cultui tabernaculi postmodum forent accommoda.   Poetarum quippe figmenta, philoso-
phorum scientia et artium liberalium disciplina, Scripturis sacris
intelligendis valde sunt necessaria."—*Ibid.* 364.

had never read a single page of Chrysostom or
Basil, of Augustine or Jerome, of Ambrose or
Hilary—if he should confess this I am of opinion
that the poor monk would cross himself, and make
off without looking behind him.

So different are the feelings of men, and I doubt
whether it is possible for any man in the present
day to form a complete idea of the state of feeling
on this subject which existed for many centuries;
but it is very desirable that it should be understood,
and perhaps it may be illustrated by a few extracts
from writers of different periods.

Pope Gregory wrote a letter to Desiderius, a
Bishop of Gaul, which begins thus:—"Having
received much pleasing information respecting your
studies, such joy arose in my heart that I could not
on any account think of refusing what you, my
brother, requested. But after this I was informed
(what I cannot repeat without shame) that you, my
brother, teach certain persons grammar.[4] At this I
was so grieved, and conceived so strong a disgust,
that I exchanged the feelings which I have described
for groans and sadness; for it cannot be that the
praises of Jupiter and the praises of Christ should
proceed from the same mouth. Consider, yourself,

---

[4] I say " teach Grammar," though it is a very absurd translation
of *Grammaticam exponere.* The reader who does not require such
an explanation will, I hope, excuse my saying, for the sake of
others, that the " ars grammatica " comprehended something much
beyond what the words would now suggest. Indeed, they might,
perhaps, be more properly translated " classical," or, what is the
same thing, " profane literature." The *Grammaticus* was, as his
name imported, a man of letters—those letters, however, to borrow
the words of Augustine, " non quas *primi magistri,* sed quas docent
qui *grammatici* vocantur."—*Confess.* L. I. c. xii. How much
those who lived in the dark ages knew of such literature, people
may dispute ; and therefore, as I know of no other alternative, I
prefer using the word " grammar," though incorrect, to the
appearance of exaggerating their knowledge, until I can show, as I
hope to do, that they were not so entirely ignorant of the classics
as some have supposed.

how sad and wicked a thing it is (quam grave
nefandumque sit) for a bishop to sing what would be
unfit for a religious layman ; and although, my most
dear son, Candidus, the priest, who came afterwards,
being strictly examined as to this matter, denied it,
and endeavoured to excuse you, yet my mind is not
satisfied. For as it is horrible that such a thing should
be told of a priest (execrabile est hoc de sacerdote
enarrari), so should the investigation of its truth or
falsehood be strict in proportion. If, therefore, the
information which I have received shall hereafter be
shown to be false, and it shall appear that you are
not studying trifles and secular literature, I shall
give thanks to God, who has not suffered your mind
to be polluted with the blasphemous praises of the
wicked, and we shall then confer, safely and without hesitation, on the subject of your requests." [5]

Our countryman, Alcwin, was probably born
about the year 735, devoted to the church as soon
as he was weaned, and brought up in it. His
biographer, who was his contemporary, or within a
few years of him, tells us that, when a child, he
frequented the daily services of the church, but was
apt to neglect those which were performed in the
night. When he was about eleven years old, it happened that a lay-brother who inhabited a cell[6]

---

[5] Lib. IX. Ep. xlviii.

[6] These cells were little establishments which rose up like offsets
round monasteries, and properly consisted of a few (perhaps from
two to half a dozen) monks placed there by the superiors of the
monastery, and living under its rule, either that they might be on
the spot for the protection and cultivation of property belonging to
the monastery— or because they desired to lead a more solitary life
than they could do in the monastery—or because applications for
admissions were so numerous, that in order to admit those who
applied it was necessary that some of the older monks should
swarm out—or because those who had given certain property had
made it a condition that monks should be settled on the spot. The
reader will imagine that, if not so originally (as in most cases it
was) the cell generally became a farm ; and often the oratory grew
into a church, a monastery, a town, &c.

belonging to the monastery was one day, by some accident, deprived of his usual companions, and petitioned the schoolmaster of the monastery that one of the boys might come up and sleep there that night, being, perhaps, afraid to pass the hours of darkness alone. Alcwin was sent, and they retired to rest, and when, about cock-crowing, they were waked by the signal for service, the rustic monk only turned in bed, and went to sleep again. Not so Alcwin, who soon perceived, with horror and astonishment, that the room was full of dæmons. They surrounded the bed of the sleeping rustic, and cried—" You sleep well, brother! " He woke immediately, and they repeated their salutation. " Why," they added, " do you alone lie snoring here while all your brethren are watching in the church ? " Quid multa ? says the historian ; and, indeed, everybody may guess what ensued. They gave him an awful drubbing, which, we are told, was not only very beneficial to him, but was matter of warning and rejoicing (cautelam et canticum) to others. In the meantime poor Alcwin, as he afterwards related, lay trembling under the persuasion that his turn would come next, and said in his inmost heart—" O, Lord Jesus, if Thou wilt deliver me from their bloody hands, and afterwards I am negligent of the vigils of Thy church and of the service of lauds, and continue to love Virgil more than the melody of the Psalms, then may I undergo such correction ; only I earnestly pray that Thou wouldest now deliver me." Alcwin escaped ; but in order to impress it on his memory, his biographer says, he was subjected to some farther alarm. The dæmons, having finished the castigation of his companion, looked about them and found the boy, completely covered up in his bedclothes, panting and almost senseless. " Who is the other that sleeps in the house ? " said the chief of the dæmons. " The boy, Alcwin, is hidden in that bed," replied the others. Finding that he was discovered, his suppressed

grief and horror burst forth in tears and screaming.
His persecutors being restrained from executing all
that their cruelty would have desired, began to
consult together. An unfortunate hiatus in the MS.
prevents us from knowing all that they said ; but it
appears that they came to a resolution not to beat
him, but to turn up the clothes at the bottom of the
bed and cut his corns, by way of making him
remember his promise.[7] Already were the clothes
thrown back, when Alcwin jumped up, crossed
himself, and sung the twelfth Psalm with all his
might. The dæmons vanished, and he and his companion set off to the church for safety.[8]

Some readers will perhaps doubt whether *all* the
monks were in the church during this scene in the
cell ; but, without arguing on the dæmonology of
the story, I quote it to show the nature of the sin
which lay on the child's conscience when he thought
that he was in the hands of devils. He was, as his
biographer had before said, even at that early age,
"Virgilii amplius quam Psalmorum amator;" but
he received a lesson which he never forgot. Speaking of him in after life, and when he had become
celebrated as a teacher, his biographer says :—" This
man of God had, when he was young, read the
books of the ancient philosophers and the lies
of Virgil, which he did not wish now to hear,
or desire that his disciples should read. ' The sacred
poets,' said he, ' are sufficient for you, and there is
no reason why you should be polluted with the
impure eloquence of Virgil's language.' Which
precept, old Sigulfus endeavoured secretly to disobey, and for so doing he was afterwards publicly
brought to shame. For, calling his sons, Adalbert

---

[7] As the passage now stands it is:—" Non istum verberibus,
quia rudis adhuc est, acris . . . . pedum tantum, in quibus
duritia inest calli, tonsione cultelli castigemus, et emendationem
sponsionis nunc suæ confirmabimus."

[8] Mab. Acta SS. Ord. Bened. tom. v. p. 140.

and Aldric, whom he was then bringing up, he ordered them to read Virgil with him in the most secret manner, forbidding them to let anyone know of it, lest it should come to the knowledge of Father Alcwin. Alcwin, however, calling him to him in his usual manner, said : ' Where do you come from, *Virgiliane?* and why have you begun and designed, contrary to my will and advice, and even without my knowledge, to read Virgil?' Sigulfus, throwing himself at his feet, and having confessed that he had acted most foolishly, humbly did penance; which satisfaction the indulgent father, after rebuking him, kindly received, admonishing him not to do so any more. The worthy man of God, Aldric, who is still alive, and an abbot, declares that neither he nor Adalbert had divulged the matter to anyone; but had, all the time, as they were directed, kept it secret from everybody."[9]

Passing over about a century, we are told by the biographer of Odo, Abbot of Clugni (who lived until 942), that he was so seduced by the love of knowledge, that he was led to employ himself with the vanities of the poets, and resolved to read the works of Virgil regularly through. On the following night, however, he saw in a dream a large vase, of marvellous external beauty, but filled with innumerable serpents, who, springing forth, twined about him, but without doing him any injury. The holy man, waking, and prudently considering the vision, took the serpents to mean the figments of the poets, and the vase to represent Virgil's book, which was painted outwardly with worldly eloquence, but internally defiled with the vanity of impure meaning. From thenceforward, renouncing Virgil and his pomps, and keeping the poets out of his chamber, he sought his nourishment from the sacred writings.[1]

---

[9] Mab. *ibid.* p. 149.
[1] Mab. *ubi sup.* tom. vii. p. 187.

After another century—that is, about the middle
of the eleventh—we find Peter Damian blaming
those monks " who go after the common herd of
grammarians (grammaticorum vulgus), who, leaving
spiritual studies, covet to learn the vanities of
earthly science ; that is, making light of the Rule of
St. Benedict, they love to give themselves up to the
Rules of Donatus ; "[2] and, very near the same time,
our Archbishop Lanfranc wrote to Domnoaldus—
"You have sent me some questions respecting
secular literature for solution ; but it is unbecoming
the episcopal function to be occupied in such studies.
Formerly, I spent the days of my youth in such
things ; but on taking the pastoral office I determined to renounce them."[3] His contemporary,
Geronius, abbot at Centule, was (his biographer
tells us) in his youth accustomed to read the heathen
poets ; and had nearly fallen into the error of
practising what he read.[4]

Honorius (about 1120), or whoever was the author
of the Gemma Animæ, says—" It grieves me when
I consider in my mind the number of persons who,
having lost their senses, are not ashamed to give
their utmost labour to the investigation of the
abominable figments of the poets, and the captious
arguments of the philosophers (which are wont
inextricably to bind the mind that is drawn away

---

[2] Ap. Mab. *ibid.* Sæc. III. P. I. Præf. No. 42, p. xvii.
[3] Ibid.
[4] " Sed, ut fieri solet, cum adolescens Grammaticæ operam
daret, et patulo sensu ipsorum jam carminum vim perpenderet,
animadvertitque inter ea quædam, quorum omnis intentio hæc est,
ut aut expletas luxurias referant, aut quomodo quis explere
voluerit, vel explere potuerit recenseant : et dum talium assidua
meditatione polluitur juvenis mens casta, tum juvenili fervore, tum
turpium verborum auditione, maxime vero diaboli instinctu ad hoc
cœpit impelli, ut ea faceret quæ tantorum Poetarum æstimabat
narratione celebrari."—*Chron. Centulen. ap. Dach. Spicil.* ii. 338.

from God in the bonds of vices), and to be ignorant
of the Christian profession, whereby the soul may
come to reign everlastingly with God.   As it is the
height of madness to be anxious to learn the laws of
an usurper, and to be ignorant of the edicts of the
lawful sovereign.   Moreover, how is the soul pro-
fited by the strife of Hector, or the argumentation
of Plato, or the poems of Virgil, or the elegies of
Ovid, who now, with their like, are gnashing their
teeth in the prison of the infernal Babylon, under
the cruel tyranny of Pluto ?   But the wisdom of
God puts the brightest honour on him who, in-
vestigating the deeds and writings of the apostles,
has his mind continually employed on those whom
no one doubts to be now reigning in the palace of
the heavenly Jerusalem, with the King of Glory."[5]

Let me add an extract from the works of a contemporary, whose name is too well-known, and
whose words are worth copying, because he was
quite a march-of-intellect man.   Peter Abelard,
after quoting the statements of Jerome, and saying
that, from the injunction laid on him, some persons
gathered that it was unlawful to read any secular
books, adds, " I conceive, however, that reading in
any of the arts is not forbidden to a religious man ;
unless it may be that by it his greater usefulness
may be hindered ; and we must do in this as we
know must be done in some other good things—
namely, the less must sometimes be intermitted, or
altogether given up, for the sake of the greater.
For when there is no falsehood in the doctrine, no
impropriety in the language, some utility in the
knowledge, who is to be blamed for learning or
teaching these things ? unless because, as I have
already said, some greater good be neglected or
omitted ; for no man can say that knowledge is,

---

[5] Prol. Bib. Pat. tom. X. p. 1179.

strictly speaking, evil. But how greatly this may
be done to our condemnation and confusion every
reflecting person may see ; since we are not only
told that 'the mouth that belieth slayeth the soul'
(Wisd. i. 11), but also that an account will be
required of every idle word. If a Christian chooses
to read for critical knowledge of phrases and forms
of speech, may he not do this sufficiently without
studying the figments of the poets and foolish tales ?
What kind of phraseology, what ornament of
language is there, which the phrase of scripture does
not supply ? Full as it is of enigmatical allegories,
and abounding as it does with mystical language,
what elegances of speech are there which may not
be learned from the mother tongue, Hebrew ?
especially when it appears that the common people
of Palestine were so accustomed to parables, that it
behoved the Lord Jesus to address them in that way
when he preached the Gospel to them. What
dainty can be wanting at the spiritual table of the
Lord,—that is, the Sacred Scripture—wherein, according to Gregory, both the elephant may swim
and the lamb may walk ? "   Then, after proceeding
to show that as much, and as good, language as can be
wanted, may be had from Jerome, Augustine,
Cyprian, and other Christian writers, he says—
" Why then do not the bishops and doctors of the
Christian religion expel from the city of God, those
poets whom Plato forbade to enter into his city of
the world ? " [6]
I might go on with extracts of this kind until we
should come again to De Rancé; but I am afraid
that the reader may think that I have already cited
more testimonies than enough on this point. Should
there, however, be anything like tautology in them,
I beg him to remember that my object in bringing
them forward is to describe and illustrate a feeling

---

[6] Theol. Christ. Lib. II. *Mart.* tom. V. p. 1238.

which existed very generally in the Christian Church before, and through, and after, the Dark Ages. That there were, even in those days, reading men, I hope to show ; and that they did not give the first place to classical or scientific learning, I allow, though I cannot admit that it was from pure ignorance of the sources of information; and the question naturally arises—What did they read ? This inquiry I hope to pursue, and to begin by showing that there were some persons—perhaps a good many—who read the Bible.

No. XII.

" Omissis igitur et repudiatis nugis theatricis et poeticis, divinarum Scripturarum consideratione, et tractatione pascamus animum atque potemus vanæ curiositatis fame ac siti fessum et æstuantem, et inanibus phantasmatibus, tanquam pictis epulis, frustra refici satiarique cupientem."—AUGUSTINUS.

THERE is no subject in the history of mankind which appears to me more interesting, and more worthy of investigation, than the actual state of the Christian church during the dark ages. It is, as I have already said, with a view to this that I have entered on this series of papers ; and having now, I trust, in some degree, cleared the way, by exposing some popular misstatements, I hope to come more directly to the point. To begin, then, with an inquiry respecting the Christian knowledge, or the means of such knowledge, which existed in those days ; and to begin this at the beginning—Did they know anything about THE BIBLE ?

I believe that the idea which many persons have of ecclesiastical history may be briefly stated thus : that the Christian church was a small, scattered, and persecuted flock, until the time of Constantine ; that then, at once, and as if by magic, the Roman world became Christian ; that this Universal Christianity, not being of a very pure, solid, or durable nature, melted down into a filthy mass called Popery, which held its place during the dark ages, until the revival of Pagan literature, and the consequent march of intellect, sharpened men's wits and brought about the Reformation ; when it was discovered that the pope was Antichrist, and that the saints had been in the hands of the little horn predicted by the prophet Daniel for hundreds of years without knowing so awful a fact, or suspecting anything of the kind. How much of this is true, and how much false, this is not the place to inquire; but I feel bound to refer to this opinion, because the necessity of describing the church during the kingdom of the Apocalyptic Beast in such a way as scarcely to admit of her visible existence, even when it has not led popular writers on the prophecies to falsify history, has at least prepared their readers to acquiesce without surprise or inquiry in very partial and delusive statements.

There is another point which I would just notice, because it has given colour to the statements of all the writers, who, from whatever motive, have maintained the entire ignorance of the dark ages,—I mean the complaints made by contemporary writers of the neglect of the word of God, as well as of the other sins of those ages. I have before alluded to something like this of a more general nature, and will here only give a single specimen; and that not so much to prove or illustrate what is plain and notorious, as because it is somewhat curious and characteristic in itself, and relates to one of the most early versions of the Scripture into the vernacular tongue.

William of Bamberg, as he is commonly called, who was a monk of Fulda, and afterwards abbot of St. Peter's by Mersburg (about the year 1070), wrote a translation, or rather a double paraphrase, of the Book of Canticles, in Latin verse and Teutonic prose, to which he prefixed the following preface :—

" When I look at the studies of our ancestors, whereby they became famous in respect of the Sacred Scriptures, I am forced to lament the depravity of this age, when almost every literary pursuit has ceased, and there is nothing going on but avarice, envy, and strife. For if there are any who, under scholastic discipline, are instructed in grammatical and dialectical studies, they think that this is enough for them, and entirely neglect the Holy Scripture ; whereas it is on account of that only that it is lawful for Christians to read heathen books, in order that they may perceive the great difference between light and darkness, truth and error. Others, however, though they are mighty in sacred learning, yet, hiding in the earth the talent committed to them, laugh at those who make mistakes in reading and chanting, though they take no pains to help their infirmity, either by instructing them or correcting their books. I found, in France, that one man, named Lantfrid[1] (who had previously been much distinguished in dialectics, but who had then betaken himself to ecclesiastical studies), had by his own acuteness sharpened the minds of many in the Epistles of St. Paul and the Psalms; and as many of our countrymen flock to hear him, I hope that. after his example, they also will produce the fruit of their industry in our provinces, to the benefit of many. And as it often happens that through an impulse given by generous steeds the half-bred horse is set a running (although I am not ignorant of the dulness of my poor genius, yet hoping to have a merciful God for my helper), I also have determined, according to my small means, to offer to the studious reader some little help towards improvement. I have determined, therefore, if God permit, to explain the Song of Songs, whose very name testifies its eminence, both in verse and in the Teutonic language, in such a way, that the text being placed in the middle, these two versions may accompany it down the sides, and thereby whatsoever is sought may be more easily found. I have added nothing of my own, but have compressed all I could find in the various expositions of the fathers; and, both in the verses and in the Teutonic translation, I have taken more pains about the sense than the words. Sometimes I repeat the same verses; for those things which the Holy Spirit has repeated in the same words, it does not appear improper for me to repeat in the same verses. I have thought it good to distribute the parts to the Bridegroom and the Bride, both in the translation and in the verses, as well as the text, not only that they may have the greater appearance of authority, but that the reader may be gratified by the persons speaking alternately. I do not know whether I am the dupe of a pleasing delusion; but if not, surely he who rained on Solomon hath also condescended to shed some few drops on me. Sometimes on reading what I have written I am as much delighted as if it was the work of an approved author. I offer this little work, as long as I live, to the correction of those who are more learned; if I have done wrong in anything, I shall not be ashamed to receive their admonitions; and if there is anything which they like, I shall not be slow to furnish more."[2]

---

[1] That is, our Archbishop Lanfranc.

[2] *M. & D.* I. 501. To this poor monk's own account of his performance, it is only justice to add the testimony of a learned Protestant :—" Paraphrasiu Willerami mire commendat Junius, autorem vocat præstantis ingenii virum, et rerum theologicarum consultissimum, qui in hac provincia administranda, et vero sensu connubialis carminis eruendo tanta dexteritate est et fide versatus,

To come, however, to the question—did people in the dark ages know anything of the Bible? Certainly it was not as commonly known and as generally in the hands of men as it is now, and has been almost ever since the invention of printing—the reader must not suspect me of wishing to maintain any such absurd opinion ; but I do think that there is sufficient evidence—(I.) that during that period the scriptures were more accessible to those who could use them—(II.) were in fact more used—and (III.) by a greater number of persons—than some modern writers would lead us to suppose.

The worst of it is, that the proof must not only be defective—for on what subject connected with that period can it be otherwise ?—but that, if by any means fully produced, it must be so voluminous as to be quite inadmissible in a work like the present. It is not by generalizing on particular cases, as has been the fault of some writers whose statements I have noticed, but by accumulating a great number of facts—facts, too, of very different descriptions, and forming totally distinct parts of the proof—that anything like a correct idea can be formed. It is absurd for Robertson to say that monasteries of considerable note had only one missal, because the Abbot Bonus found only one in the ruined chapel at Pisa. It is as absurd in Warton to tell us that " at the beginning of the tenth century books were so scarce in Spain that one and the same copy of the Bible, St. Jerome's Epistles, and some volumes of ecclesiastical offices and martyrologies, *often* served for different monasteries," [3] because old Gennadius, Bishop of Astorga, thought fit, after dividing many other books among four monasteries or oratories, which he had founded in his diocese, to give them

---

ut paucos habuerit ex antiquis illis, quos se vidisse et legisse notat, pares ; priorem fere neminem."—*Cave, Hist. Lit.* tom. ii. p. 148.

[3] Diss. ii.

his Bible and some other books as common property.[4] I think it would be quite as fair and as

---

[4] Warton refers to Fleury, L. LIV. c. liv. but adds, " See other
instances in Hist. Lit. Fr. par Rel Benedict. vii. 3." To this
book I have not access at present ; but I shall be much surprised
to find that it contains other instances sufficient to support this
assertion.

Since I wrote this note I have received a letter from a friend
whom I requested to look out the reference, in which he says, " It
is curious that you should be again sent back to your old friend,
the Homilies of Haimo ; the whole passage is not long, and I
shall, therefore, transcribe it. Hist. Lit. tom. vii. p. 3, n. 3.

" ' III. A ce defaut presque generale d'inclination pour les
lettres, qui avoit sa source dans le genie de la nation, se réunirent
plusieurs autres causes, qui concoururent à entretenir l'ignorance.
Le X siècle n'avoit pas été suffisant pour reparer *les pertes de
livres* qu'avoit souffert la France, dans les courses précédentes, les
pillages, les incendies, des Sarasins, des Normans, des Hongrois,
des Bulgares. *Quoiqu'on eût travaillé à renouveller ces livres,
comme nous l'avons montré,* ils étoient encore fort rares, ce qui
rendoit les études très-difficiles. D'ailleurs n'y aïant presque que
des moines qui s'occupoient à les copier, ils commencerent par
ceux qu'ils croïoient plus nécessaires : *la Bible* et les livres
liturgiques, les écrits des Peres, les recueils des Canons. Ainsi il
se passa du temps, avant qu'ils pussent transcrire les Historiens,
les Poëtes, les Orateurs. Et le defaut de ces ouvrages contribua
beaucoup aux mauvaises Etudes et à la barbarie qui y regnoit. On
avoit cependant de cette sorte d'auteurs : mais ils n'étoient pas
communes.—(*Mab.* an. 1. 61, n. 6). Un trait que l'histoire a
conservé touchant le prix excessif des livres en ce temps-là nous
doit faire juger de leur rareté. Encore s'agit-il d'un auteur
ecclesiastique, le recueil des Homelies d'Haimon d'Halberstat.
Grécie Comtesse d'Anjou,' &c., &c.

" The rest of the paragraph I think I sent you before ; or, at
least, you know its contents. [The reader may find it in No. V.
p. 82.] And it appears that there is nothing whatever about one
book serving many monasteries ; nay, the inference from the whole
passage is the very reverse of the statement for which it is quoted
by Warton ; and it relates, not to Spain, but to France. I therefore looked in the index of the volume, in hope that the reference
might possibly be misprinted ; but I find nothing at all like the
statement in Warton's text."

I do not wish to lengthen this note by any remarks on this
passage, which I adduce as being the authority on which Warton
relied ; but I have marked one or two words by *italics,* which
show what an important bearing it has on the subject in general,
and particularly on that part with which we are at present engaged.

foolish for me to say, "In the ninth century the
bishops used to write Bibles for their churches with
their own hands," because I find that Wicbert, who
became bishop of Wildesheim in the year 880, did
so. Still such notices are not to be passed over;
and I will here offer a few, to which, I have no
doubt, many more might be added if I had access
to more books. Though I put them first, I beg the
reader not to suppose that I consider them as the
most important part of the proof, but only offer
them as notices not entirely uninteresting in themselves, and as forming a part, though a small one,
of the proof required.

1. In the first place, then, whoever reads the
writers—perhaps I should say principally the
historians—of those ages will find them not unfrequently speaking of the Bible. I do not mean
referring to it as an authority, or quoting its
contents, or, if I may so express myself, speaking of
it in the abstract (for this is quite another part of
the subject), but incidentally mentioning the
existence of Bibles at various times, and in places
where they were accessible to many readers. I
need not repeat that the proof must be defective,
not only because we may reasonably suppose that
those copies of the Bible which happen to be thus
incidentally mentioned, in the comparatively few
documents which have come down to us, were but a
very small part of those which were in existence,
but because the instances which I can give are only
such as I happen to have met with in circumstances
not very favourable to research on such subjects.

When Aldhelm, who became bishop of Schireburn
in the year 705, went to Canterbury to be consecrated by his old friend and companion Berthwold
(pariter literis studuerant, pariterque viam religionis
triverant), the archbishop kept him there many days,
taking counsel with him about the affairs of his
diocese. Hearing of the arrival of ships at Dover,
during this time, he went there to inspect their

unloading, and to see if they had brought anything in his way (si quid forte commodum ecclesiastico usui attulissent nautæ qui e Gallico sinu in Angliam provecti librorum copiam apportassent). Among many other books he saw one containing the whole of the Old and New Testament, which—to omit the incidents for the sake of which the fact is recorded, but which are not to our purpose—he at length bought; and William of Malmesbury, who wrote his life in the twelfth century, tells us that it was still preserved at that place.[5]

In the year 780, King Offa gave to the church at Worcester, among other things, a great Bible— magnam Bibliam.[6]

It was probably soon after—for he became bishop of Orleans about or before the year 794—that Theodulfus made his great Bible, which is still in existence; at least it was so in the days of Father Sirmond, in whose works the reader may find the verses which the bishop prefixed to it, and the preface, which was written in gold.[7]

In the list of books given to his monastery by Ansegisus, who became abbot of Fontanelle in the year 823, we find " Bibliothecam optimam continens vetus et novum Testamentum, cum præfationibus ac initiis librorum aureis literis decoratis;"[8] and among those which he gave to the monastery of St. Flavian, " Pandecten a B. Hieronymo ex hebræo vel græco eloquio translatum."[9]

---

[5] Ang. Sac. ii. 21.   [6] Ibid. i. 470.   [7] Sirm. Op. tom. ii. p. 763.
[8] Chron. Fontan. ap. Dach. Sp. ii. 280.
[9] Ibid. 281. I do not know that this name was ever general, or that it was used by any writer before Alcwin. In the verses which he wrote in the copy which he corrected by order of Charlemagne (and which the reader may find in Baronius, an. 778, No. xxiii.), he says :—

" Nomine PANDECTEN proprio vocitare memento
  Hoc corpus sacrum, lector, in ore tuo ;
Quod nunc a multis constat BIBLIOTHECA dicta
  Nomine non proprio, ut lingua Pelasga docet."

As to the name *Bibliotheca*, I have already had occasion to

In a return of their property which the monks of
St. Riquier at Centule made, by order of Lewis the
Debonnaire, in the year 831, we find, among a con-
siderable quantity of books, " Bibliotheca integra ubi
continentur libri lxxii. in uno volumine ; " and also,
" Bibliotheca dispersa in voluminibus 14."[1]

In the year 843 the Normans came up the Loire,
and laid waste Nantes, and the surrounding country.
After killing the bishop in his cathedral, with many
of the clergy, monks, and laity who had sought
refuge there, they loaded their vessels with spoil
and captives, and proceeded along the Loire to an
island, where they began to divide their prey. In
doing this, they quarrelled and fought, and many of
them were killed. " The captives, however," says
the historian, " seeing the storm, all fled into the
more inaccessible parts of the island ; but among
them there was one who ventured on a very bold
stroke (magnæ invasionis audax). He took on his
back the great Bible, which is preserved to this day
[probably in or before the twelfth century] in the
great church of Nantes, and ran off to hide himself,
with the rest, in the mines." The Normans having
fought till they were tired, those who survived were
seized with a panic; in consequence of which they
gathered up the spoil, and set sail, without troubling
themselves about the captives, who at length got
safe back to Nantes, having lost much in silver, and
gold, and books, and saving only their Bible,
" solummodo Bibliothecam afferentes."[2]

It is somewhat curious that, among the little
scraps of history which have come down to us, we

---

mention that it was the common name for a Bible. It seems to
have arisen (I know not how properly) from the words of Jerome,
who, offering to lend books, says to Florentius, " et quoniam
largiente Domino, multis sacræ bibliothecæ codicibus abundamus,"
&c.—*Ep.* VI. *ad Flor.* tom. i. p. 19. I.

[1] Chron. Centul. ap. Dach. Sp. ii. 311.
[2] Frag. Hist. Armor. ap. Mart. iii. 830.

find a notice of another Bible in the same year, and
very near the same place.   In a charter cited by Du
Cange, from the tabulary of the monastery of St.
Maur, on the Loire, we find—" Donum autem con-
firmat Bibliotheca Veteris et Novi Testamenti ; " [3]
the Bible having been used, I presume, in the conveyance of some property in the way which I have
described in No. V. p. 99.   Indeed, it seems as if
they were in the habit of so using their Bible at
that monastery ; for in another charter, bearing
date 847, and conveying property to it, we find—
" Donum autem hujus rei est hæc Bibliotheca
Veteris ac Novi Testamenti." [4]

In the short interval between the dates of these
two charters—that is, in the year 845—Hamburg
was burned, and the Bible which Lewis the
Debonnaire had given to Anscharius was, with
many other books, destroyed by fire—" Bibliotheca,
quam serenissimus jam memoratus Imperator eidem
patri nostro contulerat, optime conscripta, cum
plurimis aliis libris igni disperiit." [5]

Everhard, Count of Friuli, by his will, dated A.D.
867, divided his books among his children, leaving
to his eldest son " Bibliothecam nostram." [6]   This
Count, before the time just specified, had founded a
monastery at Cisoing (a little to the south between
Lille and Tournay), and it appears that a monk
named Wulgarius, who states that he had laboured
in the monastery ever since its foundation, presented to it several books, among which we find
" Bibliothecam 1." [7]

Wicbert, who became bishop of Hildesheim in
the year 880, I have already mentioned as writing
a Bible with his own hand.   The chronicler who

[3] Du Cange in v. *Bibliotheca.*
[4] Given by Baluze Capit. Reg. Franc. tom. ii. p. 1456.
[5] Vita S. Anscharii int. add. ad Lambecii Orig. Hamburg. c.
xiv. p. 59.
[6] Dach. Sp. ii. 877.   [7] Ibid. p. 879.

records the fact, and who probably wrote in the
twelfth century, says, " Bibliothecam quæ adhuc in
monasterio servatur, propria manu elaboravit." [8]

Gennadius, who bequeathed his Bible, as part of
a sort of circulating library, to his four monasteries
or oratories, I have also already mentioned. He
describes it as " Bibliothecam totam." [9]

Olbert, who was abbot of Gembloux until the
year 1048, wrote out a volume containing the whole
of the Old and New Testament; [1] and the unfor-

---

[8] Chron. Ep. Hildesh. ap. Leib. Sc. Brun. I. 743.

[9] Mab. A. S. vii. p. 36.

[1] This is the person who, under the name of Albert, comes in for
a sneer from Warton on the page just referred to of his second
Dissertation ; " Albert, Abbot of Gemblours, who, with incredible
labour and immense expense, had collected an hundred volumes
on theological, and fifty on profane subjects, imagined he had
formed a splendid library." The " incredible labour and immense
expense," and the Abbot's own imagination of the splendour of his
library, are, I believe, as purely poetical as anything that Warton
ever wrote. Fleury, to whom he refers, says only, " Etant Abbé,
il amassa à Gembloux plus de cent volumes d'auteurs ecclesias-
tiques, et cinquante d'auteurs profanes, ce qui passoit pour une
grande bibliotheque."—Liv. LVIII. c. lii. tom. XII. p. 424. The
fact, however, is, that he was a monk of Lobbes, who was sent to
reform and restore the monastery of Gembloux, which was in a
state of great poverty and disorder—exterius ingrueret gravis rei
familiaris tenuitas, interius autem horreret grendis irreligiositas—
and he did, according to the account of his biographer, in a marvellously short time, restore discipline, build a church, and provide
many things needful for the monastery, and among others the 150
volumes of books. As to the " incredible labour," we are expressly
told that he set his monks to write, to keep them from being idle ;
and as to the " immense expense," his biographer's remark is, that
it is wonderful how one man, with such slender means, could do so
much as he did. " Non passus enim ut per otium mens aut manus
eorum torpesceret, utiliter profectui eorum providet, dum eos per
scribendi laborem exercet, et frequenti scripturarum meditatione
animos eorum ad meliora promovet. Appellens ergo animum ad
construendum pro posse suo bibliothecam, quasi quidam Philadel-
phus, plenariam vetus et novum Testamentum continentem in uno
volumine transcripsit historiam ; et divinæ quidem scripturæ plus-
quam centum congessit volumina, sæcularis vero disciplinæ libros
quinquaginta. Mirandum sane hominem unum in tanta tenuitate
rerum, tanta potuisse comparare, nisi occurreret animo, timentibus

tunate Bonus, who was abbot at Pisa at exactly the
same time, gave (as we have already seen) ten
pounds for what he describes as a " liber Bibliothece."[2]

Among the books which Thierry, who became
the first abbot of the restored monastery of St.
Evroul, or Ebrulf, at Ouche, in the diocese of
Lisieux, in the year 1050, caused to be written for
that monastery, we find, " omnes libros veteris et
novi Testamenti."[3]

Stephen, who became abbot of Beze, in the year
1088, gave the monastery a " Bibliotheca, tam
veteris quam novi Testamenti."[4]

Wicbert's Bible, twice mentioned already, did not
prevent Bruno, who succeeded him in the see of
Hildesheim in the year 1153, from presenting to
the library a glossed Bible—" contulit ad ipsum
armarium totum Testamentum novum et vetus,
utrumque glossatum "[5]—and this was followed by
another glossed Bible, very carefully elaborated,

Deum nihil deesse."—Mab. A. S. tom. viii. p. 531. The reader
will here observe that use of the phrase " divina scriptura," which
I have before noticed, and of which it would be easy to give
instances; one of the most curious is perhaps that in the Burton
Annals (Gale, iii. 264). King John is represented as saying to
the Pope's Nuncio, " unde videre potestis per *sacras scripturas*
quod beatus et gloriosus rex sanctus Edwardus contulit in tempore
suo Sancto Wulstano episcopatum Wigorniæ," &c.

[2] When I mentioned the Abbot's Bible before (No. IV. p. 47),
I gave a specimen of his latinity ; and this morsel may give me
an opportunity of suggesting to the reader that we are not, in all
cases, to take it for granted that there was nobody better able to
understand, or to describe a book, than the person who happens to
have incidentally noticed its existence, or to have made an inventory
of various things, and of books among the rest. For instance, the
list of books belonging to the church of St. James and St. Chris-
topher, at Stedeburg, which Leibnitz gives us (I. 870), begins
with " Liber Genesis Biblia," and contains " Liber in Principio et
evangeliorum secundum Marcum." I do not mention this Bible in
the text, because I do not know the date of this list. The more
modern it is, the more it is to the purpose of this note.

[3] Mab. A. S. ix. 136.   [4] Chron. Bes. ap. Dach. Sp. ii. 435.

[5] Chron. Hildesh. ap. Leib. Sc. Br. i. 747.

and presented by Berno, who succeeded to the see
in the year 1190—"contulit etiam ecclesiæ veteris
ac novi Testamenti libros glossatos et magno
scholasticæ diligentiæ studio elaboratos." [6]

To these instances I doubt not that a little trouble
would add many more; but I am afraid that the
reader has already found them tedious, and I will
here only add some notice of a correspondence
between Geoffry, sub-prior of St. Barbara, in
Normandy, and John, the abbot, and Peter, one of
the monks, of Baugercy, in the diocese of Tours,
some time between the dates just specified, and
probably about the year 1170. The sub-prior begins
one of his letters thus :—

" To his Venerable Abbot John, Geoffry, the servant of your
holiness, wishes that which is the true health. I received the
letters of your affection, which seemed to my heart to be sweetened
with the honey of love. I read them eagerly; I now read them
again gladly; and, often read over, they still please. Of this only
I complain, that you send so few and such short letters to one who
loves you, and whom you love, so much. You seldom converse
with me, and I should like the conversation to be longer. I should
like to hear something from you that might instruct us as to our
life and conversation, relieve the weariness of our pilgrimage, and
inflame us with the love of our heavenly country. I must also tell
you that the excellent Bible (Bibliothecam optimam), of which I
wrote to you long ago, you may still find at Caen, if you wish it."

The Abbot in his reply (which I presume was not
a speedy one, for he begins it with reproaching the
sub-prior that he had been so long silent) takes no
notice of the Bible, unless it be by saying at the
close of his letter, " Peter Mangot salutes you ; to
whom I wish that you would write, and comfort
him in the Lord, and among other things admonish
him about buying a Bible." It seems to have been
the custom of these two friends to add one, two, or
three couplets to their letters, in the way of
marginal notes, referring to the subjects on which

[6] Ibid. 749.

they were writing. The second of the two couplets
on this occasion is as follows :—

> " Ardenti studio sacra perlege dogmata, si vis
> Dulcis aquæ saliente sitim restringere rivo.''

This letter produced one from Geoffry to Peter
Mangot, who seems to have been a monk of Baugercy, who had undertaken and obtained permission
to build a monastery.

" To his beloved and friend Peter Mangot, brother Geoffry wishes
health and perseverance in the work begun.

" God has fulfilled your desire,—you have what you so ardently
sought. You have got what you asked from me, from the King
through me, and from the chapter of Citeaux through the King's
letters, and the help of others. These things, indeed, seemed very
difficult at first, and, from the circumstances of the case, we were
almost in despair; but God himself looked upon us with an eye of
mercy, and with a strong hand made all things plain before our
face. Go on, then, with increasing devotion in a work that was
first conceived with a devout intention, and devoutly begun ; and
carefully provide all that is necessary for it. Build up a temple
to the Lord of living and elect stones, who may receive you into
eternal habitations. I give thanks to the grace of God which
worketh in you ; I give thanks also to you, who are working
together with that grace ; for the grace of God, which without
you, wrought in you a good will, now worketh by you."

He afterwards adds :—

" A monastery (claustrum) without a library (sine armario) is
like a castle (castrum) without an armory (sine armamentario).
Our library is our armory. Thence it is that we bring forth the
sentences of the divine law, like sharp arrows, to attack the enemy.
Thence we take the armour of righteousness, the helmet of salvation, the shield of faith, and the sword of the Spirit which is the
word of God. See to it, therefore, that in your armory of defence
that which is the great defence of all the other defences is not
wanting. That defence is the Holy Bible, wherein is contained
the right rule of life and manners. There each sex and every age
finds what is profitable. There spiritual infancy finds that whereby
it may grow, youth that which may strengthen it, age that which
may support it,—a blessed hand which ministers to all, whereby
all may be saved. If therefore you have taken care to provide the
arms for this warfare, you will have nothing to do but to say to
him, ' Take thine arms and thy shield, and arise to my help.'
Farewell! and take care that the Bible, which no monastery
should be without, is bought."

To this letter three couplets are added, of which the third is as follows :—

> " Quamvis multorum multi placeant tibi libri
> Hanc habeas, sapias, sufficit ipsa tibi." [7]

It does not appear (and as our inquiry relates in a great degree to the possibility of obtaining such things in those days, it is worth while to notice the circumstance) that this recommendation to procure a Bible had anything to do with the *Bibliotheca optima* at Caen; for, in a subsequent letter, the Abbot John requests his friend Geoffry to secure it for him.[8]

All the instances which I have given refer to the whole Bible, or, as it is expressed in some of them, the *Bibliotheca integra*, or *Bibliotheca tota;* but I must beg the reader's attention to one circumstance, which is important, if we would understand matters aright. Undoubtedly Bibles were scarce in those days ; but we are not hastily to conclude that wherever there existed no single book called a Bible, the contents of the Bible were unknown. The canon of Scripture was settled, indeed, as it is now ; but the several parts of which the Bible

---

[7] The other four lines have nothing to do with our immediate subject, but I hope the reader will forgive my quoting them, as belonging to a writer of the dark ages. From his correspondence, in which the reader who is not fastidious as to style (or, rather, as to latinity), may find much that is interesting, I hope at some future time to give farther extracts. After

> " Petrus vocaris firmus esto,"

we find these four lines, or, rather, two couplets, which seem to have reference to different parts of his letter, and to have been originally unconnected with each other, as also with the third couplet quoted above :—

> " In Christo petra fidei fundamine jacto
> Spe paries surgit, culmina complet amor.
> Vivit agendo fides ; ubi non est actus amoris,
> Gignit abortivam spem moribunda fides."

[8] Mart. i. 502, 509, 514.

consists were considered more in the light of
separate and independent books than they are by
us. To copy *all* these books was a great undertaking; and even when there was no affectation of
caligraphy or costly ornament, and when we reduce
the exaggerated statements about the price of
materials to something reasonable, it was not only a
laborious but a very expensive matter. Of course,
writing and printing are very different things. I
do not pretend to speak with accuracy (for it would
require more trouble than the thing is worth), but
I am inclined to suppose that at this day a copy of
our English Bible, paid for at the rate at which law-
stationers pay their writers for common fair-copy
on paper, would cost between sixty and seventy
pounds for the writing only; and farther, that the
scribe must be both expert and industrious to
perform the task in much less than ten months. It
must be remembered, however, that the monasteries
contained (most of them some, and many a considerable number of) men who were not to be paid by
their work or their time, but who were officially
devoted to the business. Of this, however, I hope
to say more hereafter, and to show that there was a
considerable power of multiplication at work. In
the meantime, I mention these circumstances merely
as reasons why we should not expect to meet with
frequent mention of *whole* Bibles in the dark ages.
Indeed, a scribe must have had some confidence in
his own powers and perseverance who should have
undertaken to make a transcript of the whole Bible;
and that (except under particular circumstances)
without any adequate motive, supposing him to have
practised his art as a means of subsistence. For
those who were likely to need and to reward his
labours either already possessed some part of the
Scriptures, and therefore did not require a transcript of the whole, or, if it was their first attempt
to possess any portion, there were but few whose
means or patience would render it likely that they

should think of acquiring the whole at once. It is obvious, too, that when copies of *parts* had been multiplied, that very circumstance would lead to the transcription of other *parts*, which would comparatively seldom be formed into one volume. We may well imagine that a scribe would prefer undertaking to write a Pentateuch, or adding the two next books a Heptateuch, or with one more an Octateuch, or a Psalter, or a Textus containing one or more of the Gospels, or a Book of Proverbs, or a set of the Canonical Epistles, or some one or other of the portions into which the Bible was at that time very commonly divided. Of these I hope to speak hereafter, and only mention their existence now as one reason why we are not to take it for granted, that all persons who did not possess what we call " a Bible " must have been entirely destitute and ignorant of the Holy Scriptures.

No. XIII.

" Sunk in the lowest state of earthly depression, making their pilgrimage in sackcloth and ashes, pressed by every art and engine of human hostility, by the blind hatred of the half-barbarian kings of feudal Europe, by the fanatical furies of their ignorant people, and, above all, by the great spiritual domination, containing in itself a mass of solid and despotic strength unequalled in the annals of power, vivified and envenomed by a reckless antipathy unknown in the annals of the passions,—what had they [the Scriptures] to do but perish?"

HITHERTO I have spoken only of whole Bibles; and I have observed, that it would be unreasonable to expect that we should find notice of any very considerable number during the Dark Ages; not only because all books were scarce—not only because such notices, and the finding of them, are merely accidental—but because the Bible was comparatively seldom formed into one volume, and more commonly existed in its different parts. To mention all the notices which occur of these parts, and all the proofs which exist, that they must have been numerous, would be both tedious and useless; but it will tend to illustrate, not only the immediate question before us, but our general subject, if I say a few words of copies of the Gospels; at least, of some which may be worthy of notice, from their costly decorations, or from the persons by whom they were possessed, or to, or by, whom they were presented.

I have already said something on the subject of costly books; and I only refer to it here in order to correct a mistake. I stated the case of an "Elector of Bavaria, who *gave* a town for a single manuscript"; [1] whereas I should have said, that he *offered* a town for it; but that the monks, wisely considering that he could, and suspecting that he would, retake the town whenever he pleased, declined the exchange. The MS. remained in their library in the beginning of the eighteenth century; and is, for anything that I know, still there. [2]

I have before referred to St. Jerome's testimony as to the splendour of some books even in his day; and I may just mention the present of the Emperor Justin to Pope Hormisda, made between the years 518 and 523, and including a splendid copy of the Gospels—" sub hujus episcopatu multa vasa aurea venerunt de Græcia, et evangelia cum tabulis aureis, cum gemmis preciosis pensantibus lib. 15," &c. [3]

As to the period, however, with which we are particularly engaged, Leo III., who was pope when it began (having been raised to the pontificate in the year 795), gave to one church " Evangelium ex auro mundissimo cum gemmis ornatum pensans libras . . . ; " [4] and to another (as I have already stated) a copy which seems to have been still more splendid. [5]

---

[1] No. V. p. 87.

[2] I made the statement on the authority (as I thought) of Baring, who mentions the circumstance in his Clavis Diplomatica, 2nd edit. p. 5; and the word " obtulit " conveyed to my mind, from its constant use in charters, diplomas, and all the documents to which his work has reference, no other idea than that of giving —that is, offering what was not rejected. Whether he meant this, I do not know. He might be mistaken on that point, as well as with regard to its contents; for it was not a New Testament, but a book of the Gospels, as we learn from a letter dated 3rd Oct., 1717, and published by Martene in his second Voyage Litteraire. The writer says, " Le Livre aux Evangiles que je vis dans l'Abbaye de Saint Emeram, est encore une rare et très riche antiquité, c'est un don de l'Empereur Henry IV. On m'a dit que Maximilien, grand-père du Duc de Baviere d'à present, ne sçavoit assez l'admirer, et qu'il en avoit offert sa ville de Straubingen avec ses dépendances ; mais les bons moines, persuadez que ce Duc les leur reprendroit ensuite, quand il voudroit, trouverent convenable de refuser un si bel offre."—p. 177.

[3] Conc. iv. 1416.   [4] Ib. vii. 1083.   [5] See No. V. p. 92.

When the abbot Angilbert restored the Abbey of St. Riquier, in A.D. 814, he gave to it (beside two hundred other books) a copy of the Gospel, written in letters of gold, with silver plates, marvellously adorned with gold and precious stones.[6]

Ansegisus, who became Abbot of Fontenelle in A.D. 823, ordered the four Gospels to be written with gold, on purple vellum, in the Roman letter; and lived to see the Gospels of St. Matthew, St. Luke, and St. John completed.[7]

At the translation of the remains of St. Sebastian and St. Gregory to the monastery of St. Medard, at Soissons, in A.D. 826, Lewis the Debonnaire gave several rich presents; and, among others, a copy of the Gospels, written in letters of gold, and bound in plates of the same metal, of the utmost purity.[8]

Hincmar, who became archbishop of Rheims in the year 845, caused a Gospel to be written for his church in letters of gold and silver, and bound in gold, adorned with gems;[9] and another, specially for the crypt to which the remains of St. Remigius were translated, he bound in the same way (parietibus aureis gemmarumque nitore distinctis munivit[1]).

Leo IV., who became pope two years later, gave four catholic books (quatuor catholicos libros) to the church of the Virgin Mary, thirty miles from Rome (unum Evangeliorum, alium Regnorum, Psalmorum, atque Sermonum[2]), of which I do not find that they were peculiarly ornamented; but he gave to another church a copy bound in silver plates—" codex Evangeliorum cum tabulis argenteis."[3]

Of the splendid donations of his successor, Bene-

---

[6] Mab. Act. Sanct. O. B. tom. v. p. 110.

[7] Mab. ibid. tom. vi. p. 597.

[8] Ibid. viii. 388.

[9] Flodoardi Hist. Remen. l. iii. c. v. ap. Sirmondi Op. tom. iv. p. 113.

[1] Ib. c. ix. p. 119.   [2] Conc. tom. viii. p. 22.   [3] Ib. p. 27.

dict III., who became pope in A.D. 855, I have
already spoken ;[4] and I may here add that during
his time the Emperor Michael sent as a present to
St. Peter's (by the hand of the monk Lazarus,
" pictoriæ artis nimie eruditi ") a Gospel, of most
pure gold, with divers precious stones.[5]

Everhard, Count of Friuli, whose will of the year
861 has been already mentioned, beside his Bible,
bequeathed to his children a considerable number of
other books, and among them a Gospel bound in
gold—another in ivory—another in silver—another,
which is not particularly described.[6]

A charter of William, Abbot of Dijon, relating to
the monastery of Frutari, in Piedmont (and probably
of the year 1014), mentions, among the presents
made to the monks of Dijon, to reconcile them to
the withdrawment of the recent foundation from
dependence on them, " textum unum auro, gemmis
et lapidibus mire ornatum."[7]

Just in the same year we find the Emperor Henry
II., who has been already mentioned in connection
with Meinwerc, Bishop of Paderborn, making a
similar donation to the church of Mersburg ;[8] and a
few years afterwards (in 1022), on occasion of his
recovery from illness, at the Monastery of Monte
Casino, he presented to it a copy of the Gospels,
covered on one side with the most pure gold, and
most precious gems, written in uncial characters,
and illuminated with gold.[9] Returning the same
year into Germany, he had an interview with Robert,
King of France, on the banks of the Meuse, the
common boundary of their dominions; but of
all the rich presents offered by that king—presents
of gold, and silver, and jewels, beside a hundred
horses, completely and sumptuously equipped, and
each bearing a knight's armour—the emperor

---

[4] No. V. p. 92.   [5] Conc. viii. 231.   [6] II. Dach. Sp. 877.
[7] Mab. A. S. viii. 308, et Ann. Benn. an. 1003, xxxiv.
[8] Ditmar. ap. i. Leib. 399.   [9] Mab. A. S. viii. 400.

accepted only a copy of the Gospels, bound in gold
and precious stones, and a reliquary of corresponding
workmanship, containing (or supposed to contain) a
tooth of St. Vincent, for himself, and a pair of gold
ear-rings for the empress.[1]

The biographer, and almost contemporary, of
Ansegisus (who was abbot of St. Riquier, near
Abbeville, and died in 1045), informs us that he
contributed greatly to the enlargement of the
library, and specifies —

> " Librum Evangelii, Sancti vitamque Richari
> Ipsius studio mero argento decoravit.
> Est et Episto-liber-larum, atque Evangeliorum,
> Ipsius argento quem industria nempe paravit."[2]

Desiderius, who became abbot of Monte Casino in
the year 1058 (and who was afterwards Pope Victor
III.), provided his monastery with many costly
books ;[3] and the Empress Agnes, who came, as Leo
Marsicanus says, like another Queen of Sheba, from
the remote parts of Germany, to behold another
Solomon, and another temple, made many rich gifts
(dona magnifica) to the church, and, among the rest,
a copy of the Gospels, with one side (or, if I may so
speak, one board) of cast silver, with chased or
embossed work, very beautifully gilt.[4]

Paul, who became abbot of St. Alban's in the

---

[1] Glab. Rod. ap. Baron. an. 1023, iii.
[2] Mab. A. S. viii. 446.
[3] Librum quoque *Epistolarum* ad missam describi faciens, tabulis
aurea una, altera vero argentea, decoravit. Codicem etiam Regulæ
B. Benedicti pulcro nimis opere deintus comtum, a foris argento
vestivit ; similiter fecit et de Sacramentoriis altariis uno et altero,
et duobus nihilominus *Evangeliis* et *Epistolario* un." *Leo Mar.
ap. Mab.* A. S. ix. 594. After this we read, " Non solum autem
in ædificiis, verum etiam in libris describendis operam Desiderius
dare permaximam studuit ; " and in a very respectable catalogue of
these books we find, " Evangelium majorem auro et lapidibus
pretiosis ornatam, in quo has *reliquias* posuit : de ligno Domini et
de vestimentis Sancti Joannis Evangelistæ."—*Ibid.*, p. 608.
[4] Chron. Cas. Lib. iii. c. xxx. p. 609, and Mab. A. S. ix. 602.

year 1077, gave to that church " duos Textus auro
et argento et gemmis ornatos." [5]

In the same year a charter of Hugh, Duke of
Burgundy, giving the church of Avalon to the
monastery of Clugny (and containing a " descriptio
ornamenti ipsius ecclesiæ "), mentions three copies
of the Gospels, which, I presume, formed a part of
the 115 books belonging to it; " Textus unus
aureus, et unus argenteus, aliusque dimidius." [6]

In a charter of A.D. 1101, concerning the church
at Beze, we find a Textum Evangelii, " coopertum
de argento," used in the manner already repeatedly
referred to, in the conveyance of property.[7]

The author of the history of the monastery of St.
Hubert-en-Ardennes (who wrote in 1106) tells us
that in his time there was remaining in the monastery a very fine copy of the Gospels, adorned with
gold and gems.[8]

Ralph, Bishop of Rochester, in 1114, gave a
" textum pulchre deauratum " to his church ;[9] but
I do not feel certain that in this case the word
" textus " means, as it generally does when it
stands alone (as it obviously does in the cases
hitherto mentioned), a copy of one or more of the
Gospels.

There can, however, be no doubt as to the gift
of Walter, a successor in that see, who became

---

[5] M. Paris, Vit. S. Alb. Abb. tom. i. p. 51.

[6] Dach. Spic. iii. 412.

[7] Chron. Bes. ap. Dach. Spic. ii. 436.

[8] " Superest optimus sanctorum Evangeliorum textus auro gemmisque paratus ; superest psalterium auro scriptum per denos
psalmos capitalibus litteris distinctum." IV. *M. & D.* 919.
Martene adds, in a note on the word " psalterium,"—" Hactenus
servatur in Andaginensi monasterio pretiosissimum psalterium auro
elegantissime exaratum, non a Ludovico Pio, ut credit auctor, sed
a Lothario ipsius filio donatum, ut probant versus qui initio codicis
reperiuntur." The verses, and a full account of this psalter, with
a copy of the portrait of Lothaire contained in it, he has given in
his second Voyage Litteraire, p. 137.

[9] Ang. Sac. i. 342.

bishop in 1148, and gave "textum Evangeliorum aureum."[1]

Perhaps the instances which I have given are more than enough to induce a suspicion that copies of the Gospels, and even such as were of a splendid and costly description, were not unfrequently to be met with even in the Dark Ages ; and yet they are not the notices which most strongly and obviously lead to such an opinion. Some may even consider the fact that a book was given to a church, or a monastery, as implying that it was not already possessed ; and I will therefore add one or two instances, which show that churches not uncommonly (I believe I might say all churches that were at all respectably endowed and appointed) had more than one such book.

We are not, I apprehend, to suppose that the monastery of Glastonbury had no copy of the Gospels when Brethwold (who had been a monk there, and became bishop of Salisbury perhaps in A.D. 1006) sent them two.[2]

Olbert, already mentioned (p. 217), as abbot of Gembloux until A.D. 1048, gave to his monastery (beside the Bible which is there mentioned) one gold and three silver copies of the Gospels, and one silver copy of the Epistles.[3]

Among the furniture of his chapel, bequeathed by King Robert (whose present to the emperor Henry has been noticed at p. 227) to the church of St. Anian, at Orleans, were " deux livres d'Evangiles, garnis d'or, deux d'argent, deux autres petits."[4]

John, Bishop of Bath in 1160, implied a bequest of more than one copy to the Abbey church when he left to the blessed apostle St. Peter, and to his servants the monks (inter alia), all that he had collected "in ornamentis ecclesiasticis," or, as he

[1] Ibid. 345. [2] Guil. Malm. ap. Gale, tom. iii. 325.
[3] Mab. A. S. viii. 530. [4] Fleury, t. xii. p. 491.

proceeded to specify, " in crucibus, in *textibus*, in calicibus," &c.[5] I quote this instance because the reader will observe that these costly books were considered as a part of the treasure of the church, rather than merely as books ; and, indeed, the bishop bequeathed them as a distinct legacy from his whole library (plenarium armarium meum), which he also gave to the church.

For this reason, and not for this only, I will also mention another case, although—perhaps I should say because—it is nearly a century more modern than the period with which we are engaged. At a visitation of the treasury of St. Paul's, in the year 1295, by Ralph de Baudoke, or Baldock, the Dean (afterwards bishop of London), it appears that there were found twelve copies of the Gospels, all adorned with silver, some with gilding, pearls and gems ; and another, which presents an unusual feature—" Textus ligneus desuper ornatus platis argenteis deauratis cum subtili triphorio in superiori limbo continens xi capsas *cum reliquiis* ibidem descriptis." [6] I call the decoration of the Gospels with relics an unusual feature, because, though I have not intentionally suppressed it, it has appeared in only one of the cases already mentioned ; and, common as the custom might afterwards be, I do not believe that it was so (if indeed it could be said to exist as a custom at all) before the thirteenth century. I know of only one other exception, which belongs to the twelfth century, and will be noticed presently.

There is another circumstance which throws some

---

[5] Dugd. Mon. i. 186.

[6] Dugd. Monast. iii. 309, 324. Beside the parts of the Scriptures mentioned above, there were six Epistolaria, four Evangelistaria, two Bibles (one " de bona litera antiqua," and the other " in duobus voluminibus nova peroptimæ literæ"), a glossed copy of the Epistles of St. Paul, the same of the Gospels of St. Luke and St. John, two copies of St. Matthew and St. Mark, with the commentary of Thomas Aquinas, and the twelve prophets, glossed.

light on this point. It may be supposed that great
care was taken of these books ; and in fact they were
frequently kept in cases as valuable, in respect of
ornament, as themselves. Often, indeed, I apprehend, the case was the most valuable of the two,
and is mentioned among the treasure of the church
when the book which it contained is not noticed
because there was nothing uncommon about it, and
no particular circumstance as to its writer or donor
which was thought worthy of record. From some
of the notices, however, of these cases or coverings,[7]
we get farther ground for supposing that there
were not unfrequently a good many copies of the
Gospels in a church or monastery. For instance,
in the St. Riquier return, already more than once
referred to, beside the Bibles which I have noticed,
and beside three other copies of the Gospels and
five lectionaries containing the Epistles and Gospels,
we find, " Evangelium auro Scriptum unum, cum
capsa argentea gemmis et lapidibus fabricata. *Aliæ
capsæ* evangeliorum duæ ex auro et argento
paratæ."[8] A passage, too, in Ado's Chronicle,

---

[7] *Capsæ,* or *coopertoria*—for it is not necessary to speak of the
camisiæ (chemises) *librorum,* which I suppose to have been only
washable covers to keep the books clean,—or *thecæ,* or, as I have
only once found the word used, *bibliothecæ.* At the dedication of
Ripon church, Archbishop Wilfred (who lived till 711)
<blockquote>
"——— quatuor auro
Scribi Evangelii præcepit in ordine libros,
Ac *thecam* e rutilo his condignam condidit auro."
</blockquote>
(Godwin de Præs, 654.)
Or, as the prose historian who wrote soon afterwards informs us,
it was a sort of miracle such as had not been heard of before their
times, being written with the purest gold on purple vellum, and
contained in a superb case,—" necnon et *bibliothecam* librorum
eorum omnem de auro purissimo, et gemmis pretiosissimis fabre-
factam, compaginare inclusores gemmarum præcepit."—Edd. Steph.
ap. Gale, Scr. XV., p. 60. Another name was *cavea,* as the
reader may see in Du Cange, who quotes from Eckhardus, junior
(who wrote about the year 1040), " fit de auro Petri *cavea* Evangelii," &c.
  [8] Chron. Cent. ap. Dach. Spic. ii. 310.

given by Du Cange, seems to imply that the place
to which it refers had several copies, " *Viginti
capsas* evangeliorum ex auro purissimo, gemmario
opere cælatas;"⁹ and William of Malmesbury,
in the account which he gives of the chapel
which King Ina made at Glastonbury, tells us that
twenty pounds and sixty marks of gold were used
in making the " Coopertoria Librorum Evangelii." ¹
Two objections which may be made to the evidence
arising from these *capsæ*, though they do not seem
to me to be of any weight, it may be fair to mention;
—first, we are not certain that the owners always
had quite as many books as they had cases for hold-
ing them ; and, secondly, as these *capsæ* were very
costly and ornamental, those who wrote the history
of their monasteries might be tempted to pretend
that they had more than they really possessed.   If,
however, these same monkish chroniclers, in describing their premises, had told us that the abbot's
stable contained twelve or twenty stalls, we should
be apt to infer, that though some stalls might be
empty, or the number of the whole exaggerated, it
was nevertheless no very uncommon thing for an
abbot to be pretty well furnished with horses ; and
some such inference, confirmed as it is by direct
evidence, I think we may fairly draw with regard to
books.

Hitherto I have only spoken of those costly and
precious volumes which, as I have already remarked,
were considered as belonging to the treasury, rather
than to the library, of the church.   They were, I
apprehend, for the most part, brought out only on
festivals, the church being provided with others for
daily use.   Thus Berward, who became bishop of
Hildesheim in the year 993, and who was (as we
learn from his fond old schoolmaster and biographer,
Tangmar) a man skilful in the arts—if I may use

---

⁹ In v. *Capsæ*.   ¹ Ap. Gale, Scr. XV. 311.

such a word in speaking of such a period,—"fecit et ad solemnem processionem in præcipuis festis, Evangelia auro et gemmis clarissima;" [2] and Martin, the monk of Moutier-neuf, at Poitiers, tells us, that on the anniversary of their founder (Count Geoffry or William, who died in 1086), they used to perform mass in much the same way as on festivals ; and he adds, " nec aureus textus deest." [3]   Indeed, I need not say that such a style of binding could not have been adopted for books in general, or books in common use.   To have bestowed such pains and expense on books for private use, or for any use but that of the church, would have been inconsistent, perhaps, with the ideas of some strict ascetics, and at any rate it could never have become general.[4] Others, perhaps, beside Godehard (the successor of Berward just mentioned, in the see of Hildesheim), had a fancy to adorn their books (though I apprehend that here we must understand service-books) with small stones of white, or black, or red, or variegated hues, cut and polished after the manner of gems.   He used to set the children, and those

---

[2] Leib. Scr. Brun. i. 445.   Mab. A. S. viii. 184.

[3] Hist. Mon. Novi. ap. Mart. iii. 1218.

[4] Thus the Abbot Esaias, in his Præcepta, " ad fratres qui cum ipso vivebant," and in that part which is particularly addressed " ad fratres juniores," says, " Si librum *tibi* ipse compegeris, in eo ne elabores exornando.   Est enim vitium puerile."   By the way, in that same section he goes on to give directions as to the mode of receiving strangers, among which he says, " et posteaquam sederit, quomodo se habeat, quære, et nihil amplius, sed libellum ei aliquem legendum præbe;" and afterwards "Si peregre proficiscens diverteris apud aliquem, et ille domo egrediatur, et te solum relinquat, oculos tuos ne sustuleris, ut quæ ibi sunt, vasa, et supellectilem aspicias.   Fenestram, aut arcam, aut *librum* aperias, cave."—*Bib. Pat.* tom. iii. c. 887. *Ed.* 1575.   I do not pretend to decide when these precepts were written, which have perhaps nothing to do with the period, or the part of the world, to which my remarks are particularly directed ; but it must have been, I think, at some time and place where books were not extremely rare things, and where one might expect to find them lying about a room.

paupers who were not fit for other work, to collect such pebbles; and a crippled servant of the monastery, who was glad to do what little he could, was particularly useful in that matter; [5] but generally, I apprehend, the binding of books was in parchment or plain leather.

"About the year 790," says Warton, "Charlemagne granted an unlimited right of hunting to the abbot and monks of Sithiu ior making their gloves and girdles of the skins of the deer they killed, and covers for their books. We may imagine that these religious were more fond of hunting than reading. It is certain that they were obliged to hunt before they could read, and at least it is probable that under these circumstances they did not manufacture many volumes." [6] This passage I have read over many times, and I really cannot make any sense of it. *Why* should Charlemagne's grant induce such suppositions? *Why* are we to imagine that these monks loved hunting better than reading? *Why* must they hunt before they could read? *Why* is it probable that they did not "manufacture" (a strange term for binding a book, and one which looks as if Warton supposed that they were to write on buck-skin) "many volumes under *these circumstances*," the chief circumstances being (according

---

[5] " Quicquid tamen a pueris fieri vidit, quod vel sedendo vel proreptando agere potuit; in hoc se voluntaria utilitate studiosus exercuit, nec prorsus aliquod tempus, nisi cum somnum vel cibum caperet, transire sibi patiebatur, quin semper in aliquo utilis esse videretur. Consuetudo namque dilecto nostro pontifici fuit ut puerulos, vel etiam pauperes validiores saepius per plateas, vel per defossas petrarum foveas ageret, qui sibi lapillos minutos quosdam nivei coloris, vel nigri, vel rubri interdum, vel varii, deferrent: quos ipse elimatos, et politos variaque collisione vel confricatione in similitudine pretiosorum lapidum redactos, aut in altaribus, aut libris, aut in capsis honeste collocavit. In quo nimirum opere, praedictus ille pauper se privatim exercuit, et caeterorum industriam utiliter praevenit, et pro curiositate tali episcopo penitus complacuit." *Vita Godehardi ap. Leib. Scr. Brun.* i. 500.

[6] Dissert. ii. prefixed to his Hist. of Poetry.

to his account) an "unlimited" right to hunt for
leather, granted by the sovereign of such extensive
dominions? I cannot help suspecting that there
may be a meaning in the passage which I am not
acute enough to perceive, for to me the grant
appears rather to intimate that the monks who
obtained such a privilege must have done (or, to
say the least, must have been supposed to do) a
good deal in the way of book-binding.

But here, as in too many of the facetious anecdotes of the dark ages, when we turn out the
reference we find that the story is false, not only as
to the spirit, but the letter. The charter stands,
indeed, as Warton tells us, "Mab. de Re Dipl. 611,"
but as soon as we look at it, the "unlimited right"
becomes sadly circumscribed; and as to the jolly
abbot and his sporting monks, "paf—all should be
gone," like "de great Peolphan" and his spectre
train. The limitation of the grant to the woods
belonging to the monastery is express, and is
even reduced by the exception of such royal forests
as were set apart for the emperor's diversion; and
the fun of the religious hunt is entirely spoiled by
the fact that the permission is not for the *monks*,
but for the *servants*, of the monastery, to hunt for
the useful purposes specified in the charter.[7] That

---

[7] " Concessimus Autlando abbati et monachis ex monasterio
Sithiu . . . . . . ut ex nostra indulgentia *in eorum proprias silvas*
licentiam haberent *eorum homines* venationem exercere, unde *fratres*
consolationem habere possint, tam ad volumina librorum tegenda,
quamque et manicias et ad zonas faciendas, *salvas forestes nostras*,
quas ad opus nostrum constitutas habemus." The emperor then
goes on to charge all his subjects, to whom the charter is addressed
(omnium fidelium nostrorum magnitudini), that they should not
presume to oppose the exercise of this privilege by the abbot, his
successors, and their men (abbate, aut successoribus suis, seu
hominibus eorum—but nothing of the monks), " nisi liceat *eorum
hominibus* ut supra diximus ex nostra indulgentia in eorum *proprias
silvas* venationem exercere." Indeed, who that knew anything of
Charlemagne or his laws could expect to find him patronizing a
company of mere sporting monks? Let me give two short

charter, as far as I see, contains nothing which should lead us to suppose that the monks of Sithiu ever hunted at all, or that "these religious" were inferior to the modern priest who has held them up to scorn, either in the knowledge or the practice of that which their character and station required.

There is however another point relating to these costly books which must not be omitted. Their extraordinary value would of course lead to their being taken great care of—but then it would also render them peculiarly liable to destruction. It is probable that such books were among the "insignia ornamenta" of the church of St. Benignus at Dijon, when they were stolen on one of the anniversaries of the patron saint's day in the eleventh century;[8] and the soldiers who plundered Nigel, Bishop of Ely, in the time of King Stephen, thought it worth while to carry off a copy of the Gospels adorned with relics.[9] But beside downright and forcible robbery, or even fraudulent abstraction, there were many reasons why these books were liable to be destroyed. Though it does not enter into the design of this paper to refer to the present state, or even the present existence, of such manuscripts (and, indeed, I purposely avoid speaking of some, merely

---

instances from his Capitularies, one earlier, and the other more recent, than the charter in question :—" Omnibus servis Dei venationes et silvaticas vagationes cum canibus, et ut accipitres et falcones non habeant, interdicimus." This is only a repetition of previous enactments by his predecessors, made probably quite at the beginning of his reign. In 802 we find " Ut episcopi, abbates, presbyteri, diaconi, nullusque ex omni clero canes ad venandum, aut acceptores, falcones, seu sparvarios habere præsumant ; sed pleniter se unusquisque in ordine suo canonice vel regulariter custodiant. Qui autem præsumpserit, sciat unusquisque honorem suum perdere. Cæteri vero tale exinde damnum patiantur ut reliqui metum habeant talia sibi usurpare."—*Capit. edit. Baluz.* tom. i. 191, 369.

[8] " Latronum fraude in ipsius sancti festivitate, occisis custodibus furto fuerunt asportata."—*Mab. A. S.* viii. 301.

[9] Ang. Sac. i. 622.

because they are known to be now in existence, and
therefore belong to another part of the subject), yet
as I have mentioned the Bible presented by Lewis
the Debonnaire in the year 826, I may here add that
Mabillon tells us that it was still in existence, with
silver plates, which had been supplied by the Abbot
Ingrannus in the year 1168, to replace the original
golden ones which had somehow disappeared.

Of course, various things—charity and need, as
well as cupidity,—were likely to produce what was
then termed *excrustation*, and to risk, if not almost
to ensure, the destruction of the manuscript itself.
Charity,—as when all the valuables (omne ornamen-
tum in auro et argento) belonging to the church of
St. Benignus of Dijon were sacrificed to provide
relief for the poor in the famine of A.D. 1001;[1] or
when, five years afterwards, Odilo, Abbot of Clugni,
having exhausted all other sources, was obliged to
apply the sacred vessels to the same object.[2] Need,
—as when, in order to meet the heavy tax laid by
William Rufus to raise money for the purchase of
Normandy, Godfrey, Abbot of Malmesbury (*pessi-
morum usus consilio, quos nominare possem, si peccan-
tium societas crimen alleviare posset magistri*, says
William the historian), stripped no less than *twelve*
copies of the Gospels;[3] or when William de Long-
champ, who became bishop of Ely in the year 1190,
contributed one hundred and sixty marks towards
the redemption of King Richard, and, to raise the
money, pawned *thirteen* copies of the Gospels,
including one of great value which had belonged to
King Edgar.[4]

That books thus pawned did not always find their

---

[1] Mab. A. S. tom. viii. p. 300.

[2] " Exhaustis in egentium usus horreis et ærariis, sacra etiam
vasa confregerit."—Mab. Ann. an. 1006, tom. iv. 170.

[3] Die uno xii. textus Evangeliorum, viii. cruces, viii. scrinia
argento et auro nudata et excrustata sunt,"—*Vita Aldh. ap. Ang.
Sac.* ii. 44.

[4] Ang. Sac. i. 633.

way back may be imagined; and indeed we are told
that three books, adorned with gold and silver and
precious stones, were lost to the Abbey of Laurisheim
about the year 1130, owing to their advocate,
Bertolf, having been allowed by the abbot, Diemo,
to raise money upon them. Whether these copies
of the Gospels ever ran a risk of having the inside
as well as the outside falsified, and a false reading
or gem substituted for a true one, I do not know;
but it is certain that a " textus aureus " belonging
to the church of Ely was once pledged to the Jews
of Cambridge. This, however, belongs rather to the
dangers arising from cupidity, if we may trust
Richard of Ely, who mentions the circumstance in
his long list of the depredations committed by
Nigel, already mentioned.[5] This source of danger
is indeed obvious enough; and I will here give only
one other instance, which I am unwilling to omit
because it refers to a considerable number of copies.
The historian who relates the destruction of Hide
Abbey, near Winchester, tells us that Henry, who
was bishop of that see from A.D. 1129 to 1174, got
the monastery into his hands. After it had been
burned in the year 1141, the monks got out of the
ashes sixty pounds of silver, and fifteen pounds of
gold, and various other things, which they brought
to the bishop, who subsequently committed the care
of the monastery to Hugo Schorchevylene, a monk
of Clugni, whom he made abbot. This monk

---

[5] " Item pro parvo *textu aureo* et pro ansa argentea dedit v.
marcas cuidam de Thetford; et præterea uno anno abstulit de
Sacristaria xxiv. marcas et vi. solidos. Antea vero prædictam
crucem et *textum* similiter pro nummis transposuerat Judæis apud
Cantebrigge, quæ gloriosus rex sæpe dictus Edgardus ob signum
libertatis suæ et munificentiæ ibi donavit : et ne tanto muniminis
titulo frustrarentur, Monachi dederunt cc. marcas per manus
Willelmi prioris."—*Hist. Elien.* ap Ang. Sac. i. 625. As to the
importance of the Jews of Cambridge a few years before this time,
see Fuller's History of the University, p. 4, § 11, 12 ; but in his
quotation from Peter of Blois he omits his testimony that a
principal object of Gislebert's preaching was the refutation of

having, by the bishop's direction, dispersed thirty
out of the forty monks, laid hands on the treasures
of the church, and stripped *ten* copies of the
Gospels.[6]

It may probably be said, that too many of those
who gave and received these costly volumes thought
more of the outside than the inside, and even forgot
that the rich cover enclosed the more precious Word
of God;—it may have been so, though I hope not
always,—but I beg the reader to take care that he
does not fall into much the same error. I hope he
will not forget that, whether in sackcloth and ashes,
or in gold and silver, each of the books which I
have here spoken of was the Gospel of Christ.
Should he think that, although tiresome for their
sameness, these instances are not in fact very
numerous, I would repeat that they are only such
as have occurred to me, in circumstances not the
most favourable for research ; and I must add, that
while I have met with these notices of the Scriptures,
and with many others which I hope to bring forward
in this argument, I have *not* found anything about
the arts and engines of hostility, the blind hatred of
half-barbarian kings, the fanatical fury of their subjects, or the reckless antipathy of the popes. I do
not recollect any instance in which it is recorded that

Judaism ; and that, in fact, several Jews were converted by it.
" Verbum Dei ad populum prædicans . . . contra Judaicum
errorem maxime disputabat . . . cumque nonnulli increduli et
adhuc Judaica perfidia cæcati ad ejus verba in sinum matris
ecclesiæ, relicto penitus suo pristino errore, compuncti accurrerunt,"
&c.—*Pet. Bles. ap. Rer. Ang. Scr.* tom. i. p. 114.

[6] " Manum in sanctuarium Domini extendens, cruces quinque,
scrinia decem, *textus totidem* auro argento gemmisque pretiosis
ornatos, . . . excrustavit."—*Dug. Mon.* i. 210. One cannot
suppose that this sort of spoliation was known to the bishop, whose
taste for costly ornament was so fully proved. In particular,
Giraldus Cambrensis tells us that " Cathedralem ecclesiam suam
palliis purpureis et olosericis cortinis et aulæis preciosissimis,
textis, philateriis, crucibus aureis . . . usque ad regum invidiam
exornavit."—*Ang. Sac.* tom. ii. p. 421.

the Scriptures, or any part of them, were treated with
indignity, or with less than profound respect. I know
of no case in which they were intentionally defaced
or destroyed (except, as I have just stated, for their
rich covers), though I have met with, and hope
to produce several instances, in some of which they
were the only, and in others almost the only, books
which were preserved through the revolutions of the
monasteries to which they belonged, and all the
ravages of fire, pillage, carelessness, or whatever
else had swept away all the others. I know (and in
saying this I do not mean anything but to profess
my ignorance, for did I suppress such knowledge I
might well be charged with gross dishonesty) of
nothing which should lead me to suppose that any
human craft or power was exercised to prevent the
reading, the multiplication, the diffusion of the
Word of God. When, therefore, after having
written almost all the foregoing pages, a periodical
work fell into my hands containing the passage
which stands at the head of this paper, I could not
resist the temptation to borrow it as a motto. In
so using it I mean no offence to the gentleman from
whose tercentenary sermon it purports to be an extract, but only to call the attention of the public to
the different views which are held, and the different
statements which are made, on a very interesting
subject, in the hope that truth may be thereby
elicited.

Whether, however, the Scriptures were exposed
to this treatment in the dark ages, or not, I hope to
show as the next step in the argument that there are
still in existence many copies which belonged to that
period; and in the meantime to draw the reader's
attention to some circumstances which, to my own
mind, render it a matter of astonishment that we
possess so many.

No. XIV.

" Still I am not satisfied; and the stubborn fact of *scarcity* inclines me to suspect that the pens of the monks were less constantly employed than many would induce us to believe."— BERINGTON.

WITHOUT entering into any question here as to what may, or may not, be properly called *scarcity*, in regard to ancient manuscripts, let us assume that its existence is a stubborn and undeniable fact; yet that fact may, perhaps, admit of some explanation. Suppose there are but few manuscripts in existence, it is no proof that but few were written; and, indeed, I must say, that from what I have been able to learn respecting the real number, of which this surviving *scarcity* consists, and the circumstances under which they have been preserved, I can only wonder that we have so many—or, I am almost tempted to say, that we have any—manuscripts seven or eight hundred years old. It is, however, quite clear, that if we would form any opinion of the state of literature, or means of knowledge, in the Dark Ages, we must, in some degree, enter into this question, and cannot pass it over with a slight allusion to the ravages of time. It is necessary to our design ; and I am inclined to hope, that a short and superficial sketch, such as the nature of these essays admits, may not be altogether uninteresting. As a great part of my illustrations will be drawn from the reports of some literary travellers, I will first give some notice of them, in order that I may hereafter refer to them with more brevity, and that such of my readers as are not acquainted with the books may understand my references.

Between the 16th of April and the 10th of June, 1682, Dom Mabillon, accompanied by his brother

Benedictine, Michael Germanus, made a journey through Melun, Sens, Auxerre, Dijon, Verdun, Chalons sur Saone, and Autun, to Lyons, and returned by way of Moulins. In the course of this excursion they visited Citeaux, Clugni, and many other monasteries, and overhauled their manuscripts; the object of their journey being to examine, or to search for, some documents relating to the royal family. How far this was openly avowed, and whether it was known even to the younger of the two travellers, I cannot tell; but Mabillon's acknowledged supremacy, in all such matters, naturally pointed him out to the minister Colbert as the fittest person to be sent on such an errand. That he executed it with skill and fidelity, and, at the same time, took an opportunity of doing a little business in his own way, of antiquarian research, nobody will doubt. Two years after, he drew up an account of his tour; and it was subsequently printed under the title of " *Iter Burgundicum.* " [1]

The next year, they went, by the same order, through part of Germany, taking the route of Basil, Zurich, Augsburg, Munich, &c. They set out on the 30th of June, and appear to have returned in October. Mabillon prefixed an account of this journey to his " Vetera Analecta," under the title of " *Iter Germanicum.* " [2]

In the year 1685, at the suggestion of Le Tellier, Archbishop of Rheims—the brother of the minister who had succeeded Colbert, and the owner of 50,000 volumes—Mabillon was sent, at the royal cost, to investigate the libraries of Italy, and to procure books for the king's library. He set out, with the same companion as before, on the 1st of April, and returned in the June of the following year. The royal library was enriched by the addition of 3,000 volumes; and Mabillon published an account of the

---

[1] It will be referred to as, It. Burg.   [2] It. Germ.

journey, in the first volume of his "Museum Italicum," under the title of "*Iter Italicum*."[3]

Again this father set out in the year 1696, accompanied by another Benedictine—the well-known
Ruinart ; and, between the 20th of August and the
10th of November, they travelled through most of
Alsace and Lorraine, conducting themselves, in
respect of all libraries which they could meet with,
in the way which might be expected from them.
Ruinart drew up an account of the journey, which
he entitled, "*Iter Litterarium in Alsatiam et Lothar-
ingiam*."[4]

When Father Montfaucon had completed the
Benedictine edition of "Athanasius," he became
convinced that the Greek fathers could not be
properly edited without first ransacking the libraries
of Italy for manuscripts ; and therefore (permissu
superiorum) he and Father Paul Brioys set off for
that purpose on the 18th of May, 1698, and did not
return until the 11th of June, 1701.   In the course
of the next year he published his "*Diarium Italicum*;"[5] which was, I believe, the year after, translated into English.

The Benedictines of St. Maur—that learned body,
to which all the travellers hitherto mentioned belonged
—having determined to undertake a new edition of
the "Gallia Christiana," resolved to send one of their
number to collect what materials he could, for correction and addition, from the various libraries, churches,
and monasteries of France. "La resolution,"says Dom
Edmund Martene, "en fut prise à Marmoutier au
chapitre general de 1708, et comme j'étois sur les lieux,
et qu'on sçavoit que Dieu m'avoit donné quelque petit
talent pour lire les anciennes écritures, je fus un
des premiers sur lesquels on jetta les yeux."
Nothing could be more natural, as it respects the
Chapter ; and, perhaps, as to Martene, though he

[3] It. Ital.   [4] It. Alsat.   [5] Diar. It.

might sincerely feel all that he says of the vastness of the undertaking, nothing more agreeable. He set out accordingly on the 11th of June, and travelled until the 23rd of December, when he got back into winter quarters at Marmoutier, just in time to avoid being exposed to a more inclement season than any which the oldest persons living could remember. Being informed that he must set out again as soon as Easter was past, he begged to have a companion. This request being granted, he chose Dom Ursin Durand, and they set out together on the 4th of April. In short—for I am not writing the history of their travels—that year, and the four which succeeded (except when they were in winter quarters), were spent in making various circuits, in the course of which they visited a great part of France; the whole time, from Martene's first setting out to their joint return on the 16th of Nov., 1713, being five years and a half; or, so far as travelling was practicable, we may perhaps more correctly say, six years. Martene tells us, that they visited about a hundred cathedrals, and at least eight hundred abbeys; in which they failed not to examine whatever manuscripts they could find. In so doing, they not only fulfilled their commission, as it regarded the " Gallia Christiana," but met with a vast quantity of unpublished matter, of various sorts, which they gave to the world in the year 1717, in five folio volumes, under the title of "*Thesaurus Novus Anecdotorum;* " and it is the work which (having explained myself in No. II. p. 34 *n.*) I have since frequently quoted, under the brief reference "*Mart.*" In the same year that this large work was brought out, Martene published an account of these six journeys, in one volume quarto, entitled, "*Voyage Litteraire de deux Religieux Benedictins de la Congregation de Saint Maur;* " and it is to this which I now refer.[6]

---

[6] I. Voy. Lit.

Having published these collections of his journeys, there was nothing, Dom Martene tells us, which he less expected than to set out again on his travels : yet so it was.　A new edition of the ancient historians of France was projected ; and our two travellers were requested to go and look for materials, to render it as full and correct as possible. They accordingly set out on the 30th of May, 1718, from the neighbourhood of Paris ; passed through Soissons, Rheims, Amiens, Brussels, Liege, Aix-la-Chapelle, Dusseldorf, and penetrated as far into Germany as Paderborn—returned by Cologne, Treves, Luxembourg—and got back in January, 1719.　By that time, the scheme of publishing the early historians had been abandoned ; but the travellers had accumulated a great quantity of curious matter.　Their former labours, and the published fruits of them, had brought them invitations to ransack Germany and Spain ; and though they could not accept them, yet literary contributions poured in from those quarters : much, also, that Mabillon had previously collected, but not published, was thrown into the common stock ; and when the work came forth in 1724, the editors felt justified in calling the nine folio volumes, " *Veterum Scriptorum et Monumentorum historicorum, dogmaticorum, moralium, amplissima collectio.*"　It is the work which I have quoted by the reference " *M. & D. ;* " but at present, our business is with the single quarto volume in which Martene gave an account of this journey.　He published it under the same title as the former ; but, for the sake of distinction, I shall refer to it as his *second* literary tour.[7]

From these sources, it would be easy to show that there are—or, at least, that there were, a little more than a hundred years ago, which is quite sufficient for the purposes of our inquiry—a good

---

[7] II. Voy. Lit.

many ancient manuscripts in existence; but for that fact there are better proofs; and it is not my present object to prove it. I quote these literary tourists, not to show that manuscripts are numerous; but as incidentally furnishing illustrations of the reasons why they are so few, and why we may reasonably wonder that they are not fewer still. It is grievous, for instance, to read such notices as those which both Mabillon and Martene have given of the state of things at Clugni. They found the old catalogue (Mabillon says four, Martene five or six, hundred years old), written on boards three feet and a half long, and a foot and a half wide, and covered with parchment—grandes tablettes, qu'on ferme comme un livre—but of the books which it contained (ex copiosissimo illo numero), they could find scarcely one hundred. "On dit," says Martene, that the Huguenots carried them to Geneva; but be this as it may, they were gone somehow.[8] Such was the case, also, at Nonantula, where, of all its former riches (ex multis quos celeberrima olim illa Abbatia habebat veteres codices), Mabillon found but two manuscripts.[9] At Rebais, Martene says, "Il y avoit sans doute autrefois beaucoup de manuscrits dans l'abbaye, mais après des révolutions si étranges, à peine y en reste-t-il quelques-uns;"[1] and, at the Abbey of Beaupré, "Il y avoit autrefois beaucoup de manuscrits; mais nous n'y en vîmes que deux ou trois."[2]

But the fact that the manuscripts were gone in places which had possessed considerable collections, will be sufficiently proved incidentally; and my wish is rather to call up to the reader's mind those causes which may account for it, by a brief and superficial enumeration of them.

I.—I hardly know how to arrange these causes; but, as it is of little consequence, I will first advert

---

[8] It. Burg. 22 ; I. Voy. Lit. 227.   [9] It. Ital. 202.
[1] I. Voy. Lit. P. ii. 73.   [2] Ib. 166.

to one of the most powerful, but one which, through
the distinguishing mercy of God, can hardly be
appreciated among us. No man living has known
anything like war in our country; and even in
modern Europe generally, the mode of warfare, the
circumstances of places taken by siege or by storm,
as to their liability to be burned or utterly destroyed,
and the fact that most books are now produced by
hundreds or thousands at a time, make so great
a difference, that we can scarcely institute a
comparison. When, however, the word WAR is
mentioned, it will readily occur to the reader, that
among the desolations of fire and sword, manuscripts
did not escape destruction; but I wish to raise a
more particular idea of the dangers to which they
were exposed, and the destruction which they
actually suffered from certain wars during and since
the period with which we are engaged.

Think, in the first place, of the ravages of the
Danes and Normans in the ninth century; accounts
of their cruel desolations meet us at every turn in
monastic history. It may easily be conceived, that
at all times,—at least, all early times,—monasteries
and churches were likely to form a nucleus, both
from their being the places most likely to contain
spoil, and from their being (next to those which
were regularly fortified) the places of greatest
strength. Hence they became peculiarly obnoxious
to destruction, and particularly to destruction by
fire. As to the desolation of monasteries by these
barbarians, however, the shortest way to give some
idea of them would be to copy the article
"Normanni," in the index of the third volume of
Mabillon's Annals, in which he gives a list of the
monasteries of his own order which were pillaged
or destroyed. Even that, however, would be too
long to insert here; but it begins, "Normanni,
monasteria ab eis incensa, eversa, direpta, —;
Amausense, —; Arulense, —; Arvernense S. Illidii,
—; Autissiodorense sancti Germani, —; Barden-

eiense,—," &c. ; and so the index goes on through the alphabet, naming between seventy and eighty Benedictine monasteries. It is impossible to doubt, and, indeed, in some cases it may be proved, that there was a great loss of books. When, for instance, the Abbey of Peterborough, in Northamptonshire, was burned by the Danes in the year 870, there was a large collection of books destroyed—sanctorum librorum *ingens bibliotheca*.[3] The language of Ingulph may provoke a smile; and I assure the reader that I do not want to make mountains of mole-hills, or to catch at a word in any writer of the dark ages. But I cannot consent to sneer away the statement to nothing; and the rather because, though it may not be easy to say what the abbot's idea of an "ingens bibliotheca" was, yet, as will presently appear, he uses no such expression in speaking of the library of seven hundred volumes belonging to his own monastery which was burned in his own time—that is, in A.D. 1091.

Again, " when the black swarm of Hungarians first hung over Europe, about nine hundred years after the Christian æra, they were mistaken by fear and superstition for the Gog and Magog of the Scriptures,—the signs and forerunners of the end of the world."[4] There would be no use in detailing

---

[3] Ingul. ap. Gale. V. Scr. p. 23.

[4] As it is a principal part of my design to draw attention to the misrepresentations of popular writers, I cannot help offering a remark or two on the note which Gibbon adds to his words which I here quote (Dec. and Fall, vol. v. p. 548):—" A bishop of Wurtzburg submitted this opinion to a reverend abbot ; but *he* more gravely decided, that Gog and Magog were the spiritual persecutors of the church ; since Gog signifies the roof, the pride of the Heresiarchs, and Magog what comes from the roof, the propagation of their sects. Yet these men once commanded the respect of mankind. Fleury, Hist. Eccles. tom. xi. p. 594, &c." I do not know why Gibbon says " a bishop of *Wurtzburg*," when his authority Fleury and D'Achery (Fleury's only authority) say *Verdun ;* nor do I know how he learned that " *these* men " ever commanded the respect of mankind, for it seems as if there was

such particulars as are handed down to us; it is
always the same horrid tale of barbarous outrage
and destruction.   I will here only refer to one case,
partly out of respect to our friend the Abbot Bonus,

---

some doubt who the bishop was—and as to the "reverend abbot,"
I believe no one pretends to guess who he was, or of what country.
Could it be shown, therefore, that these two persons, whoever they
might be, held a foolish opinion on a very obscure point, and maintained it by mere nonsense, yet that would not go far towards
showing that the respect of mankind in the tenth century was
misplaced, in so far as it was given to bishops and abbots.   The
document exists, however, merely as "Epistola cujusdam Abbatis
Monasterii S. Germani ad V. Episcopum Virdunensem de Hungris."
Neither the bishop nor the abbot seem to have given any credit to
the notion of the Hungarians being Gog and Magog.   In writing
to the abbot, the bishop appears (for I believe his letter is not
extant, and is only known by the answer) to have mentioned that
the idea was current in his diocese, and to have desired him to
look at the prophecy of Ezekiel, and let him know what he
supposed to be its meaning.   That the bishop did not express or
imply any belief in the opinion, may be presumed from the terms
in which the abbot (after saying that it was current in his part of
the world also) sets it down as mere nonsense—frivolam esse et
nihil verum habere—contrasted with the language of deep respect
and affection in which he addresses the bishop.   But farther—the
sarcasm can scarcely be said to touch either of the parties; for the
abbot gives the notion about Gog and Magog being the roof, and
the heretics, &c., as the exposition of Jerome, without the
expression of any opinion as to its correctness; unless indeed we
may find something like apology in the language of the single
sentence of comment which he bestows on it—"quæ quia a B.
Hieronymo exposita sunt, et brevitas epistolæ plura de his dicere
non permittit."   He then goes on to inquire who the Hungarians
really were, whence they came, and how it happened that they had
not been mentioned in history, considering the extent of the Roman
conquests and researches—had they been known under some other
name?   "sicut solent mutari urbium vel locorum seu fluminum
nomina.   Nam Tiberis quondam Albula dicebatur.   Unde Virgilius
' amisit priscum Albula nomen;' et Italia prius Saturnia dicebatur;
sicut idem poeta, ' et nomen posuit Saturnia tellus,'" &c.   The
letter, on the whole, is such as that I cannot but hope that the
writer did command the respect of his age.   Whether the wretched
infidel who thought fit to sneer at him will command the respect
of those who take the trouble to look out his authorities, they who
see such a specimen as this may fairly question.   Fleury refers to
Dac. Spic. xii. 349; in the folio edition it is at tom. iii. 368.

who was brought up there, though it was before his time, in the days of Abbot Leopard, who presided there from the year 899 to 912 ; and principally because, as I have just said, Mabillon found only two manuscripts at Nonantula.[5]   In the first or third year of Abbot Leopard, after a great battle on the river Brenta, in which many thousands of Christians were slain, the pagans advanced to Nonantula, killed the monks, burned the monastery with many books (codices multos concremavere), and ravaged the whole place.

I pass over the irruption of the Saracens into Italy; but, though it is lamentable to carry on the history of desolation as the work of Christians, yet truth requires me to notice what may be called religious, or, more properly and emphatically, irreligious, wars.   Happily the books which I have mentioned as furnishing illustrations relate chiefly to France, and we will not at present look elsewhere. The Dean and Chapter of *St. Theudere, near Vienne,* says Martene, "nous comblerent d'honnêteté, et nous communiquirent, de la meilleure grace du monde, ce qui leur reste d'anciens monumens de la fureur des heretiques.   Car ces impies brûlerent en 1562. toutes les chartes." [6]   "Nous fûmes de là à Tarbe, où nous ne trouvâmes pas grand travail, l'église cathédrale et tous les titres ayant été brûlé par les Calvinistes, qui, dans toute le Bearn et dans la Bigorre, ont laissé de funestes marques de leur fureur." [7]—"Pour l'abbaye de *St. Jean* [at *Thoüars*], elle est beaucoup plus ancienne, mais les ravages qu'y ont fait les Calvinistes le siecle passé, en ont dissipé la plûpart des monumens." [8]   *Grimberg* I must reserve for another purpose, and here only mention that it had been destroyed and its library

---

[5] Of course I do not mean that they had none in the meantime. I hope under another head to show that they had many, of whose fate fire and sword were guiltless.
[6] I. Voy. Lit. 252.   [7] I. Voy. Lit. P. ii. p. 13.   [8] Ib. p. 5.

burned by the Huguenots; and as I do not wish to
repeat the same cases, even for the illustration of
different points, I here only mention the neighbour-
ing monastery of *Dilighen,* of which Martene says—
" Cette abbaye a éprouvé le même sort que celle de
Grimberg. C'est à dire, qu'elle a été ruinée par les
heretiques. Aujourd'hui on la rétablit, et on lui a
rédonné son premier lustre; " except, of course, in
one respect, for he adds, " L'église est fort jolie
. . . . . la bibliotheque assez bonne, mais il n'y a
que très-peu de manuscrits qui ne sont pas de consequence." [9] At another monastery (near *Ferte sous
Jouarre,* not far from Meaux), Ruinart says,
" Sperabamus nos ibi in archiviis aliquid forte
reperturos . . . . . at monasterii chartas a Calvin-
ianis penitus combustas fuisse nobis responsum
. . . . . . supersunt in bibliotheca aliquot codices
manuscripti; " and, after specifying a good many
works, he adds, " quæ non sunt magni momenti." [1]
Much the same injury had been suffered at the
monastery of *Fleury,* where Mabillon found but a
few relics of the vast collection which had been
destroyed in the religious wars of the preceding
century.[2] The effects of war were, indeed, too
frequently visible; but not to tire the reader with
repetition,—yet without repetition how can I
impress on him the extent of the mischief?—some
other notices of the destruction produced by what
may be termed general or common warfare shall be
thrown into a note, and I will proceed to speak of
another cause of destruction.[3]

---

[9] II. Voy. Lit. 112.   [1] It. Alsat. 415.

[2] " Penes quos quidam adhuc reliqui sunt ex innumera illa
veterum librorum copia, quæ superiori sæculo, furente hæresi,
direpta est." It. Burg. 30.

[3] Take the following instances—Of the abbey of *Brunwillers,*
Martene says, " Comme le monastère a beaucoup souffert par les
guerres, et qu'il a été sujet comme les autres aux revolutions, on
ne doit pas être surpris s'il n'y a plus qu'un manuscrit des lettres
de Ciceron." (II. Voy. Lit. 269.) " Le Roi Louis XIV. ayant

II. I need not insist on the liability of manuscripts to be destroyed by accidental FIRE, especially at a time when so many were kept in wooden buildings. Our travellers, however, continually furnish us with such notices as these, most of which are quite modern. At *Rheims*, "L'église cathédrale et l'archevêché ayant été brûlez dans le douzième siècle, toutes les archives furent pour lors consumées par le feu."[4]—At *Gembloux*, "Nous passâmes la matinée à voir ce qui restoit de manuscrits de l'incendie generale du monastère."[5] —At the monastery of the Jacobins at *Liege*, "Il y avoit autrefois une assez bonne bibliotheque ; mais il y a quelques années que tous les manuscrits périrent dans un incendie, qui consuma entièrement le monastère."[6]—At *Lucelle*, "L'incendie qui consuma tout le monastère en 1699 nous priva du plaisir d'y voir une très-riche bibliotheque en manuscrits, que les flammes ont reduit en cendre, avec le religieux qui y étoit entré pour tâcher de les sauver."[7]—"Ce que nous venons de rapporter nous fait voir que les *six incendies* qui sont arrivées à *S. Wast*, n'ont pas tout consumé, et nous font aisé-

---

soûmis Luxembourg à la force invincible de ses armes, l'abbaye de *Munster* éprouva une seconde fois le sort de la guerre, et fut entièrement rasée . . . . . après tant de revolutions on ne pouvoit pas s'attendre à faire des découvertes dans la bibliotheque. En effet, nous n'y avons trouvé que cinq ou six manuscrits." (II. Voy. Lit. 302.) St. *Arnoul* at *Metz*, "Cette abbaye . . . . . fut entièrement rasée avec celles de Saint *Clement*, de Saint *Symphorien*, de Saint *Pierre*, et de Sainte *Marie*, au siege de Mets formé par l'empereur Charles-quint." (I. Voy. Lit. P. ii. 112.) At *Othmersheim*, "Cette abbaye, étant exposée au theatre de la guerre, a perdu ses anciens monumens, et nous n'y trouvâmes rien qui dût nous arreter." (I. Voy. Lit. P. ii. 143.) *La Chartreuse*, by Liege, "Il y avoit autrefois beaucoup de manuscrits ; mais le monastère ayant esté entièrement réduit en cendres dans les dernières guerres, ils ont tous esté consumez dans les flammes. Il n'y a que les sermons de Jacques de Vitry, en quatre ou cinq volumes, qui ayent échappé à l'incendie." (II. Voy. Lit. 183.)

[4] I. Voy. Lit. P. ii. 79. [5] II. Voy. Lit. 117.
[6] II. Voy. Lit. 182. [7] I. Voy. Lit. P. ii. 141.

ment juger des trésors immenses que nous y trou-
verions, si nous avions tout ce que les flammes nous
ont ravi." [8]—The abbey of *Loroy*, " Qui ayan tété
entièrement brulée il y a environ quarante ans, n'a
conservé aucun de ses anciens monumens." [9]

I do not wish to be tedious on this point, but I
am irresistibly tempted, first of all, just to allude
to the conflagration of the monastery of *Teano*, near
Monte Casino, which was burned, as Leo Marsicanus
says, "cum omnibus operibus suis," in the year
892, because, among those "opera" it is said that
the original copy of the Rule of St. Benedict
perished,[1] and then to give one or two anecdotes
respecting what may be called accidental burning
of monasteries, as contra-distinguished from those
conflagrations which took place in the wars. I give
them not as proofs that such things happened, for
that is naturally to be supposed, and is sufficiently
attested by history, but as stories illustrative both
of one particular point and of our general subject.

Thieto, who was abbot of *St. Gall's*, in the year
937, was a strict disciplinarian; and this was very
sensibly felt, not only by the monks, but by the
school-boys. St. Mark's day being a holiday, some
of the latter had got into mischief (quædam
errata commiserant) which the monitors (censores
scholarum quos *circatores* vocabant) reported to the
masters. Sentence having been passed on the
guilty, one of them was sent to the upper part of
the building to fetch rods. By way of anticipatory
revenge for his flogging, or as a desperate resource
to avoid one, the boy took a brand from a fire and
placed it under the dry wood which was next to the
roof. This quickly took fire, and the flames, driven
by the wind, soon seized the tower of the church.
The monastery was almost entirely burned, and

---

[8] II. Voy. Lit. 65.   [9] I. Voy. Lit. 36.
[1] Mab. Ann. tom. iii. p. 263.

many books were lost (multi libri amissi), though
they were in time to save the church bells and
furniture. The writer who relates the story, adds,
"that from this mischief, the monks of St. Gall
took a great dislike to the scholars, and some
thought that the school ought to be entirely given
up, but he suggests that the loss which the
monastery sustained by this occurrence was more
than counterbalanced by the credit which it had
gained through the scholars whom it had sent
forth." [2]

If it had not happened in the same year, I should
not have mentioned the burning of the famous
monastery of *Fulda*, because I do not know how
it happened, and cannot prove that the library was
burned ; and where there are cases enough of
positive evidence, it is not in general worth while
to notice that which is merely presumptive, however strong it may be ; and of this monastery and
its library I hope to find a fitter occasion to speak.

"Towards the evening of that day," says the
historian of the monastery of *Lawresheim* or Lorsch
(a few miles east of Worms), speaking of the 21st
of March in the year 1090, "after that, following
the example of the carnal Israel, the people had sat
down to eat and to drink, and risen up to play, it
happened that, among other games, a disc, set on
fire at the edge in the usual way, was whirled in
the air by a soldier.[3] Being driven round with
great force, and presenting the appearance of a
circle of fire, it forms a spectacle which pleases,

---

[2] Mab. iii. Ann. 407.

[3] " Inter cætera ludorum exercitia discus in extrema marginis
ora (ut solet) accensus, militari manu per aera vibrabatur ; qui
acriori impulsu circumactus, orbicularem flammæ speciem reddens,
tam ostentui virium quam oculis mirantium, spectaculi gratiam
exhibet." I do not quite understand this, but I suppose it must
have been some kind of circular wheel or circular frame, whirled by
a strong arm, and presenting some such appearance as a Catherine
wheel.

not only the eye by its appearance, but as an exhibition of strength. This being whirled by someone who did not keep sufficiently fast hold, it flew, by his unintentional cast, on the top of the church. Sticking fast there, between the wooden tiles and the old beams, it set fire to the place. What need of many words ? In the first place, the flame seized on the tower, which was made with admirable woodwork,[4] and in which were the bells, and their ropes being burned they could not be used to give the alarm. It then seized all the upper part of the building, the towers, and the porches. At length the dropping of the melted lead, with which all the roof was covered, rendered it utterly impossible to go in or get anything out. Then was the face of things miserable—so many excellent buildings, of the church as well as of the whole monastery—so many fine ornaments devoured by the sudden ravages of the flames, a few only saved with great exertion and risk, either snatched with the hand or broken away with the axe or hatchet from the very midst of the fire." [5]

I hope to give the reader another story somewhat similar, and more graphic; but, though I am not apprehensive of his thinking it tedious, it would extend this paper to an unreasonable length ; and therefore, in the meantime, and before I speak of some other causes, I will take the opportunity of briefly adverting to a point which cannot be fairly passed over.

It is somewhat anticipating to say so, but in fact

---

[4] " Castellum mirabili dolatura fabrefactum." I do not undertake to decide the precise meaning of *dolatura* in this place, and therefore translate by general terms only ; but I suppose that we may in fact understand it to refer to those small, neat, wooden tiles (if I may use the expression, as I have done above, in translating *tegulas,* because the historian tells us that all the roof was covered with lead) which, in some parts of Europe, may still be seen forming the roofs or fronts of houses.

[5] Chron. Laur. ap. Freher. p. 81. Edit. 1600.

there are still so many manuscripts of some sorts in
existence, that it has been very warmly contended
by some learned men that a great part at least must
be forgeries, because it is impossible that so many
should have survived the perils to which such things
have been exposed. On such an occasion as this, I
must only just glance at what have been called the
Bella diplomatica, and my sole reason for referring
to them at present is, to show that those causes of
destruction which I have already specified have
been considered by learned men as sufficient to
account for (indeed, I may say, to require) a
greater *scarcity* of manuscripts than actually exists.
" They say," says Ludewig, " that since all the
kingdoms of Europe have carried on so many wars,
and Germany in particular has been subject to such
intestine commotion, no doubt all ancient documents
have thereby perished, which led to the forging of
new and supposititious ones. But, as nobody
doubts respecting the destruction of manuscripts
through these causes, so there were also reasons
why they might escape. For soldiers, intent on
gold and silver, and other things which they could
turn to account, were, as they are now, careless
about writings, especially considering the ignorance
and contempt of letters which then prevailed among
them. To this we may add, that even amidst the
outrages of war, the soldiers were restrained by
superstition from laying hands on the literary
treasures of the bishoprics." He goes on afterwards to speak of fire, and represents his opponents
as saying that there is scarcely to be found a city, a
monastery, or a habitation of any confraternity of
any kind which has not been more than once the
subject of a conflagration, in which all its documents
have perished. " This also," he replies, " is most
true; for my own part, I declare that I have never
been in any archives in Germany, though I have
visited them without number, where the keepers
have not attributed their deficiencies to fires which

S

had destroyed those very documents which were most important." [He adds in a note, " The keeper at Mayence told the same story in 1705. When I inquired for their documents of earlier date than the period of Frederic I., he answered, ' that they had all perished when the castle and the court, which were of wood, were burned.' "]   " But," he goes on to say, " even in the most tremendous fires, the first care is commonly to preserve the public archives from destruction ; nor do I hesitate to commend the prudence of the celebrated Maskowsky, Chancellor of Darmstadt, who, when the castle and principal palace were on fire, proposed and paid a reward to those who, at the risque of their lives, went into the lowest story, which was well arched, and brought the written documents out of the archives, which were thus saved like brands plucked from the burning. The same thing we may reasonably suppose to have been done in older times by prudent keepers." [6]

I did not like to pass over this point without some notice ; but the reader will at once perceive that there is an important difference between the case of which I am speaking and that to which Ludewig refers. Indeed, so far as our subject is concerned, I really have the suffrage of both parties in this diplomatic war in my favour. Those who contend that wars and fires must have destroyed the diplomas, charters, deeds, and other comparatively small and portable manuscripts of the dark ages, will readily grant that books were not likely to escape ; and those who reply, as Ludewig justly does, that such documents would be kept with peculiar care, and saved first, and at all hazards, in case of danger, would not think of extending their argument to such manuscripts as we are concerned with.

---

[6] Reliq. Manuscript. Pref. p. 84, 85.